THE MITRE &
THE CROWN

THE MITRE & THE CROWN

A HISTORY OF THE ARCHBISHOPS OF CANTERBURY

DOMINIC AIDAN BELLENGER
& STELLA FLETCHER

SUTTON PUBLISHING

First published in the United Kingdom in 2005 by
Sutton Publishing Limited · Phoenix Mill
Thrupp · Stroud · Gloucestershire · GL5 2BU

British Library Cataloguing in Publication Data
A catalogue record for this book is available from the British Library.

ISBN 0-7509-3121-3

Typeset in Photina MT 10.5/15 pt
Typesetting and origination by Sutton Publishing Limited.
Printed and bound in England by
J.H. Haynes & Co. Ltd, Sparkford.

CONTENTS

ILLUSTRATIONS

Black and white plates between pages 76 and 77

FOREWORD

One of the most distinguished Anglican scholars of the twentieth century, Dom Gregory Dix, wrote some sixty years ago of the way in which the bishop's office in England had varied over the centuries – from the 'tribal wizard' of Anglo-Saxon days to the gentleman-politician of the eighteenth century and the reforming headmaster of the Victorian age. He had no great opinion of the bishops of his own era, it must be said. But his perception is an acute one: the reality of episcopal ministry may be pretty continuous, but its embodiments have been wildly diverse. And what goes for bishops in general is emphatically true for the primates of all England.

The modern incumbent has to balance the urgencies of mission and witness in England with the increasingly complex needs of a worldwide network – as well as still struggling to maintain the heart of the work as a pastor to the parishes of east Kent. But the study of the office's history, so comprehensively and elegantly set out in these pages, is a good defence against nostalgia for past glories. There may be an unregenerate flicker of mourning for the long-lost days when the job was regarded by at least some governments as an appropriate semi-retirement for prelates of failing strength and faculties. But being at the centre of British politics has always been a somewhat risky enterprise, and no contemporary primate is likely to feel much regret that his chances of a violent end at the hands of monarchs or rebels or invaders are a bit reduced.

Yet that history of involvement with the institutions of this society leaves its mark – not only on the office but on the society. England cannot be understood historically without understanding how and why the Church contributed to its very identity – while at the same time returning constantly to the vexed theme of how that Church defined itself as something more than a chaplaincy to the governing elite. The history of the archbishops is not only one of involvement with the nation's institutions but one of argument and critical engagement – from Becket to Sancroft to William Temple's extra-ordinary role in creating something of the consensus on which postwar welfarism could grow.

This admirable book does what any good piece of church history should: it concentrates our minds upon the strange mixture of solidarity and distance that always characterises the Church's relation with the specific social worlds in which it finds itself. The questions that arise from trying to understand that mixture are among the most theologically serious that there are. This is therefore a deeply worthwhile study, and I hope that it will do its job in stimulating those deeper questions – as well as fascinating and instructing its readers.

Rowan Cantuar

ACKNOWLEDGEMENTS

W hen James Whistler was obliged under cross-examination to defend the asking price of 200 guineas for his *Nocturne in Black and Gold: the Falling Rocket*, a work 'knocked off' in a couple of days, he maintained that the figure was asked 'for the knowledge I have gained in the work of a lifetime'. In a similar fashion, our first collaboration, *Princes of the Church: a History of the English Cardinals* (2001), was 'knocked off' quite briskly, but built upon the knowledge of *two* lifetimes. Research was little more than an exercise in filling in the gaps. Our readers proved to be far kinder to the book than Ruskin was to Whistler and the *Falling Rocket*, and their generous response duly resulted in the notion that we might like to produce a comparable volume about the archbishops of Canterbury. This time, though, the gaps in our knowledge were much wider, both chronologically and geographically. We were, for instance, more familiar with the churches and palaces of Rome than with those of Kent or Surrey. For the present book, therefore, we have found it necessary to seek advice and information, and are pleased to acknowledge the assistance so readily and cheerfully given by Cressida Annesley (Canterbury Cathedral Archives), Alexandra Berington, Brenda Bolton, Joy Cooper (at Abergwili), John Crook, Alan Crosby, Claire Cross, Alan Foster (at Farnworth), Anne and George Holmes, Doreen Holyoak (at Higham Ferrers), Jeanne and Bruce Males (at Addington), John McManners, Denise Mead (at Croydon), Angela Moore (Flintshire Record Office), Edward Norman, Daniel Rees, Jonathan Riley-Smith, Michael Riordan (St John's College, Oxford), Deborah Saunders (Centre for Kentish Studies) and Richard Sharp. More mundane but no less valuable help has been provided by Sue Corke, Charles Fitzgerald-Lombard, Brenda and Frank Fletcher, Carolyn and Steve Gordon, Marjory Holt and Melissa Mahon. Particular thanks must go to Clare Brown, assistant archivist at Lambeth Palace, for guiding us so skilfully through the resources of Lambeth Palace Library and for introducing us to Archbishop Laud's tortoise. The scale of the present work means that we have inevitably skimmed surfaces, most particularly with regard to those archbishops who doubled up as cardinals and have been treated at greater length in *Princes of the Church*. We hope that the result is sufficient to remind readers of the rich traditions embodied by the archbishop of Canterbury as heir to the monk Dunstan, the reformer Lanfranc, the theologian Anselm, and the martyr Becket, as well as to more recent defenders of ecclesiastical liberties against lay encroachment, episcopacy against Dissent, and Christianity itself against secularism. We are delighted that the weight of so much tradition has not prevented Archbishop Rowan Williams from contributing the foreword to this book.

Stella Fletcher
Dominic Aidan Bellenger

ARCHBISHOPS OF CANTERBURY AND ARCHBISHOPS-ELECT

In most cases the first date refers to the year of consecration or enthronement, rather than that of election. Archbishops-elect appear in italics. Adapted from P. Collinson, N. Ramsay and M. Sparks, *A History of Canterbury Cathedral*, Oxford, 1995, pp. 563–4.

Augustine	597–604x9	Byrhthelm	959
Laurence	604x9–619	Dunstan	959–988
Mellitus	619–624	Æthelgar	988–990
Justus	624x31–653	Sigeric	990–994
Honorius	627x31–653	Ælfric	995–1005
Deusdedit	655–664	Ælfheah (Alphege)	1006–1012
Wigheard	*666/7–668*	Lyfing	1013–1020
Theodore	668–690	Æthelnoth	1020–1038
Berhtwald	692–731	Eadsige	1038–1050
Tatwine	731–734	Robert of Jumièges	1051–1052
Nothhelm	735–739	Stigand	1052–1070
Cuthbert	740–760	Lanfranc	1070–1089
Bregowine	761–764	Anselm	1093–1109
Jænberht	765–792	Ralph d'Escures	1114–1122
Æthelheard	792–805	William of Corbeil	1123–1136
Wulfred	805–832	Theobald	1139–1161
?Feologild	832	Thomas Becket	1162–1170
Ceolnoth	833–870	Richard of Dover	1174–1184
Æthelred	870–888	Baldwin	1185–1190
Plegmund	890–923	*Reginald FitzJocelin*	*1191*
Athelm	923x5–926	Hubert Walter	1193–1205
Wulfhelm	926–941	*Reginald*	*1205–1206*
Oda	941–958	*John de Gray*	*1205–1206*
Ælfsige	*958–959*	Stephen Langton	1207–1228

Walter de Eynesham	*1228–1229*	Thomas Cranmer	1533–1553
Richard le Grant (Wethershed)		Reginald Pole	1556–1558
	1229–1231	Matthew Parker	1559–1575
Ralph Neville	*1231*	Edmund Grindal	1576–1583
John of Sittingbourne	*1232*	John Whitgift	1583–1604
John Blund	*1232*	Richard Bancroft	1604–1610
Edmund Rich (Edmund of Abingdon)		George Abbot	1611–1633
	1234–1240	William Laud	1633–1645
Boniface of Savoy	1245–1270	William Juxon	1660–1663
Adam Chillenden	*1270–1272*	Gilbert Sheldon	1663–1677
Robert Kilwardby	1273–1278	William Sancroft	1678–1690
Robert Burnell	*1278*	John Tillotson	1691–1694
John Pecham	1279–1292	Thomas Tenison	1695–1715
Robert Winchelsey	1294–1313	William Wake	1716–1737
Thomas Cobham	*1313*	John Potter	1737–1747
Walter Reynolds	1313–1327	Thomas Herring	1747–1757
Simon Mepham	1328–1333	Matthew Hutton	1757–1758
John Stratford	1333–1348	Thomas Secker	1758–1768
John Offord	*1348–1349*	Frederick Cornwallis	1768–1783
Thomas Bradwardine	1349	John Moore	1783–1805
Simon Islip	1349–1366	Charles Manners Sutton	1805–1828
Simon Langham	1366–1368	William Howley	1828–1848
William Whittlesey	1368–1374	John Bird Sumner	1848–1862
Simon Sudbury	1375–1381	Charles Thomas Longley	1862–1868
William Courtenay	1381–1396	Archibald Campbell Tait	1868–1882
Thomas Arundel	1396–1397	Edward White Benson	1883–1896
Roger Walden	1397–1399	Frederick Temple	1896–1902
Thomas Arundel (restored)		Randall Thomas Davidson	
	1399–1414		1903–1928
Henry Chichele	1414–1443	Cosmo Gordon Lang	1928–1942
John Stafford	1443–1452	William Temple	1942–1944
John Kemp	1452–1454	Geoffrey Fisher	1945–1961
Thomas Bourchier	1454–1486	Michael Ramsey	1961–1974
John Morton	1486–1500	Donald Coggan	1974–1980
Thomas Langton	*1501*	Robert Runcie	1980–1991
Henry Deane	1501–1503	George Carey	1991–2002
William Warham	1503–1532	Rowan Williams	2002–

INTRODUCTION

They have been reviled and ridiculed, suspended and sequestered, impeached and imprisoned, deprived and degraded, exiled and excommunicated. They have met violent deaths by order of the Crown and of Parliament, and at the hands of revolting peasants, opportunistic knights and drunken Danes. Only the drunken Danes were not even nominally Christians. Apart from the more gory episodes, many archbishops of Canterbury have suffered daily martyrdoms in their witness to the Christian faith, and yet their office has survived – with a break in the mid-seventeenth century – for over 1,400 years. The archbishopric is older than the English nation, let alone the monarchy, and has endured the vicissitudes of both ecclesiastical and secular history. It has survived military and ideological invasions, and revolutions in Church and State. Royal dynasties have come and gone, but the archbishops of Canterbury have been there to crown monarchs, both before and since the creation of the Established Church. Survival was only possible with adaptation to changing circumstances. When status was determined by wealth and ownership of land, the archbishops were important landowners in south-east England, with a string of manors across Kent and Surrey; but when that socio-economic phase passed, they relinquished their estates and received instead a clerical stipend set at a suitably lordly rate. Britain's *ancien régime* came to an orderly conclusion, but the archbishops of Canterbury nevertheless retained their position within the ruling elite. The nature of their jurisdiction – or jurisdictions – has evolved over the centuries and can be charted in the rise and fall of diocesan, provincial and legatine courts. To select just three examples, the Court of Arches[1] survives from the thirteenth century, the Court of Audience disappeared in the seventeenth, and the court of High Commission was created in the aftermath of the sixteenth-century break with Rome, but abolished by the Long Parliament in 1640-1.[2] The geographical area under the archbishop's jurisdiction has also been subject to change: at diocesan level this can be illustrated by the temporary addition of Calais to the Canterbury diocese between 1375 and 1558; at provincial level it can be traced in the threat posed by the short-lived province of Lichfield in the eighth century, and also through the suppression and creation of dioceses on numerous occasions.

The earliest holders of the see of Canterbury were appointed by the pope and travelled to Rome to receive confirmation of that appointment in person. As a symbol of his metropolitan status – exercising authority over the various dioceses of which his province was composed[3] – the archbishop received a pallium from the pope. This circular band of white wool, embroidered with black silk crosses, is worn over liturgical vestments and has pendants hanging to the front and back. In the Anglo-Saxon world, in particular, the pallium was charged with great power. The authority of the pope lay in the bones of Peter, a power extended to the bishop through the pallium. It is placed on or near St Peter's tomb before being conferred, thus bringing the touch of Peter himself and becoming a relic of the apostle. When archbishops of Canterbury ceased to visit the papal court in person, the pallium was sent to them in England. That practice ceased in the sixteenth century, though the symbolic value of the pallium was retained in the Anglican archbishops' coats-of-arms. In pre-Reformation Canterbury the monks of Christ Church formed the cathedral chapter and claimed the right to elect the archbishop, who was their nominal abbot; the bishops of the province of Canterbury also claimed the same right. In practice the monks were bound by the wishes of the king, and were not free to elect anyone until they had obtained from him a *congé d'élire* ('permission to elect'). Freedom of episcopal election from lay involvement was at the head of Magna Carta in 1215, but the assertion of this right had little impact on royal intervention, which itself came into conflict with the pope's claim to provide bishops to vacant sees and not merely confirm capitular elections. The appointment of Archbishop Simon Mepham illustrates the complexity and the length of the process: on 11 December 1327 he was elected by the Canterbury chapter; royal assent was signified on 2 January 1328; papal confirmation followed on 25 May and consecration by Pope John XXII at Avignon on 5 June; the temporalities (estates) of the see were 'restored' to him on 19 June; he was finally enthroned at Canterbury on 22 January 1329. From the death of Archbishop Walter Reynolds on 16 November 1327 the entire process had taken nearly fourteen months.

When, from the sixteenth century onwards, reference was no longer made to Rome the appointment procedure was considerably shortened. In the nineteenth and twentieth centuries it fell to the prime minister to select the bishops of the Church of England.[4] Any number of swift appointments could be cited, but that of John Bird Sumner may be taken as typical: Archbishop William Howley died on 11 February 1848; Lord John Russell selected Sumner, the bishop of Chester, and his appointment was officially confirmed at St Mary-le-Bow on 10 March. Sumner's enthronement at Canterbury followed on 28 April, just eleven weeks after Howley's death. Since 1976 the powers of appointment have been vested in the Crown Appointments Commission and the dynamics of patronage have been replaced by those of bureaucracy. The Vacancy-in-See Commission appoints the four-member Crown Appointments Commission, which shortlists candidates and forwards two names to the prime minister who, in turn, commends one name to the monarch. Only then do the dean and chapter of Canterbury – heirs to the monks of Christ Church – elect the name with which they have been provided. From the announcement in January 2002 of Archbishop George Carey's intention to resign to the enthronement of Archbishop Rowan Williams on 27 February 2003 was a period of over thirteen months: closer to fourteenth- than to nineteenth-century practice.

Although St Augustine of Canterbury enjoyed metropolitan status, received the pallium from Pope Gregory the Great and created suffragan bishops of London and Rochester, the first holder of the see of Canterbury to be styled 'archbishop' was Theodore of Tarsus, nearly a century after Augustine's arrival in Kent in 597. Theodore's successor Berhtwald was the first archbishop of Canterbury to be specifically designated 'primate', which literally means 'holder of the first see' *(prima sedes)*.[5] A primate holds authority not only over the bishops of his own province but also over several provinces and metropolitans, rather like exarchs in the Eastern Church. Primates exist by privilege rather than by right. This ecclesiastical one-upmanship, which acknowledged the archbishop of Lyon as primate of the Gauls, and those of Esztergom and Toledo as primates of Hungary and Spain respectively, has largely dwindled into a matter of historic interest in the Roman Catholic world, leaving concern with the position and powers of primates to the Church of England and the Anglican Communion. As metropolitans of the northern province, the archbishops of York were also primates, and disputes about precedence became a recurring feature of

English church history. One particularly virulent outbreak occurred in the twelfth century between William of Corbeil and Archbishop Thurstan of York, in consequence of which the accord of Winchester (1127) made the subtle distinction between the archbishop of York as 'primate of England' and Canterbury as 'primate of *all* England'. In 1874 there was talk of Archbishop Tait achieving a higher status yet. When the second Lambeth Conference visited Canterbury he addressed the assembled bishops from the throne of St Augustine, the marble chair, and appeared to some as *orbis Britannici Pontifex* or even as *Papa alterius orbis*, a true pope of empire.[6] At the beginning of the twenty-first century, in relation to the question of authority that besets the Church of England and the Anglican Communion, *The Times* can still ask, 'Do Anglicans need a pope?'

One archbishop who rather thought they did was Edward White Benson in the late nineteenth century. However circumscribed his ecclesiastical powers in reality, Benson could be in no doubt of his social standing, as Debrett's *Peerage* assured him that he was

> the first peer of England next to the Royal Family, preceding not only all Dukes, but all the great officers of the Crown. The Bishop of London is his provincial Dean, the Bishop of Lincoln his Chancellor and the Bishop of Rochester his Chaplain. 'It belongs to him to crown the King', and the Sovereign and his or her Consort, wherever they may be located, are *speciales domestici parochiani Arch. Cant.* (parishioners of the Lord Archbishop of Canterbury). The Archbishop is entitled to the prefix of 'Your Grace' and styles himself 'By Divine Providence Lord Archbishop of Canterbury'.[8]

To this admirably clear statement of his position, it may be added that the archbishop is formally addressed as 'The Most Reverend and Right Honourable the Lord Archbishop of Canterbury', a combination that recognises both his clerical status and his position as a peer of the realm. He signs himself 'Cantuar', a shortened form of the Latin for 'Canterbury'.

The primate of all England presides over a Church wedded to the State and exercises a primacy of honour among the leaders of the worldwide Anglican Communion, but he still traces his ecclesiastical ancestry back to St Augustine, the missionary monk sent to bring the English people into the Roman Church at the end of the sixth century. No archbishop was more conscious of this than Matthew Parker, the man appointed in 1559 to put the Elizabethan Settlement into practice. While more zealous reformers sought to sever all connections with anything that smacked of 'popery', Parker emphasised the importance of continuity between the pre- and post-Reformation English Church, and did so through the compilation of a history of the archbishops of Canterbury: *De antiquitate Britannicae ecclesiae et privilegiis ecclesiae Cantuariensis cum archiepiscopus eiusdem* (1572). It is a work of antiquarian scholarship typical of its time and can serve as an English parallel to the lives of popes and cardinals compiled by Girolamo Garimberti and Alfonso Chacón in the same period.[9] Parker followed the story through from St Augustine to his own immediate predecessor, Reginald Pole, and carefully enumerated a total of sixty-nine archbishops. His list does not include Ælfsige and Byrhthelm in the tenth century or Roger Walden in the fourteenth, all of whom are counted in the official Church of England list that makes Rowan Williams the 104th holder of the office.[10] At the same time, Parker does recognise the archbishops-elect Reginald FitzJocelin and John Offord, in the twelfth and fourteenth centuries respectively. These discrepancies almost cancel out one another: if Parker's list is brought up to date, there have been 103 archbishops of Canterbury in total, rather than 104. On the other hand, the number rises to as many as 117 if all the archbishops-elect are included in the calculation; it declines to a maximum of eighty-three for anyone who refuses to recognise Anglican Orders.

Historiographically, Parker's successor was Walter Farquhar Hook, a long-serving vicar of Leeds in the mid-nineteenth century, who took violently against what he regarded as the 'Romish' practices of E.B. Pusey in the neighbouring parish of St Saviour. From 1859 Hook was dean of Chichester and his twelve-volume *Lives of the Archbishops of Canterbury* (1860-76) began to appear the following year. It is a monumental work, with much attention devoted to somewhat surprising details. Hook was a self-confessed enemy of 'Romanism', an admission that must be borne in mind when reading his heavily laboured account. Considerably more accessible is A.E. McKilliam's one-volume history of the archbishops up to Randall Davidson, *A Chronicle of the Archbishops of Canterbury* (1913), replete as it is with anecdotes and biographical details. Edward Carpenter's *Cantuar: the Archbishops in their Office* first appeared in 1971 and has been through three editions, the most recent (1997) with a new introduction and lively additional chapter by Adrian Hastings. Carpenter was a 'modern churchman', dean of Westminster from

1974 to 1985, and the biographer of Archbishop Geoffrey Fisher; Hastings was on the liberal wing of Roman Catholicism. *Cantuar* is heavily weighted towards the Anglican period in the history of the archbishops, which gives the present authors scope to appreciate the pre- and post-Reformation periods as parts of a unified whole. When Carpenter produced his first edition, the Church of England was still bolstered by all the certainties of Establishment. Establishment remains, but in just a generation or so the 'certainties' have effectively disappeared, providing a considerably more challenging environment in which the archbishop of Canterbury endeavours to preach the Christian message of love and forgiveness, hope and reconciliation.

With over a hundred principal players and an extensive supporting cast of popes and monarchs, bishops and nobles, statesmen, families and friends, the present volume cannot provide more than a fairly impressionistic account of each archbishop and his career. Its format does, however, permit the tracing of four intertwined strands through fourteen centuries. The strongest of these, binding together all six chapters, is that provided by the relationship between Church and State, a relationship that began with Augustine's mission to King Æthelberht of Kent in 597. As a single English kingdom evolved, so the primacy of Canterbury became a reality, confirmed by the archbishop's part in the coronation rite. The post-Conquest period, from the time of Lanfranc in the eleventh century to that of Boniface of Savoy in the thirteenth, witnessed the full spectrum of Church-Crown relations. These ranged from Lanfranc's restructuring of the English Church and close co-operation with the Conqueror through to the violent conclusion of Henry II's feud with Thomas Becket. In the period covered by the third chapter, competing papal and royal claims to appoint candidates to vacant benefices were interspersed with bouts of conflict between pope and king over clerical taxation. With the Avignon popes enjoying the support of England's French enemies and the post-Avignon papacy seriously weakened by schism, many of the fourteenth- and fifteenth-century archbishops of Canterbury found it expedient to distance themselves from Rome and become loyal servants of the Crown. Simon Sudbury and Henry Chichele provide prime examples of this policy. Chapter four takes the Canterbury saga from Cardinal Morton in the late fifteenth century to William Laud in the seventeenth; in so doing it seeks to emphasise continuity in the service of the archbishops to the Tudor and early Stuart monarchs, whether or not those monarchs acknowledged papal supremacy. The emergence of the Church of England as the ecclesiastical arm of the State redefined the archbishop's position, so that he became that pillar of the Establishment described in Debrett. During the Anglican centuries there have been differences of opinion over individual pieces of legislation and unimaginative newspaper headlines about 'turbulent priests' speaking out against particular government policies. However, since the restoration of episcopacy in 1660, the most serious breach between the primate and either the Crown or Parliament was as long ago as the deprivation of Archbishop Sancroft in 1690. Royal coats-of-arms displayed prominently in churches continue to provide ample visual evidence of the Church of England's Established status, but of greater relevance in the present context are the pairs of churchwardens' staffs of office found in Anglican parish churches, topped as they are by miniature mitres and crowns.

As references to papal authority indicate, the history of even so English an institution as the Canterbury archbishopric cannot easily be told in isolation from the wider world. Stifling insularity is avoided in the present account by weaving in the second of our four strands, that of the archbishops' international role, whether in the context of pre-Reformation Christendom, post-Reformation imperialism, or in the world of scholarship unconstrained by national boundaries. Scholarship brings us to the third strand, that of literary and material remains: the archbishops as writers, collectors of books, builders and restorers of churches and palaces, and occupants of tombs. In each of these capacities, their contributions must necessarily be accounted for in only the briefest of terms, but their publications and building projects can at least serve as convenient indices of their vision of the Church and understanding of their mission.

The fourth strand deals with the 'anatomy of leadership' and accounts for the experience that individuals brought to the office of archbishop in terms of their geographical and social background, their education and the networks of contacts they acquired prior to holding senior office. For the pre-Conquest period this is more or less confined to a tentative exploration of the monastic world to which so many of the archbishops belonged, even before becoming abbots of Christ Church. Between the eleventh and thirteenth centuries, monastic networks gradually gave way to university ones, based on the Oxford-Paris axis. Oxford remained the intellectual home of the fourteenth- and fifteenth-century primates, among whom there developed a marked consciousness of whether or not they were born into England's ruling elite. The early modern period witnessed the eclipse of the Oxford canon lawyers, the rise to episcopal prominence of Cambridge theologians and then the return of Oxonians with heightened theological awareness, a sequence otherwise known as the English Reformation. Among the post-Restoration archbishops, from Juxon to Howley, university-based networks remained significant, but episcopal careers were in large measure determined by the patronage of the aristocratic elite. Dynasticism of the ecclesiastical variety comes to the fore in the history of the nineteenth- and twentieth-century archbishops of Canterbury, the privileged world of the Taits, Davidsons, Bensons and Temples only gradually giving way to the more suburban milieu of Runcie, Carey and Williams. Archbishop Williams makes headlines as do few other church leaders today, and this presents a useful opportunity to explore and reflect on the careers of his predecessors, the princes and the statesmen, the exiles and the martyrs.

597–1070: CONVERSION AND CONSOLIDATION

Anglo-Saxon England was steadily transformed by the consolidation of its new Christian identity. Opportunities for artistic and technical expression provided by the Church furnished an exquisite series of works of art and maintained a spiritual integrity which defied the Viking raiders and illuminated what was never really such a 'dark' age. At an historical and cultural level, arguably the greatest innovation introduced by Christianity was the art of reading and writing, essential for the dissemination of the Word, and resulting in the production of those written records from which the past may be partially reconstructed. The story these records tell is of an increasingly unified people in which the ecclesiastical structure of metropolitan and bishop gradually encompassed and redrew the frontiers of the highly competitive English kingdoms. The Christian Church created a new national identity and, beyond that, an awakening to an inheritance of faith associated with the Roman Empire and an enticing world of cities and civilisation. The establishment of the see of Canterbury was central to bringing the English people, who lived towards the edge of the known world, into close, creative and lasting relations with the other provinces of Christendom. The Channel was not so much a barrier between England and continental Europe as a means of access to ports which, like all roads, ultimately led to Rome.

Christianity had made its mark in Britain since at least the third century, as can be seen in remaining fragments which incorporate such characteristically Christian images as the *chi-rho* symbol. A Kentish example of this early Christian art can be found in the wall paintings of the Roman villa at Lullingstone near Eynsford. In addition to the archaeological evidence, written records provide tantalising hints at an original diocesan structure from which a delegation of British bishops, those of York, London and

Caerleon-on-Usk, was sent to the Council of Arles in 314, an assembly called by the first Christian emperor, Constantine (d. 337), to counter the Donatist heresy. A century later, in 410, the imperial authorities abdicated responsibility for Britain's defences, leading to the settlement of southern and eastern parts of the island by Angles, Saxons and Jutes from what is now Denmark and northern Germany. Christianity may well have become practically invisible in south-east Britain, but further west the native authorities stabilised their position in the late fifth century and remained in close contact with the Mediterranean world until the middle of the following century. The Celtic Church, for all its cultural singularity, remained thoroughly Roman in creed and origin; it was less an independent phenomenon and more that branch of the Universal Church which happened to exist in Celtic-speaking Britain. Irish monasticism, ascetic and wandering, flourished in the sixth century and, shortly before Augustine's arrival in England, the Hibernian monk Columbanus began his series of great continental monastic foundations, including Luxeuil (590), near Vesoul, and Bobbio (612), some 40 miles inland from Genoa. Among the correspondents of Columbanus was Pope Gregory the Great (590-604).[1]

Pope Gregory is remembered as the apostle of the English and the founder of the archbishopric at Canterbury. Bede celebrated him thus:

> We can and should by rights call him our apostle, for though he held the most important see in the world and was head of churches which had long been converted to the true faith, yet he made our nation, till then enslaved to idols, into a church of Christ, so that we can use the Apostle's words about him: 'If he is not yet an apostle to others, yet at least he is one to us, for we are the seal of his apostleship in the Lord'.[2]

In the wider Church his name became renowned as the last of the four Latin Doctors, joining Ambrose (d. 397), Jerome (d. 420) and Augustine of Hippo (d. 430) as interpreters of the faith. Gregory was born into an aristocratic Roman family with two recent popes as kin. Following a classical education he served for some years (c. 572–4) in the important civic office of *praefectus urbi*, prefect of the city, before rejecting worldly wealth and embracing the monastic life, transforming his residence on Rome's Caelian Hill into a monastery dedicated to the apostle Andrew. The city of Rome was in long-term decline, caused in no small measure by Constantine fixing his capital at

Byzantium – Constantinople – in 330. By Gregory's time imperial rule in Italy was mediated through the exarch of Ravenna, leaving the popes to rule Rome by default. In 579 Gregory was sent to Constantinople by Pope Pelagius II (579–90) as part of a united effort between Rome and Constantinople to counter the encroachment of German Lombard power in Italy. He stayed there until 585 and met Leander of Seville (c. 550–600), whose conversations inspired Gregory's great book of biblical scholarship, the *Moralia*, a commentary on the book of Job. He returned to Rome as secretary to Pope Pelagius and, on his patron's death in 590, was himself elected to the papal office. However great his worldly success and skill in human affairs, Gregory's aspirations remained focused on personal sanctification and citizenship of the heavenly Jerusalem. He was convinced that the day of judgement was close at hand and that, as supreme pontiff, he had an urgent obligation to preach the Gospel to the ends of the world. His surviving writings, which include some 850 letters as well as the *Liber regulae pastoralis (Book of Pastoral Care, c.* 591), written for all those who exercise the cure of souls, are replete with pastoral sensitivity and an awareness of the urgency of the task. It is within this context that the mission to the English makes most sense.

Gregory's first biographer, a monk of Whitby who wrote about a century after the pope's death, was the first to record the story about Gregory encountering the English boys in the Roman slave market. The 'Non Angli, sed angeli' anecdote is also recorded by Bede. Both authors place the incident long before Gregory became pope, suggesting a long gestation for his English mission plan. In 596 he sent a party of forty missionaries from Rome to the court of King Æthelberht of Kent (d. 616x18), where the queen, Bertha, was a great-granddaughter of Clovis (d. 511), the first Christian king of the Franks. As Clovis had been in part converted by his Burgundian wife Clotilde (d. 545), so Bertha and her Frankish chaplain, Bishop Liudhard (d. c. 603), were harbingers of Christianity in Kent. Thus 'an English king who wanted to become a Christian and a pope with an overwhelming desire to save the world' became linked through 'the Frankish royal court, provider of information and later, through the bishops, of practical help' for the nascent English Church.[3]

Gregory's chosen instrument was Augustine, a Roman monk who was serving in 596 as prior of Gregory's monastery in Rome. Little is known about his background or personality other than Gregory's commendation of his knowledge of Scripture in a letter of 601 to Æthelberht and the evidence of some understandable faintheartedness in responding to Gregory's invitation to embark on such an ambitious mission. As Bede relates, Augustine landed in Thanet, that portion of north-east Kent separated from the rest by the River Stour (or 'Wantsum', as Bede names it), and sought out Æthelberht, whose capital was at Canterbury, formerly the Roman town of Durovernum Cantiacorum. Canterbury had been deserted in the fifth century, but began to function again as an urban centre in the sixth and seventh centuries. When Augustine arrived its most conspicuous building was the Roman theatre, an eminently suitable tribal meeting-place. Æthelberht's Kentish kingdom was enjoying a temporary pre-eminence in Britain for, in spite of being one of the smaller tribal realms, Æthelberht exercised some measure of overlordship over the other kingdoms south of the Humber. Kent also enjoyed a gateway status, exploiting the trade routes that ran to London from the French and Frisian ports. In the encounter between Augustine and the Kentish king, the conversion of Æthelberht himself was crucial: 'if the conversion of the king could be secured, then that of his nobility and their retainers was virtually assured'.[4] This objective had been achieved by 601, in which year Gregory dispatched a supplementary group of missionaries led by Abbot Mellitus and including Paulinus, the future bishop of York.

Augustine's success in converting Æthelberht did not help him in his attempt to come to terms with the existing Christian priests and people in Britain. The missionary's agenda contained efforts to restore a lost province to the Roman Church and to build in England a new Rome. Gregory flattered Æthelberht in his letters, casting him as a new Constantine and Bertha as a new Helena. Canterbury, barbaric and dilapidated, slowly came back to life, transforming itself (in Bede's rather overstated phrase) 'into the metropolis of [Æthelberht's] empire'. Royal power and influence duly ensured that Christianity gradually permeated northwards from Canterbury with new bishoprics at Rochester and London (from 604) forming the nucleus of an expanding Church. Mellitus was the first bishop of London and another Roman missionary, Justus, that of Rochester. Gregory the Great planned his English Church with twin metropolitan centres at London and York, cities which had gained distinction as centres of Roman civic government and military organisation respectively, and which remained strategically important. There were to be twelve bishoprics in each of the two provinces. Augustine himself failed even to reach London and the patronage of Æthelberht ensured that Canterbury duly became England's ecclesiastical centre.

The Anglo-Saxon centuries are represented in Canterbury's archaeological record by a deep layer of dark earth. While Roman stone structures, not least the city walls, survived, the wooden buildings of the Anglo-Saxon period have not. The street pattern, on the other hand, is almost entirely Anglo-Saxon, the Roman gridiron having been rejected. Within the walls, in the north-east quarter of the city, Æthelberht provided an existing church for Augustine's use. This became Augustine's cathedral, served by monks and dedicated to the Holy Saviour, Our Lord and God, Jesus Christ. Its dedication as Christ Church has survived throughout its entire history. As adapted by Augustine, it is thought to have been a building of simple design, consisting of a nave and apsidal sanctuary.[5] Close to Christ Church but outside the city wall, lay the land donated by Æthelberht for a second monastic foundation, dedicated to Sts Peter and Paul, the patrons of Rome, reminding us of the pleasure Bede expressed when he noted how closely Canterbury's customs accorded with those of Rome. This second foundation later became St Augustine's Abbey, named in honour of its founder, and was designed to act as a mausoleum for both kings and archbishops. Royal mausolea provided architectural opportunities for dynastic display and, in the case of Christian monarchs, for clear affirmations of their commitment to Christianity. The burial church endowed by Clovis outside the walls of Paris was a case in point. Reflecting the dual significance of Christ Church as *locus* of the archiepiscopal *cathedra* and St Augustine's as the burial place of canonised archbishops, the hagiographer Goscelin of Saint-Bertin (d. after 1107) stated 'there he rules, here he dwells'. St Augustine's, thoroughly ruined at the Dissolution, has been excavated to reveal the various levels of its building from the seventh century onwards. The first burial places of the kings and early archbishops are visible and marked. The new shrine area, where Augustine and his successors were translated in 1091, has entirely disappeared. Within a century of the twin foundations, though, the seeds were sown of centuries-long discord between the archbishop, who was effectively abbot of Christ Church, and the community at St Augustine's, for a papal privilege granted by Pope Agatho (678–81) gave the monks of St Augustine's exemption from all but papal authority and the freedom to elect their own abbot. At the time it seemed like an honour for a singularly successful monastery, but the long-term consequence was to create a monastery exempt from the archbishop's jurisdiction just yards from his own cathedral.

Augustine's English career was relatively brief, for he died between 604 and 609, but it established the themes which can be traced through the lives of his successors up to the Norman Conquest. At the most fundamental level, the archbishops' position was firmly tied to the fluctuating fortunes of the English kings and kingdoms. External forces were highly varied, ranging from the devastation caused by Viking raiders to the considerably more benign influence of the distant popes, without whose confirmation an archbishop-elect could not exercise authority. Even in Augustine's lifetime, the foundations of an English episcopal framework were laid; the evolution of that episcopal system can be traced through the careers of his successors. At its heart lay the city of Canterbury and its two great monastic houses, with both of which the archbishops remained intimately connected. Like Augustine, many of the archbishops were themselves monks and their careers cast important light on the nature of English monastic history. First, though, something must be said about the relatively limited number of written sources through which each of these threads can be traced.

The first nine holders of the see of Canterbury – from Augustine to the election of Tatwine – together with its first unconfirmed and unconsecrated archbishop-elect, Wigheard, were memorialised by Bede the Venerable. The archbishops' modern historian is inevitably struck by the contrast between the thoroughness of Bede's coverage of the 130 years or so after the arrival of Augustine in Canterbury and the relative paucity of information about the archbishops who lived during the following two centuries. It is only post-Bede that serious doubts arise about the identities of the archbishops and their personal histories. Bede was an early member of the Wearmouth monastery founded in 674 by Benedict Biscop and subsequently, from 682, a founder member of Biscop's house at Jarrow. While his mental world was seemingly boundless, his relatively limited physical travels took him only as far as York. Biscop, by contrast, was an inveterate traveller, visiting Rome five times, and it was his library that made possible Bede's *Historia ecclesiastica gentis Anglorum* (completed 731). For Canterbury material he owed most to Albinus, abbot of Sts Peter and Paul (St Augustine's), his 'principal authority and helper, a man of universal learning' (like Bede himself) who collated the Canterbury sources and was very helpful on Roman documentation. Although Bede's narrative provides much of our information about the English Church of his time, his native Northumbria inevitably emerges in sharper focus. Similarly, although Gregory the Great in distant Rome is presented as the hero of the second book of the *Ecclesiastical History*, Robert Markus reminds us that Bede's writings, with their strong emphasis on wonders and miracle stories, display 'an emblematic picture of the tensions between the continental model of the Christian Church, organised on a territorial basis with bishops in charge of dioceses, and a British model, monastic and charismatic in its emphasis.'[6]

The miraculous was indeed central to the history of the early archbishops of Canterbury, all of whom attracted cults based on their tombs. It was only with the confused conditions of the ninth century that these localised cults grew more obscure and that it became an option for an archbishop *not* to be recognised as a saint. In the centuries after Bede, the tradition of writing saints' lives, and even of setting them in their historical context, was not quite lost, but the disappearance of libraries and the secularisation of property which followed the Viking raids made it a tenuous line of literary descent. The *Anglo-Saxon Chronicle*, the single most important source for the history of England in that period, provides some chronological framework, but it was not until the eleventh century that the archbishops of Canterbury received more detailed biographical attention. The Latin lives of the monastic reformers like Dunstan, whose life was recorded by 'B' and Adalhard, were supplemented by a group of writers who breathed new life into the great men of Canterbury. Goscelin began his monastic life in the Benedictine house of Saint-Bertin at Saint-Omer, but travelled in southern and central England from 1058 and settled at St Augustine's, Canterbury, from 1090. Goscelin was a skilled hagiographer and a passionate defender of Canterbury's authority over York, which had had its own archbishop since 735. Osbern (d. *c.* 1072) produced accessible lives of Archbishops Ælfheah (Alphege) and Dunstan. Although most directly associated with the epoch-making life of his contemporary Anselm, Eadmer (d. *c.* 1128) also wrote widely on the English saints. William of Malmesbury (d. *c.* 1143) was the author of important histories of the English nation and the English Church, and neglected no opportunity to discuss the native saints or to further their cults.

Augustine's four immediate successors were not only buried in what became St Augustine's and honoured as saints; they were all Italian monks who arrived in England in the missionary waves of 597 and 601. Laurence had been sent back to Rome as Augustine's intermediary, but returned to England in time to be named by Augustine as his successor. Bede passes sketchily over the pontificate of Laurence until the death of King Æthelberht in 616 or 618 and the succession of the pagan Eadbald. An anti-Christian reaction overwhelmed the fledgling Church. Bishops Mellitus of London and Justus of Rochester fled into exile and Laurence was on the verge of following their example when he saw himself in a dream being flogged by St Peter for his cowardice and resolved to stay in Kent. According to Bede, the crisis soon passed and Eadbald converted to Christianity. The miraculous looms no less large in the Northumbrian's coverage of the five-year pontificate of Mellitus, who came to the primacy with missionary experience among the East Saxons of his London diocese and diplomatic experience as Laurence's envoy to Rome. Bede prefers to concentrate on the story of how a devastating fire spread through the city of Canterbury and raged close to the church of the Four Crowned Martyrs. Mellitus was old and infirm but requested his attendants to carry him to this place, where he prayed that the city might be delivered from the flames. The wind thereupon changed direction and the conflagration was quelled. Justus (d. 627), the fourth archbishop of Canterbury, had been bishop of Rochester since 604, so clearly ranked next to Mellitus in seniority. Although the date has been disputed, the consecration of their missionary colleague Paulinus as bishop of York has traditionally been placed in 625, making it likely that Justus was his consecrator and therefore the episcopal godfather of the Northumbrian Church. When Justus died in 627, Paulinus was left as the only bishop in the whole of England. It therefore fell to him to consecrate Honorius (d. 653), another of Gregory's Roman monks, as the fifth archbishop of Canterbury.

Bede's attention was understandably distracted from Canterbury by the baptism of King Edwin (d. 633) of Northumbria at Easter 627, a somewhat delayed consequence of his marriage with the Christian princess Æthelberga of Kent (d. 675). Northumbria had become a single kingdom with the coalition of the rivals Deira (between the Humber and the Tees) and Bernicia (between the Tees and the Firth of Forth). It reached the peak of its power in the middle of the seventh century under Edwin and his nephew Oswy (d. 670). The only power they could not vanquish was that of Mercia, under the leadership of King Penda (d. 655). Although Bede insists that Penda was not overtly hostile towards Christianity, which was accepted by his son Paeda as a condition of marriage with a Northumbrian princess, it was only after Penda's death that the Mercians embraced the Christian faith. While Northumbria experienced a monastic and cultural golden age in the seventh and eighth centuries, epitomised by the Lindisfarne Gospels (c. 696–8), Mercia was militarily ascendant. By c. 800 the Mercian kingdom controlled not only the whole of central England as far as Offa's Dyke to the west and a line between the Mersey and the Humber to the north, but also the former kingdoms of the East Angles, East Saxons, South Saxons and Kent. The death of Æthelred II in 762 and the short reign of Eadberht II marked the effective end of the Kentish ruling dynasty and the Mercian king Offa (d. 796) was in control of the former kingdom by 765. Mercian supremacy was short-lived and Kent was annexed by the next ascendant kingdom, Wessex, in *c*. 825. The archbishops of Canterbury worked with whichever power happened to be dominant in the region: they were all Christian. The Norwegian Vikings, on the other hand, did not accept Christianity until the tenth century and began raiding towns and monasteries along the British coast from 793 onwards. The Danes were still largely pagan until the later ninth century and were predominant in raids on the coastline of eastern England. Canterbury was sacked in *c*. 851. Northumbria, East Anglia and a large part of Mercia fell to the Scandinavian invaders. By 876 York had become the capital of a Danish kingdom, covering most of Deira, while Bernicia remained in native hands with Bamburgh as its capital. The West Saxons, led by Alfred the Great from 871 until his death in 899, put up tougher resistance, preventing the complete conquest of the island and laying the foundations for the united kingdom of the English. The defeat of Erik Bloodaxe in 954 marked the expulsion of the invaders from Deira, Lindsey and East Anglia, though Viking raids and widespread disorder resumed later in the century. Edgar of Mercia and Northumbria became the first king of a united English kingdom in 959. For a while, tenth-century Canterbury ceased to be vulnerable to attack and benefited from the relative stability of Anglo-Saxon government, while the archbishops could concentrate on their pastoral commitments. The Danes returned and duly invaded most of England, Cnut the Great (d. 1035) incorporating it into his short-lived empire around the shores of the North Sea. This time, the invaders were fellow Christians, just as they were in 1066, after the reign of the English king Edward the Confessor.

When the ecclesiastical map of southern Britain is superimposed on that of the fluctuating native kingdoms and the waves of invaders and settlers from overseas, the role of the archbishops of Canterbury naturally appears to be more prominent. In the seventh century it was Honorius who sent the Burgundian missionary Felix (d. 647) to convert the East Angles and become their bishop. His see was fixed on the coast at Dunwich, which remained a bishopric until the late ninth century. Honorius was less involved in the evangelisation of the West Saxons, which was entrusted to Birinus by Pope Honorius I (625–38). In 634 Birinus established his *cathedra* at Dorchester-on-Thames, near Oxford, but Wessex soon acquired bishops at Winchester (from 660) and Sherborne (*c.* 705), and Dorchester fell under Mercian rule. In 644 Archbishop Honorius made English ecclesiastical history by consecrating Ithamar as bishop of Rochester, the first native Englishman to attain episcopal status. The first English archbishop of Canterbury was Honorius's immediate successor, a West Saxon called Frithowine or Frithona, who took the name Deusdedit and was consecrated by Ithamar on 12 March 655. The events of Deusdedit's pontificate are largely obscured by the prominence accorded by Bede to the Synod of Whitby, summoned by King Oswy of Northumbria in 664 to iron out the discrepancies between the Celtic practices emanating from Ireland and Iona, on the one hand, and those of Rome, which reached his realm via Canterbury and York, on the other. The 'Roman' delegation was led by Bishop Agilbert of Wessex and Abbot Wilfrid (d. 709) of Ripon, rather than a direct representative of Canterbury, but it nevertheless persuaded Oswy to choose Roman practices, most notably the dating of Easter, over those of the marginalised Celtic Church.[7] Wilfrid's reward was the bishopric of York, his consecration taking place in Frankish territory and by Frankish bishops because he considered the Celtic bishops to be in schism.

Deusdedit died soon after the synod, but a potential successor could not be found for some time. The chosen candidate was Wigheard, a monk of Christ Church, Canterbury. Bede relates that the kings of Northumbria and Kent jointly decided to send Wigheard to Rome to receive consecration from the pope, though the delay and the Roman mission also suggest that Wigheard's position among his fellow bishops may not have been too secure. Wigheard died in Rome and Pope Vitalian (657–72) selected his replacement. The pope's first choice was Hadrian the African, an abbot in Italy and a scholar celebrated for his knowledge of monastic and church discipline. Hadrian rejected the offer but recommended instead Theodore of Tarsus, a Greek monk of relatively advanced years. It was 669 before Theodore reached England, where he found the Church in need of effective leadership, not least because plague had removed a number of bishops. Never before had Canterbury experienced so protracted a vacancy. Although aged sixty-five at the time of his appointment, Theodore proved to be an energetic and far-sighted prelate, whose activities are known to us from Bede. He began with a thorough visitation designed to sort out anomalies. By 672 a sufficient degree of order had been restored for Theodore to call and preside over the first general synod of the English Church. As if to underline the geographical inconvenience of Canterbury for anything but access to the coast, this was held at Hertford on 24 September 672 or 673. This was not only the first all-English ecclesiastical council; it was the first all-English assembly of any kind. Theodore's main task was to secure geographically fixed sees for the English tribal kingdoms, whose borders fluctuated under political pressure. It was agreed that bishops should not intervene in the affairs of other dioceses and an order of precedence among bishops, based on practice found elsewhere in the Church, was established. York was not yet a separate province, so Theodore was perfectly able to interfere in its affairs, dividing it into three dioceses and incurring the ire of Bishop Wilfrid, who went to Rome to appeal to the pope. To ensure the continuity of synodical practice, provision was made for further councils to be held at an intriguingly unidentifiable place called Clovesho (or Clofesho), somewhere in the Mercian sphere of influence. Another council certainly met at Hatfield in 679, but that was concerned with doctrinal matters and declared its rejection of the short-lived Monothelite heresy. Theodore has sometimes been credited with too much – the creation of the parish system as we now know it, for example – but his quest for unification of the disparate elements of the English Church was so successful that Bede was able to conclude that 'the English churches made more spiritual progress during his archbishopric than ever before'.

After a two-year vacancy, Theodore found a worthy successor in Berhtwald, abbot of Reculver on the north Kent coast, who was elected as archbishop on 1 July 692. He was consecrated at Lyon in 693 and went on to receive the pallium from Pope Sergius I. Berhtwald remained on good terms with King Withred, who reigned from 691 to 725. This gave him a secure power base from which to put Archbishop Theodore's vision of the Church into practice. Berhtwald himself enjoyed considerable respect and, like Theodore, was accorded such titles as 'archbishop of the whole of Britain'. Canterbury's role as head of the English Church was being gradually enhanced, but it came at a price, and that price was paid by Bishop Wilfrid of York, a man of great ability and a clear rival of Berhtwald for the Canterbury see. 'As an apostolic pioneer, a monastic founder, a builder of churches and patron of art, and as a person of remarkable fortitude and persistence, inspired by grandiose ideals and imaginative vision, [Wilfrid] deserves to be considered one of the most important men of the Old English Church.'[8] When Wilfrid left York after disagreements with the Northumbrian king, Berhtwald decreed that the bishop should retire. A second time Wilfrid took himself and his case to Rome; a second time the pope declared in his favour. After decades of hostility with his archbishops, Wilfrid finally accepted a form of retirement in his monastery at Ripon.

Tatwine and Nothhelm, Berhtwald's two immediate successors, seem to have been appointed under the influence of the newly dominant kingdom of Mercia. Tatwine was a Mercian monk and Nothhelm a priest of London. Mercian influence might also be detected behind the election of Cuthbert in 740 for, although he was a monk of Lyminge in Kent, it seems that he was possibly bishop of Hereford, on the very edge of Mercian territory, from 736. No less doubt hangs over the figure of Archbishop Bregowine, who is said to have originated in Saxony and travelled to Canterbury to study at the school founded by Theodore and Hadrian. By way of contrast, the next archbishop – Jænberht – was certainly of Kentish origin and served the Church as abbot of St Augustine's, Canterbury. It was that strong regional identity that defined Jænberht's opposition to Mercian dominance and was reflected in Offa's brief loss of control over Kent after the battle of Otford in 776. In spite of this, Offa exercised a greater influence over the English Church than did the archbishop. As the reputed founder of abbeys as far apart as Bath and St Albans – the latter in an effort to atone for the murder of King Æthelberht of the East Saxons in 794 – Offa had as great an impact on the ecclesiastical map of England as he did on the political one, and never more so than in 787 when he created a short-lived third English province, York having become a province fifty-two years earlier. Offa's province was based at Lichfield, in the Mercian heartland, and consisted of the sees of Dunwich and Elmham in East Anglia, Hereford, Leicester, Lichfield, Lindsey and Worcester. This was a personal snub to Jænberht, whose reduced Canterbury province was left with the suffragan bishoprics of London, Rochester, Selsey, Sherborne and Winchester.[9] This division was determined at the 'contentious synod' of Chelsea, which also decided in favour of the first English consecration of a king, that of Offa's son and heir Ecgfrith (d. 796), probably by the Mercian bishop Hygeberht. Again, Jænberht was sidelined.

The pontificates of Æthelheard (792–805) and Wulfred (805–32) were full of incident. Abbot Æthelheard (possibly of Lydd or of Louth in Lindsey), seems to have been a protégé of Offa, resented in Kent and not consecrated until two years after his appointment. On Offa's death in 796 Mercian hegemony was dissolved, Eadberht Præn led a Kentish revolt, and Æthelheard was forced into temporary exile. Plans to make London the metropolitan see of southern England would have resolved the rivalry between Kent and Mercia for control of the Church, but they were not given papal approval and Æthelheard, re-installed in his cathedral city in 798, urged all his fellow bishops to look to Canterbury, 'where, by the direction of the blessed Gregory the order of ecclesiastical office is administered to us all'.[10] With the exception of Gilbert Foliot's attempt to further London's archiepiscopal claims at the height of the Becket crisis, Canterbury's metropolitan authority was never seriously threatened and the Mercians' attempt to reconstruct the English Church in their own political image floundered, the province of Lichfield being suppressed in 803. Wulfred served as Æthelheard's archdeacon at Canterbury and was chosen to succeed him, probably the first member of the Christ Church community to be elevated to the archbishopric since Wigheard in the 660s. It is with Wulfred that the extent and significance of the archiepiscopal estates in south-eastern England begin to come into focus. Perhaps most significantly, he acquired from the abbess of Minster-in-Thanet an important estate at Harrow in Middlesex. By such means were laid the foundations of one of the richest medieval bishoprics in the whole of Christendom. Wulfred sought to secure the financial future of both the archbishopric and the monastic communities of Christ Church and St Augustine's. All three institutions thus gained a greater measure of financial independence, which aroused royal resentment, but at the same time cushioned them from such hostility. Wulfred took his cue from Rome, which was then insisting on the strengthening of espiscopal power and ecclesiastical exemption from lay ownership and lay control. At the 816 Synod of Chelsea, Wulfred reminded his bishops that they had the power to choose abbots and abbesses in their dioceses without royal or noble interference. It made for uneasy relations with King Cenwulf of Mercia (d. 821), but Wulfred weathered this and adapted the more easily to West Saxon domination over Kent from c. 825. Obscurity reigns over the identity of Wulfred's short-lived successor. Even his name is in doubt: some sources suggest Suithred, others Feologild. Perhaps there was a disputed election.

From his election in 833 to his death in 870, Ceolnoth's Canterbury pontificate was the longest yet. It also witnessed fewer disputes with the lay powers because Ceolnoth recognised the need to maintain good relations with the kingdom of Wessex, while steadily edging away from the declining power of the Mercian kings. It was during his time that the Viking sack of Canterbury took place. Like Ceolnoth, Archbishop Æthelred may have been a Christ Church monk, though later monastic chronicles were too ready to identify men as monks on little or no evidence. The Viking assaults continued into the time of Archbishop Plegmund (890–914), who may have been of Mercian origin (it is argued that the hamlet of Plemstall in Cheshire means 'holy place of Plegmund') but owed his rise to being one of the scholars attracted to the court of King Alfred of Wessex. Plegmund worked closely with Alfred, not least in connection with the erudite king's English translation of Gregory the Great's *Liber regulae pastoralis*, but perhaps most significantly in the administrative restructuring of the southern kingdom in response to the Viking attacks. A new emphasis on easily defended urban centres presented valuable opportunities for the Church and, in 898, Plegmund and Alfred were both in London for the creation of the new borough. In *c.* 909 Plegmund divided the Wessex dioceses of Winchester and Sherborne into five: Crediton, Ramsbury, Sherborne, Wells and Winchester, Alfred's capital. This rearrangement has survived with remarkably little change: in 1050 the south-western see was transferred from Crediton to a safer location at Exeter; Ramsbury was united with Sherborne in 1058, and that in turn was transferred to Old Sarum in 1075.

Archbishops Athelm and Wulfhelm reinforced Canterbury's identification with Wessex, for both were bishops of Wells who had been translated to the archbishopric. For two centuries (if the curious case of Cuthbert as bishop of Hereford is discounted) the English Church had observed the ruling of the Council of Nicaea that bishops could not be translated from one see to another. In reality this practice increased, so it became all the more incumbent upon the archbishops to travel to Rome and receive the pallium in person. When a more or less united English kingdom emerged under King Athelstan (d. 939), the powers and position of the archbishops of Canterbury were subject to significant redefinition. They lost the right to mint their own coins, and became closely linked to the ruling dynasty through the anointing of kings in increasingly elaborate rites and through attendance at the annual *witan* or national assembly. Wulfhelm's successor, Oda (d. 958), was promoted from the see of Ramsbury and served as trusted counsellor of Kings Athelstan, Edmund (d. 946) and Eadred (d. 955). Oda was an East Anglian of Danish parentage and a convert to Christianity. After Oda's death Ælfsige did not get beyond the status of archbishop-elect, and Archbishop Byrhthelm also died before the year was out. A crisis in the upper echelons of the English Church is also apparent in the rapid promotion of Dunstan to Worcester in 957, London in 959 and Canterbury in 560, in succession to Byrhthelm. All these promotions came courtesy of the patronage of King Edgar (d. 975).

Dunstan (d. 988) was one of the outstanding archbishops of Canterbury and was perhaps the first to hold the office whose biography and personality can be traced with any precision. He was born at Baltonsborough, near Glastonbury, and was of noble birth. Educated at Glastonbury Abbey, he joined the household of his uncle, Archbishop Athelm. He moved to the court of Athelstan and seemed destined for a successful and eminently forgettable worldly career. A little on the wild side, perhaps, he was expelled from court in 935, but then changed direction, took private monastic vows and was ordained priest on the same day as his friend Æthelwold (d. 984), later bishop of Winchester. Dunstan began his religious life as hermit-craftsman in Glastonbury, where he worked on painting, embroidery and metalwork. Later he was sometimes shown holding the devil by the nose with a pair of tongs which he had made. King Edmund (d. 946) recalled Dunstan to the active life and made him abbot of Glastonbury, where both Edmund and his successor Eadred were duly buried. Dunstan enjoyed positive relationships with all the kings of his time, but the most mutually beneficial was that with Edgar, who collaborated in Dunstan's reforms of the English Church and at whose 'imperial' coronation at Bath in 973 Dunstan and Archbishop Oswald of York jointly officiated. Dunstan inspired many of England's laws and even with the anti-monarchic reaction which set in following the death in 978 of Edgar's son, Edward, Dunstan's protégé, and the accession of King Æthelred 'the Unready' (d. 1016), the archbishop continued to exercise quiet authority.

Dunstan's two immediate successors are relatively obscure figures, although both came from his monastic circle and were monks of Glastonbury, at that time England's richest and most splendid religious house. The first, Æthelgar, made his way eastwards to Canterbury in the course of his career, via Winchester, where he was a member of Æthelwold's circle, and as bishop of Selsey from 980. He received the pallium in Rome but little is recorded of his fifteen-month pontificate. Sigeric was abbot of St Augustine's, Canterbury, by 975 and bishop of Ramsbury by 986. Sigeric's journey to and from Rome to receive the pallium was recorded in detail and could easily form the basis for a guide to the tenth-century monastic landscape. On the return journey he passed through Sutri, Viterbo, Siena and Lucca, reaching the Po at

Piacenza in thirty-eight stages. He then passed through Pavia, where St Augustine of Hippo and the philosopher Boethius (d. *c.* 524) are buried in the church of S. Pietro in Ciel d'Oro, and on to Vercelli and Aosta, and crossed the Alps via the Great St Bernard pass. Beyond the Alps, Sigeric's itinerary took him to Lausanne, Besançon, Reims and Laon, and he finally embarked for England at the Channel port of Wissant.[11] This odyssey complete, Sigeric's pontificate is notable for the resumption of Viking raids on Kent and other English coastal regions.

Kent having been reduced from a kingdom to an earldom, Sigeric's successor, Archbishop Ælfric, was the son of an earl of Kent. He had been a monk of Abingdon and a reforming abbot of St Albans before his consecration as bishop of Ramsbury. There were only nine diocesan bishops of Ramsbury, three of whom were translated to Canterbury, a proportion which no other see comes close to rivalling. Of the next archbishop, Ælfheah (alternatively known as Alphege), considerably more has been recorded. This is accounted for by the circumstances of his death, owing to which he became of interest to hagiographers who probably embroidered facts and filled in missing details. Ælfheah was a monk of Deerhurst and lived as a solitary before being appointed abbot of Bath by Archbishop Dunstan. He succeeded Æthelwold as bishop of Winchester in 984 and Ælfric as archbishop of Canterbury in 1005. Between 991 and 1016 there were eight significant Danish raids in southern England. In 994 Sigeric saved his cathedral church from destruction by borrowing money to buy off the invaders. In 1011 the invaders were in less compromising mood, sacking the cathedral and taking Archbishop Ælfheah hostage. A vast ransom of £3,000 was demanded, but Ælfheah refused to allow this exorbitant sum to be levied on his people and thus he was killed at Greenwich on the site, it is said, of the present church of St Alphege. The lives of Canterbury's first martyred archbishop relate that he was the victim of a drunken feast; his murderers attacked him with the bones of oxen before an axeman delivered the final merciful blow. Ælfheah became both a saint and a national hero. His cult stalled at the Conquest, but Anselm considered him a true martyr, a martyr for justice rather as John the Baptist was a martyr for truth. In 1105 it was discovered that his body was incorrupt and in 1170, as he faced his own martyrdom, Thomas Becket commended himself to God and St Alphege. Thereafter, Becket's own cult overshadowed that of his murdered predecessor.

There followed a year's vacancy, after which another Dunstanian monk was selected for Canterbury. This was Lyfing (or Elfstan), abbot of Chertsey and bishop of Wells. After an unsteady start during what remained of Æthelred's reign and the brief reign of Edmund Ironside, from 1016 Lyfing found a useful ally in Cnut, who needed the Church to give his barbarian roughness a religious validation. He was crowned and anointed by Lyfing. Æthelnoth, archbishop from 1020 until his death in 1038, continued to benefit from Cnut's patronage. As a reflection of Cnut's importance in northern Europe as a whole, Æthelnoth was grandly received by Pope Benedict VIII (1012–24) when he went to Rome to receive his pallium. During the pontificate of Pope John XIX (1024–32), Cnut cemented the relationship between Rome and England by making a personal pilgrimage to Rome.

The last three archbishops before the Norman Conquest – Eadsige, Robert of Jumièges and Stigand – were less distinguished or less lucky men. Eadsige, a secular clerk and a protégé of Cnut, became a monk in order to ease his eventual appointment to Canterbury and was appointed as an effective coadjutor to Æthelnoth. His position was threatened by the death of Cnut in 1035 before he assumed office and by the fact that, between 1035 and 1066, English politics centred on the fortunes of the families of the three earls whom Cnut had left to govern his kingdom during his absences. As leader of the English Church and customary consecrator of the monarch, the archbishop of Canterbury could hardly avoid becoming involved in the power struggle between them. Eadsige's ill-health led him to appoint an Abingdon monk, Siward, as his coadjutor, but Siward predeceased him. Edward the Confessor, king from 1042, favoured Norman appointments and overruled the Christ Church choice of a monk and kinsman of the Earl Godwin, heir to the childless king, instead appointing Robert of Jumièges as the new archbishop: 'The Metropolitan see had in fact become a political football in the wider contest for the English throne.'[12] Robert of Jumièges, formerly prior of Saint-Ouen at Rouen and abbot of Jumièges in Normandy, was made bishop of London in 1044. Hardly had Robert been appointed than Earl Godwin and his sons were exiled and the duke of Normandy recognised as heir to the English throne. Just months later, in 1052, fortunes were reversed: Godwin was back in England, Robert was exiled and Stigand became archbishop in his stead. Historians came to regard Robert as Edward the Confessor's evil genius and the ambiguities of the king himself, canonised and entombed at Westminster Abbey, are important in understanding the chaos of the pre-Conquest years. Frank Barlow, a writer always sympathetic to the Anglo-Saxon point of view, characterised the Confessor thus:

> Impressed and formed by his long exile, simple in his habits, rustic in his pleasures, kind and, up to a point, loyal to his friends, martial in temper, terrible in his anger, easily vindictive, rash and passionate when his interest was aroused or his interests involved, sometimes capable of manipulating forces, sometimes if not patient at least long-suffering, mindful of his father's fate, without great aims or noble intentions, without real ambition . . . inclined to rely on others. . . . The English Church was ruled by the king but to little purpose and to no true ecclesiastical end.[13]

The reputation of Stigand, the last pre-Conquest archbishop of Canterbury, was damaged both by his chronological proximity to the reformer Lanfranc and the saintly Anselm and by Anglo-Norman hagiographers who saw him as the personification of the weakness of the Anglo-Saxon Church. The English Church under Edward the Confessor was not without good bishops but Stigand's leadership, administratively competent as it might have been, lacked moral authority. He was probably an East Anglian of Scandinavian descent (his name is Old Norse) and he emerged in the reign of Cnut as an astutely political secular clerk. He was bishop of Elmham by 1043 and of Winchester, already the richest of the English sees, by 1047. Following the deposition of Robert of Jumièges, he created a dangerous innovation by accepting Canterbury in plurality with Winchester and compounded his difficulties by receiving the pallium from the schismatic 'Benedict X' (anti-pope 1058–9). Though both Winchester and Canterbury were monastic sees, Stigand was no monk. He remained a pluralist and a worldling until his removal from office in 1070. Indeed, by the mid-eleventh century the archbishopric had acquired a considerable number of lucrative estates in south-eastern England, making it particularly attractive to a man of Stigand's acquisitive nature. Among the richest of these estates were Aldington and Chartham in Kent, Harrow and Hayes in Middlesex, Croydon and Mortlake in Surrey, and South Malling in Sussex. Reconstructing the development of this endowment, by means of charter evidence of varying reliability, is not easy, but F.R.H. Du Boulay suggests that, by the time of the Conquest, the archbishopric had an endowment 'great even by comparison with Continental church lordships'.[14] In addition, Stigand also acquired personal properties in his native East Anglia and in Gloucestershire. It can be argued that Stigand was a spokesman for the Anglo-Saxon cause, but he was first and foremost a self-seeker. There is a ring of truth about the story of Stigand ingratiating himself with Edward the Confessor's heir, Harold Godwinson instead of ministering to the dying king who had, in any case, never trusted the man he regarded as a usurper. Stigand accumulated much wealth and Gervase of Canterbury recorded how, after his death, a small key was discovered on his body which opened a vault full of treasure. He was a great patron of the arts and of church fittings in particular, but no one took him for a holy man. Attempts to portray him as a patriotic hero, hiding in the fens with Hereward the Wake, are as fanciful as the later excessive accounts of his infamy.[15] The fact that he crowned Harold – and appears by name and portrait on the Bayeux Tapestry – was enough to undo him in the eyes of the new regime. William the Conqueror was crowned by Archbishop Aldred of York. The new king tolerated Stigand until 1070, when he was brought before a council at Winchester and deprived of both his sees. He was kept in custody at Winchester until his ignominious death two years later.

Stigand's sad end was an unfortunate coda to a crucial period in the history of the Canterbury archbishopric, an era of saints and reformers inspired by the monastic model. From Augustine to Æthelnoth, at least eighteen archbishops of Canterbury became the objects of official or unofficial cults. In later centuries only Anselm (d. 1109), Becket (d. 1170) and Edmund of Abingdon (d. 1240) were added to their number. Most of the Canterbury saints were honoured as confessors, suffering for their faith, but not to the extent of martyrdom. Their shrines were seen as places of healing, where the body of the dead saint acted as an intermediary between heaven and earth. In his work on relics, the twelfth-century monk Eadmer described the monks of Canterbury, both at St Augustine's and Christ Church, as custodians of the saints' earthly remains. The living archbishop was somehow the personification of his sainted predecessors and thus had particularly significant custodial responsibilities, which he could demonstrate through care for Canterbury's monastic communities, their buildings, landed endowment, spiritual well-being and intellectual reputation.

Unlike Augustine's cathedral, which was adapted by his successors and finally perished in the fire of 6 December 1067, the intellectual reputation

created in the first century of the Canterbury archbishopric has survived the
test of time. When Hadrian the African rejected the invitation to become
archbishop, he nevertheless consented to assist Archbishop Theodore of
Tarsus and to serve as abbot of St Augustine's. It was there that he presided
over its school for some forty years, a school which became the most
celebrated in England. Theodore was no remote or disinterested patron of this
initiative, for his vision of a unified English Church was expressed as much
through the calling of annual synods as by the promotion of learning, which
was centred in Canterbury at Christ Church but especially at St Augustine's.
Theodore was the first archbishop of Canterbury to have a European
reputation for learning. He became celebrated as the founder of the modern
penitential system and was a distinguished biblical commentator. The school
at St Augustine's taught Latin and Greek, scriptural exegesis and astronomy
as specialities, the last assisting in the fine art of ecclesiastical computation,
the calculating of movable feasts. The most celebrated alumnus was St
Aldhelm (d. 709), a fine poet, abbot of Malmesbury, the first bishop of
Sherborne and the founder of monasteries at Frome and Bradford-on-Avon.
Other students included several future bishops and St Ceolfrith, successor to
the founder Benedict Biscop as abbot of Wearmouth and Jarrow. Ceolfrith (d.
716) was a great scholar who commissioned the *Codex Amiatinus*, the oldest
surviving Latin Bible in one volume (now in the Biblioteca Laurenziana in
Florence). Michael Lapidge suggests that it is 'legitimate to regard the
seventh-century school of Canterbury as one of the high points, perhaps the
acme, of intellectual culture in the early Middle Ages'.[16] The famous school of
York, of which Alcuin (d. 804) was the most famous product, was not
founded until the following century.

Although Cuthbert was only the eleventh archbishop, he found that St
Augustine's was not large enough to continue as the archiepiscopal
mausoleum. Thus, in the mid-eighth century, he built the church of St John
the Baptist, as close as possible to the cathedral sanctuary, designed as a
baptistery and burial place for the archbishops. It, too, soon required
expansion and adaptation. Cuthbert was therefore the first archbishop to be
buried at Christ Church rather than St Augustine's. Until the Conquest all his
successors except Jænberht, abbot of St Augustine's before he became
archbishop, were buried in their cathedral church. The next phase of building
work at Christ Church is known to have taken place in the time of
Archbishop Wulfred in the early ninth century, but his rebuilding may have

been confined to the monastic buildings. Defence against the Viking raiders came at a heavy cost and by the tenth century the religious foundations of the early Anglo-Saxon period were in ruins. In Archbishop Æthelred's time learning and manuscript production were, understandably, at a low ebb. There is, however, archaeological evidence – including the bronze Canterbury Cross brooch – to prove that urban life recovered in the ninth century, presumably after the first sack of Canterbury in *c.* 851. One of the archbishops with whom this urban revival may be associated was Plegmund, who shared King Alfred's commitment to this cause. Plegmund was among those archbishops honoured in Canterbury as a saint, as reflected in a thirteenth-century martyrology, which places his feast day on 2 August.[17] Plegmund's deliberate contribution to the cult of saints was to acquire from Rome relics of St Blasius (Blaise) – the fourth-century martyr associated with curing throat problems – which were enshrined at Canterbury.

The next archbishop to make a recorded contribution to the fabric of the cathedral church was Oda in the mid-tenth century, enlarging the building and translating the relics of St Wilfrid there from Ripon. Of more enduring significance for Christ Church and for the wider English Church, was Oda's commitment to monastic revival. It was possibly in 936 that Oda took the monastic habit at Fleury, on the Loire, a centre of the monastic revival that took its inspiration from Cluny. The monastery of Cluny, in Burgundy, had been founded in 909/10, and soon began setting a high standard of monastic observance. Through Oda this revival reached Canterbury and was continued by his nephew Oswald (d. 992), a monk of Fleury, archbishop of York and, together with Dunstan and Æthelwold, one of the great English monastic reformers of the tenth century. Oda encouraged Dunstan as abbot of Glastonbury and provided him with a model in all his pastoral work. When the latter duly became archbishop himself, he never passed Oda's tomb in the cathedral without kneeling. Dunstan's bequest to Christ Church was a succession of archbishops who had been monks of Glastonbury and abbots of various reformed houses; for his part Archbishop Sigeric bequeathed books for the revived scriptorium.

The last significant royal benefactor to Canterbury before the Conquest was Cnut, who sanctioned the translation of Ælfheah's relics from St Paul's to Christ Church and, together with his consort, Emma, provided the Christ Church community with many important gifts, including an arm of St Bartholomew and, more prosaically, the port of Sandwich. Like the archbishop himself, the community had received numerous estates in south-eastern England as a consequence of lay benefactions; by 1066 these included Meopham and Monkton in Kent, Merstham in Surrey and Monks Risborough in Buckinghamshire. It was also during Cnut's time that the western end of the cathedral was reconstructed to include an oratory of St Mary, or Lady Chapel.

When Eadmer recorded the cathedral's layout from memory, following the fire of 1067, he described a building with apses at both the east and west ends, with the high altar in the eastern apse flanked by the tombs of Ælfheah (Alphege) and Oda. Dunstan was enshrined in the crypt, the location being marked by a stone column or pyramid in the choir above. By 1066 the cathedral, a complex of chapels and buildings, was probably the largest church in England, an English version of the Constantinian basilica of St Peter's in Rome. 'Imitation of Rome, a liturgy that was becoming ever more elaborate and more explicitly Benedictine, and the burial of the growing number of venerable [and] saintly archbishops – these seem to have been the dominant ideas that had shaped the Cathedral's development over the five centuries that separated St Augustine from the Norman Conquest.'[18]

Though the Anglo-Saxon cathedral was destroyed in the fire of 1067, the spirit of the Anglo-Saxon Church continued in the monastic life, of which so many of the sainted Anglo-Saxon archbishops were practitioners. St Boniface, an English monk and missionary to the Germans, considered the monastic life best validated by action:

Of the two wives of Jacob, whom spiritual writers regard as the biblical types of the contemplative and active lives, Rachel was beautiful, but Liah was the fertile one. Gregory [the Great] himself thought he had married Rachel when he became a monk; but being pope was like waking up in the night to find himself in the arms of Liah. It was a shock, but while there were those who still lacked the Christian faith, it was a necessary shock.[19]

Gregory the Great was one of the principal influences on the development of the monastic order and he, like his disciple Augustine of Canterbury, is often described as 'Benedictine'. Gregory was indeed Benedict's first biographer and, in the Middle Ages, the abbey of St Augustine at Canterbury was given a precedence of honour among the English black monks. Yet, while there was nothing 'unBenedictine' (as David Farmer puts it) in Canterbury monasticism, the monks there were not professed 'according to the Rule'.[20] It is probable that the Rule was known in southern England by the middle of the seventh century but the early monasticism of Canterbury was not juridically Benedictine. This came only in the tenth century. Later Benedictine historians, fighting their corner for Benedictine superiority, made much of Augustine's Benedictinism. The missionary-minded monks of the revived English Congregation in the seventeenth century identified Augustine as their model. In the *Apostolatus Benedictinorum in Anglia* (1626), a work of wide-ranging erudition, Dom Clement Reyner claimed that Gregory and Augustine were both Benedictines and that England's conversion was the work of monks. This remains a happy thought.[21]

As abbot of Glastonbury, Dunstan was one of the revivers of monastic life in England, using the Benedictine Rule as his model. From 940 until the dissolution of the monasteries by Henry VIII six hundred years later Benedictine monasticism was a formative influence in English religious life. As archbishop, Dunstan reformed the English Church using monasticism as his instrument. He personally supervised the reform of such religious houses as Bath, Muchelney and Westminster and had reforming monks (notably his friend Æthelwold and nephew Oswald) appointed bishops. Together, they are sometimes said to have spearheaded a 'tenth-century reformation' of the English Church. Dunstan had spent some time at the abbey of St Blandin in Ghent, a house influenced by the reform of Gorze, an abbey near Metz which, unlike Cluny, believed that the ecclesiastical and secular powers should act in unison to promote the Christian commonwealth in their respective spheres. The *Regularis concordia* (*c.* 970), promulgated by Dunstan if not actually compiled by him, was a clear statement of his monastic ideal, whose salient features have been identified by Douglas Dales:

. . . the respect for longstanding English tradition, mediated by the authority of the archbishop of Canterbury, coupled with the fervour of reform; the enhanced role of the monarch and his consort; the sense of the past seen in the light of Bede's *Ecclesiastical History*; the need for direct political action and sustained episcopal resolution to effect lasting change in the Church; and finally the sophisticated Christian political theory by which the role of monarchy, episcopacy and monasticism in Christian society was addressed and articulated.[23]

Dunstan was a model diocesan bishop and a stickler for the details of Christian life, whether in marriage laws or fasting. He was almost eighty when he died and spent his last years among the Christ Church community.

Dunstan towers above the other Anglo-Saxon bishops in his personality and his achievement. His posthumous reputation was considerable, not only as an artist and an artisan, but as a musician (Kyrie VII, *rex splendens*, in the Vatican Gradual was long attributed to him) and as a wonder worker. He transformed the Church of his time.

His example helped to inspire a massive transfer of landed resources from the secular aristocracy to a religious aristocracy; it made possible a revival of scholarly, religious, pastoral and cultural standards in later tenth-century England that gave a distinctively monastic character to the English church and hierarchy. Some of the results of that transformation are with us still.[24]

Taken as a whole, the Anglo-Saxons experienced a prolonged period of Christianisation in which the archbishops of Canterbury played a central part. For much of the seventh century, relations between England and the continent resulted principally in the introduction into England of cultural, educational and religious skills. By the end of the century, however, the movement was in the opposite direction and the English began to send out missionaries, especially to the north and east of the Rhine. In its last generation, the Anglo-Saxon Church had to come to terms with a new continental influence. The Normans, descendants of the Viking invaders of Normandy, introduced a newly vitalised form of Christianity into England, but the foundations of the English Church had been laid and the pre-eminence of Canterbury established.

1070–1270: ECCLESIA ANGLICANA REFORMATA

The story of Christendom between the eleventh and thirteenth centuries is one of expansion, triggered by the sort of favourable climatic conditions that made famine and pestilence comparatively rare. Within its bounds, the expanding population was compelled to drain fens and fell trees to increase the amount of land under cultivation, and to cluster in settlements with such tell-tale names as Villeneuve, Neustadt and Newtown. On the fringes of Christendom, expansionism came at the expense of the Muslim powers, whether in Sicily, which was conquered by the Normans in 1090, or in Spain, where the Christian Reconquista presented generation after generation of crusading opportunities. By 1275 only the kingdom of Granada remained in Muslim hands. From 1098 crusading fervour took knights from western Christendom to the Holy Land, leading to the establishment of the relatively short-lived Latin states along the eastern Mediterranean seaboard. While Englishmen participating in the Second Crusade stopped short of the Holy Land to settle in Lisbon in the 1140s, Italian merchants opened up the Mediterranean and Black Seas to commerce, and trade links were established with parts of Asia, although the first archbishop of Peking was not appointed until the 1290s. The successors of William the Conqueror (1066–89)[1] and of Archbishop Stigand participated fully in this world of expanding opportunities: however dysfunctional the Angevins as a family, Henry II (1154–89) ruled an empire that stretched from the Scottish border to the Pyrenees; however frequently archbishops of Canterbury were forced into exile, the English Church flourished economically, organisationally and in terms of its architectural grandeur.

There were thirteen archbishops and as many as seven archbishops-elect in the two centuries between Lanfranc's consecration in 1070 and the death of Boniface of Savoy in 1270. In comparison to the archbishops of other periods, they were cosmopolitan in background: in addition to Boniface's clearly non-insular origins, Lanfranc was born in *c*. 1010 at Pavia in Lombardy and should not be confused with St Lanfranc of that city, Anselm was from Aosta, and William of Corbeil was a Frenchman; Ralph d'Escures, Theobald and Richard (prior) of Dover were all Normans. Thomas Becket was a Londoner of Norman parentage. The other English-born archbishops were also natives of the Canterbury province: Baldwin of Forde was from Devon, Hubert Walter from Norfolk, Stephen Langton probably from Lincolnshire, Richard le Grant (or Wethershed) from Sussex, and Edmund Rich from Abingdon, now in Oxfordshire.

Of their family backgrounds little can be said for certain, such details being thought of interest only for archbishops of noble birth or saintly reputation. Indeed, so little is known of Archbishop Richard Wethershed that he is remembered more for his physical stature – 'grand' or 'grant' – than for his family. The saints of the period were Anselm (who never received formal canonisation but who, since 1720, has nevertheless been acknowledged as a Doctor of the Church), the martyr Becket and Edmund of Abingdon. Boniface's tomb in the Cistercian abbey church at Hautecombe, the mausoleum of the House of Savoy, attracted a localised cult and, in 1838, Pope Gregory XVI beatified him. Boniface was more closely related to the ruling dynasties of western Christendom than any other archbishop of Canterbury, before or since. His father was Thomas I, a particularly dynamic count of Savoy, whose daughter Beatrice married the neighbouring count of Provence. As Dante records in the *Paradiso*, Beatrice was the mother of four daughters, every one of them a queen: of France, Germany, Sicily and England. The last was Eleanor of Provence, wife of Henry III (1216–72). Belley was the first bishopric over which the counts of Savoy gained control and Boniface was appointed as its ordinary in 1234. His translation to Canterbury resulted from the royal marriage of his niece, which provided a range of economic and cultural opportunities for Savoyards and Provençals in England. Nor was this an unparalleled distinction for this exceptionally well-connected dynasty, for Boniface's brother Philippe was archbishop of Lyon from *c*. 1246 to 1267, when dynastic needs forced his return to the lay state. For two decades, therefore, the primate of all England and the primate of the Gauls were brothers both in Christ and in blood. Among the other Canterbury archbishops of non-English birth, Anselm and Theobald are known to have belonged to the landowning or knightly class. Among the

Englishmen, Hubert Walter was probably born with the most significant worldly advantages, for he came from a family of East Anglian landowners and was brought up in the household of his uncle, Ranulf de Glanville, a great lawyer and chief justiciar of England for the last nine years of Henry II's reign.[2] The hagiographical lives of Edmund of Abingdon relate that he was he the eldest son of Reginald and Mabel Rich, that his parents belonged to the merchant class and that, appropriately enough, they were noted for their piety.

Thomas Becket's education took him first to Merton Priory in Surrey, then to London and Paris, after which Archbishop Theobald, to whose household he belonged, sent him to study law at Bologna and Auxerre. This career encompassed the full range of educational opportunities available to a secular clerk of his generation. In the twelfth century, the monastic and cathedral schools, which had long been important centres of learning and international culture, slowly lost their dominance to those corporations of masters that became the universities. Archbishop Baldwin's early career illustrates something of this transition, for he began by sitting at the feet of the great canonist Bartholomew of Exeter in the cathedral school there and continued his legal studies at Bologna, which gained university status in 1200, a few decades after Baldwin's time there. He became a distinguished canon lawyer and served as a papal judge delegate and possibly assembled part of the important Worcester Collection of canon law texts.[7] In the mid-twelfth century Paris emerged as the most influential school in western Europe and it was there that Stephen Langton studied under the renowned theologian Peter the Chanter and that Edmund of Abingdon was partly trained. The Oxford masters formed themselves into a university in c. 1190 when war with France made Paris inaccessible to English scholars.[8] Oxford's basic administration and curriculum were soon in place, and Edmund of Abingdon was among the first regent masters, teaching the arts curriculum in the 1190s. Edmund was the first Oxonian archbishop of Canterbury and the last to be canonised. St Edmund Hall, Oxford, was named after him, a distinction enjoyed by none of the other Canterbury primates in either of the English universities. Although its earliest history is obscured by the fact that such halls, unlike colleges, required no foundation charter, St Edmund Hall certainly existed by the early fourteenth century; it gained a reputation as a nest of Lollard heresy in the early fifteenth.[9] Edmund retained his Oxford connections to the end, being attended on his deathbed by Richard Wych

(St Richard of Chichester), the first person to gain a doctorate in canon law at Oxford, who went on to be bishop of Chichester from 1244. Shortly after Edmund's death, the university petitioned the pope in support of his canonisation and one of the greatest Oxford scholars of the thirteenth century, the polymath Robert Grosseteste, who became bishop of Lincoln in 1235, was a member of the commission that investigated his life and posthumous miracles.

Edmund's writings also provided evidence of his suitability for canonisation. These were commentaries on Scripture and works of devotion, most notably *Speculum ecclesiae*, which proved to be accessible and popular. Lanfranc and Langton were also biblical commentators, and the latter is credited with the present chapter divisions of the Bible. They were both scholars of international renown, Lanfranc's principal contribution being his *De corpore et sanguine Domini*, written at Bec in the 1060s, in which he took issue with the Eucharistic teaching of his contemporary Berengar of Tours. Of considerably greater intellectual distinction was Anselm, a pupil of Lanfranc and his successor both as abbot of Bec and as archbishop of Canterbury. Anselm was the most notable theologian to hold the see of Canterbury and the only Doctor of the Church to do so.[10] His scholarship was that of a philosopher and mystic, seen most characteristically in the *Proslogion* (1078), which presents the ontological argument for the existence of God, and in the treatise *Cur Deus homo* ('Why [did] God [become] man?', 1097–8) on the Atonement of Christ. Kings William Rufus and Henry I (reigned 1089–1100 and 1100–35 respectively) did not operate on the same intellectual or spiritual plane and had no obvious regret in forcing Anselm into two periods of exile from England. This had the unforeseen consequence of bringing him into renewed contact with other leading theologians and in 1098 he attended the Council of Bari, at which representatives of the Latin and Greek Churches debated the Double Procession of the Holy Spirit, 'from the Father and the Son' (the *Filioque* clause in the Nicene Creed, added by the Latins and rejected by the Greeks). Archbishop Baldwin was another writer of serious theological works, and Langton is now generally regarded as the originator of the Pentecost sequence *Veni, Sancte Spiritus*.

Anselm, Theobald, Becket and Langton each experienced periods of exile from their province; other archbishops of the twelfth and thirteenth centuries went on time-consuming journeys to Rome or otherwise chose to absent themselves from Canterbury. All of these primates thus came into direct contact with the latest initiatives in church reform, initiatives which they helped to foster in England. Reform of the *Ecclesia Anglicana* was administrative and jurisdictional, but the monastic variety was probably closest to the hearts of the archbishops, whether because some of them were members of religious orders or because all of them were nominal abbots of Christ Church, Canterbury. Thomas Becket, Hubert Walter, Richard le Grant, and Edmund of Abingdon were secular clerks, but Lanfranc, Anselm, Ralph d'Escures, Theobald and Richard of Dover were all Benedictine monks; William of Corbeil was an Augustinian canon, Baldwin a Cistercian and Boniface of Savoy had a Carthusian background.

In the eleventh, twelfth and thirteenth centuries, wave upon wave of monastic reform broke upon England's shores. The influence of Cluny was felt in English monasticism well before the Conquest, but fully fledged Cluniac houses only acquired an organisational structure, dependent on the mother house, in the late eleventh and early twelfth century. Lewes Priory, the first English Cluniac house, was founded in 1077. Houses not directly attached to Cluny were nevertheless influenced by its life and customs, and these customs became a template for twelfth-century Benedictinism, in particular exerting a profound influence on liturgical development: Archbishop Lanfranc drew up monastic constitutions inspired by the revived Norman monasticism and, beyond that, by Cluny. Among the monks, Cistercians arrived in England in 1128–9 and Carthusians in 1178–9. Much influenced by their greatest exemplar, Bernard, abbot of Clairvaux (d. 1153), the Cistercians sought a radically simple version of the Benedictine Rule and became great colonists, both of underused land on the edge of cultivation and as propagandists of the crusading movement. One of the four original foundations (1114) from the mother house at Cîteaux in Burgundy was Pontigny, which stands about 100 miles south of Paris. The present church there dates from the middle of the twelfth century. It was in the heart of country dependent on the king of France and provided refuge for three archbishops of Canterbury between the 1160s and 1240. Thomas Becket was in exile at Pontigny while the church was under construction. Stephen Langton spent five years there from 1208 to 1213 while England was under papal interdict, and made a perpetual grant to the monastery, to be paid annually from the Canterbury revenues, in recognition of the hospitality he received there. Edmund of Abingdon confirmed the grant and was buried at Pontigny following his death at nearby Soissy. Baldwin, a monk of Forde in Dorset, was the only Cistercian to become archbishop of Canterbury, but neither he nor those archbishops who sympathised with the Cistercian reform, enjoyed easy relationships with the more traditional Benedictines of Christ Church. The silent Carthusians, founded by St Bruno in 1084, were too ascetic to be a threat to anyone, though the would-be crusader Archbishop Boniface of Savoy was a novice at the Grande Chartreuse. It seems strange to find a Carthusian leaving that solitude to pursue an episcopal career, as Boniface did 'with tears of sadness'[11] in 1234, but this move was not without precedent, for St Hugh of Lincoln (d. 1200) had left the Grande Chartreuse when Henry II invited him to establish the English Charterhouse at Witham in Somerset, a move followed by his appointment to the bishopric of Lincoln in 1186. In spite of his worldly reputation, Archbishop Hubert Walter proved to be a valuable benefactor to Witham.

Along with the Cistercians, the Augustinian canons regular spearheaded monastic reform in the twelfth century, living a communal life according to the Rule of St Augustine of Hippo. They arrived in England *c.* 1100, and included the future archbishop William of Corbeil, who was prior of their house at St Osyth in Essex. The young Edmund of Abingdon also spent some time with their community at Merton in Surrey. The Premonstratensian canons of St Norbert followed in *c.* 1143. Known in England as the White Canons from the colour of their habits, they attained a total of thirty-five English houses in a short space of time, among them West Dereham in Norfolk, endowed on one of his family's estates in the 1180s by the future archbishop Hubert Walter when he was dean of York, the most senior position in the English Church below episcopal rank. Among the various orders of canons regular were the native English Gilbertines, founded *c.* 1131 by Gilbert of Sempringham (*c.* 1083–1189). Unusual in having double houses for male and female religious, the Gilbertines were patriotically supported by the English kings. Archbishop Hubert Walter was instrumental in persuading Pope Innocent III (1198–1216) to canonise Gilbert in 1202. The Order of Trinitarians, who specialised in the ransoming and rehabilitation of captives, first appeared in England *c.* 1200 but made less of an impact there than they did in the Mediterranean region. The military orders of Templars and Hospitallers of St John of Jerusalem, stood at the opposite end of the monastic spectrum to the contemplative Carthusians and first began to acquire properties – known as preceptories – in England in *c.* 1128 and *c.* 1144 respectively.[12] They represented a vastly different religious life, having chosen, as part of their Christian vocation, the obligation to go to war and, if required to do so, to kill their adversaries. The Fourth Lateran Council, summoned in 1215 by Innocent III, put a brake on the proliferation of religious orders. The last reforming wave to reach England was thus of a quite different nature: as originally conceived, the mendicants were itinerant preachers and confessors, exempt from episcopal control and owning no property in common. The Dominicans arrived in England in 1221, the Franciscans following in 1224, the Carmelites in 1242 and the Austin Friars in 1248–9.

To appreciate the relationship between the archbishops of this period and the monks of Christ Church, Canterbury, one must trace the story back to Lanfranc's decision in 1042 to abandon the life of a wandering scholar and join the abbey of Bec, which was then in its first springtime of vitality. Bec proved to be seminal to the Anglo-Norman Church. Its founder was Herluin, a former knight, who established his community near Brionne, midway between Lisieux and Rouen, around 1034. Life there was a struggle.[13] Lanfranc's arrival transformed the impoverished community. He soon attracted pupils. Among them was a future pope, Alexander II (Anselm of Lucca, though not the saint of that name; pope 1061–73), together with Lanfranc's immediate successor at Canterbury, Anselm of Aosta. It was Alexander II who granted the banner of St Peter to the Normans who ousted the Muslim rulers of Sicily and again in 1066 at William the Conqueror's invasion of England. Around 1044 Lanfranc became Herluin's prior and in 1063 was appointed abbot of Duke William's new foundation at Caen, planned as the ducal mausoleum. Over a short period Normandy became a duchy of many abbeys, most of them following the Benedictine Rule. Rouen was becoming a model monastic province.

Lanfranc moved to Canterbury in 1070 following the deposition of Stigand and was about fifty-five years old at the time of his consecration.[14] The move disturbed his Benedictine *stabilitas loci*, but he retained the vowed status of a Benedictine monk and regarded Christ Church as the focus of his life and activity. The Anglo-Saxon Church had perfected the institution of the cathedral-monastery with the bishop as nominal abbot, and Lanfranc's community at Christ Church stood alongside Winchester, Worcester and Sherborne in this respect. He oversaw the rebuilding of the fire-damaged cathedral church, which was completed by 1077, and provided the community with regulatory *Monastic Constitutions*.[15] Some French-speaking monks accompanied Lanfranc to Canterbury and were appointed to senior posts within the community, but the new archbishop was not entirely insensitive to tradition, for the earthly remains of Dunstan and other revered figures from Canterbury's past were reburied close to the high altar in the rebuilt church. Under Lanfranc the community at Christ Church grew to a hundred in number and, like an English Bec, its influence was felt across the country. The two new cathedral-monasteries of Durham and Rochester adopted his constitutions, as did St Albans, the most senior English religious house. At Lanfranc's death in 1089 he was described by one of the monks of St Augustine's, Canterbury, as 'the father and protector of monks'. After his death the see remained vacant for four years.

Thanks to his conscientious biographer Eadmer, the Anglo-Saxon monk of Christ Church, Anselm appears to posterity as the most complete fully-rounded character among the archbishops of this period. Eadmer was Anselm's close companion, his spiritual director and his 'minder'; from Eadmer we can actually hear the reported speech of Anselm.[3] Eadmer provides us with the first great life of a Canterbury archbishop. Like any good archivist or historian, Eadmer quietly disobeyed Anselm's instructions to destroy his correspondence and his *Vita Anselmi* (1109–25) and *Historia novorum in Anglia* (1109–14) reflect the biographer's sharp historical judgement.[4] In one of his letters, to Eulalia, abbess of Shaftesbury, Anselm confessed: 'I am so harassed in the archbishopric that if it were possible to do so without guilt, I would rather die than continue in it.' Many of his successors have doubtless felt the same. Anselm was monastic and holy in a way that the utterly practical Lanfranc could never be, and when he reluctantly accepted the see of Canterbury from the equally reluctant William Rufus, he saw himself as 'a weak old sheep' being yoked to 'an untamed bull'. Anselm lived out to perfection the Benedictine charism of listening. Although twice driven into exile, he retained a strong local commitment to Canterbury, where he saw himself as the guardian of a rich and cultured tradition, a bishop incorporated into the 'persona' of the church's saints.

Archbishop Ralph d'Escures was appointed after a five-year vacancy following Anselm's death in 1109. Monk and abbot of Saint-Martin at Séez in Normandy, Ralph had a reputation for eloquence and wit, which the judgemental monastic chronicler William of Malmesbury considered synonyms for frivolity. His period in office was marked by a severe decline in his health, leading to virtual paralysis. Neither this misfortune nor the lengthy archiepiscopal vacancies prevented the cathedral, both as a building and as a community, experiencing great growth and prosperity in the late eleventh and twelfth centuries. For this a number of gifted priors were responsible. Ernulf of Beauvais (prior 1096–1107), a monk of Bec and a great scholar, was the effective founder of the Christ Church scriptorium and library, which benefited from the scriptorium already established at St Augustine's, despite the tradition of rivalry between the two houses. Prior Conrad (prior 1107–26) was a great builder and although his choir was gutted by fire in 1174 its ground plan determined that of the present cathedral. It was the consecration of Conrad's church in 1130 that provided William of Corbeil with the most notable event of his thirteen years as archbishop (1123–36). Prior Conrad's building was the setting for a splendid cathedral liturgy, the Benedictine ideal in its greatest English setting.[16]

The fifth of the Anglo-Norman archbishops was Theobald, who succeeded William of Corbeil in 1139 after a vacancy of two years. Although he followed in the tradition of Lanfranc and Anselm in having previously been abbot of Bec, Theobald was not a figure of European significance. At first Theobald's position was compromised by the power and personality of Henry of Blois, King Stephen's brother, who combined his bishopric of Winchester with the office of papal legate. Theobald was Stephen's choice and the king's will prevailed. Although Theobald was a Benedictine, he relied more on his own household for support than on the Christ Church monks. Medieval archbishops were surrounded by an ecclesiastical protocol and administration which took on the character of a court. What began as a *familia*, the immediate circle and aides of the archbishop, developed into a *curia*, a fully fledged administration and court, a local reflection of the court of Rome. Like the archbishops of Canterbury themselves, their households became less monastic and more bureaucratic with the passage of time. In 1174 Pope Alexander III (1159–81) reminded Archbishop Richard that, as a monk himself, he should have some monks in his household. Like a monastic community, the archbishop and his household were expected to provide hospitality. According to his hagiographers, Becket was a model of personal austerity while his generosity to others was legendary, entertaining rich and poor alike. The household and its guests were provisioned from the archbishop's estates in south-east England, which were still based on the Anglo-Saxon endowments. At the Conquest these had suffered short-term damage, especially through the depredations of Odo, bishop of Bayeux, half-brother to William the Conqueror, but were recovered after Lanfranc's arrival in 1070. By the time of Domesday Book (1086) the *corpus* of the Canterbury estates had been re-established. Archbishop Theobald's household was a nursery of talent: four archbishops and six bishops were apprenticed there and several went on to perform significant roles in Church and State. His secretary was the notable historian and humanist scholar John of Salisbury (d. 1180), who undertook missions to Rome for the archbishop and rose to become bishop of Chartres.

Another of Theobald's closest associates was Thomas Becket, whose early career he oversaw and who became his archdeacon in 1154. Margaret Gibson has highlighted the stark contrast between the resentment with which the Christ Church monks regarded Becket in life – a secular clerk who sympathised with the Cistercian reform and spent three-quarters of his eight-year pontificate in exile – and their feelings for the martyred St Thomas of Canterbury, whose cult they nurtured for 370 years.[17] In 1163, during the brief time that Becket spent at Canterbury, Anselm's relics were translated and an attempt made to have him canonised. A wall painting in St Anselm's Chapel was probably commissioned by Becket to mark this occasion. In Eadmer Anselm may have found his Boswell, but for sheer quantity of documentary sources, none of the Canterbury archbishops could match Becket, of whom there are at least eleven more or less contemporary lives;[5] nearly all those who memorialised him were clerks or monks committed to making a saint of a man whose canonisation was due not to his heroic virtue but to his martyrdom. Becket has been fortunate in his more recent biographers, notably Anne Duggan (2004), Frank Barlow (1986) and Dom David Knowles (1970),[6] and in one of his celebrated dramatists, T.S. Eliot, who captures much of his spirit in *Murder in the Cathedral*, which was first performed at the Canterbury Festival in 1935. By contrast, Jean Anouilh's play *Becket* (1961, filmed in 1964) tells us more about the author's attitude towards the occupation of France during the Second World War than it does about the ideological maelstrom of the twelfth century.

After Becket's death the see remained vacant for more than two years and the choice then fell to what was perceived as a safe pair of hands, those of Richard, prior of St Martin's, Dover, a Norman by birth but a monk of Christ Church. In the year of his appointment the cathedral suffered another disastrous fire, which led to the rebuilding of the choir in the Gothic style of northern France, under the direction of William of Sens and William the

Englishman. In stone, glass and sheer architectural audacity, the great cathedrals of this type were exuberant expressions of the reality of the Church's dominance and authority. Building work on the choir or Trinity Chapel continued until *c.* 1180 and that on the 'corona' beyond lasted into the pontificates of Baldwin and Hubert Walter.

Archbishop Baldwin, the formidable Cistercian abbot of Forde and bishop of Worcester, brought to Canterbury the wider monastic dispute between the corporately wealthy Benedictines and the austere Cistercians. His disagreement with the monks of Christ Church was pastoral and led him to found a college of secular canons at St Stephen's, Hackington, to the north of Canterbury. By this means, Baldwin intended to separate the monks from their privilege of electing the archbishop and create a new electoral college on the lines of the Sacred College of cardinals in Rome. The dispute between Baldwin and the monks blighted his relatively brief archiepiscopate, involved each side appealing to Rome against the other, and possibly reached its lowest ebb when Baldwin had the monks besieged in their monastery for months, in the hope of reducing them to submission. The Hackington scheme failed but an alternative was devised in the construction of a new collegiate church, dedicated to Sts Stephen and Thomas, by the Thames at Lambeth. This land for this project was donated by Gilbert de Glanville, Bishop of Rochester, and was the initial step towards the creation of the archbishop's London palace. Across the river from Westminster, Baldwin's new church and college could almost have fulfilled Gregory the Great's plan for a London metropolitan see.[18] Baldwin's real interest, however, was the liberation of the Holy Land, and his charismatic preaching of the Third Crusade was recounted in vivid detail by his friend Gerald, the archdeacon of Brecon – better known as Gerald of Wales – who accompanied him on his preaching mission.[19]

When word arrived in Canterbury that their crusading archbishop had died in Acre on 19 November 1190, the monks of Christ Church were all the more determined to assert their recently threatened right of election. With the king also on crusade they enjoyed more freedom than usual and chose the bishop of Bath, Reginald FitzJocelin. Reginald was the son of Jocelin de Bohun, bishop of Salisbury, and served as his father's archdeacon there.[20] The monks elected him on 27 November 1191 and he began his journey from Bath to Canterbury the following month. By 24 December he had reached Dogmersfield in Hampshire, where he was struck by paralysis and died two days later. With reference to Baldwin's college of Sts Stephen and

Thomas, it was observed that Reginald died on the feast of St Stephen and was buried on that of St Thomas, 29 December.

In 1193 the electoral dilemma was finally resolved when King Richard named as archbishop Hubert Walter, the man who had visited him in his Austrian prison and negotiated his ransom. As a secular clerk Hubert – *laicus et illitteratus* in the eyes of his detractors – was no particular friend to the Benedictines and conflict with the monks continued, even if less intensively than in Baldwin's day. His contribution to the Christ Church precinct was the great hall of eight bays to the north west of the cathedral. Only Westminster Hall was larger. This structure confirmed the archbishop's position as more of a noble and less of a monk. It was completed by Archbishop Langton, but demolished during the Commonwealth period. Building work also resumed at Lambeth in 1196 and it was suspected that Hubert intended to have a residence for himself alongside the collegiate foundation. It would certainly have been conveniently close to Westminster and the court, to which Gerald of Wales considered him too much addicted: 'like a fish out of water [in the Church], he cannot live without the court and secular care'.[21] Lambeth was also attractive because it remained the property of Hubert's kinsman, the bishop of Rochester. On the order of Innocent III, and in an attempt to halt the dramatic quarrel which threatened to discredit the Church, the Lambeth building was demolished in 1199, though Hubert's compromise offer of a new Premonstratensian house on the site came to nothing.

At Hubert Walter's death there was a contested election, when the monks chose Reginald, their own sub-prior, and King John sought to impose on them John de Gray, bishop of Norwich. Innocent III's solution was to send Stephen Langton as a troubleshooter from Rome. The monks accepted him and were promptly exiled by the king. The entire community of this revered house crossed the Channel and stayed for five years at the monastery of Saint-Bertin, another of Becket's former refuges. Archbishop Langton rewarded them lavishly for their loyalty by having Becket's remains translated to a new shrine, dedicated on 7 July 1220. It stood in the Trinity Chapel, to the east of the high altar, dominating the cathedral's interior. For three centuries pilgrims were exposed to the grand opera of medieval religion: 'After making their way to the Trinity Chapel from the site of the martyrdom and the crypt, many on them crawling on their hands and knees and prostrating themselves before the shrine, the climactic moment came for the canopy to be raised on its pulleys and the glistening casket revealed.'[22] The pilgrimage inspired perhaps the first great masterpiece of English literature, Geoffrey Chaucer's *Canterbury Tales*, and was a crucial source of income for the ever more splendid cathedral until 1538, when the shrine was demolished following a royal proclamation of Henry VIII that Thomas Becket was no saint but a traitor.[23] The archbishop's cult was brought to an ignominious end. Shadows of the shrine's glory linger in the cathedral to this day. The 'Opus Alexandrinum' pavement remains at what was once its foot and, more surprisingly, significant portions of the stained glass depiction of the miracles of St Thomas survive in the ambulatory windows.[24] The iconic status of Thomas as a martyr for the freedom of the Church ensured that images of him, from manuscript to wall-painting, were systematically obliterated in England. By way of contrast, across Europe, from Iceland to Sicily, the extent of his cult was startling. In the province of Rouen alone fifty-nine chapels or churches were dedicated to him and at Chartres two windows in the cathedral were devoted to his cult. At Sens both windows and a collection of relics commemorated his martyrdom. Forty-eight Limoges enamel Becket 'chasses' or relic boxes survive as physically far apart as Trondheim in Norway and Toledo in Spain. At Marsala, in Sicily, it was claimed that the saint's relics themselves, shipwrecked at the Reformation while on a secret journey to the Holy Land, found a final resting place, although such a tradition probably owes more to Marsala's strong wine than to historical accuracy.

Langton's successor, Richard le Grant (Wethershed), was papally provided to Canterbury in 1229, after the monks asserted themselves by electing one of their own number, Walter de Eynesham. Le Grant survived just two years thereafter, dying in Umbria in August 1231, at which the monks tried again, their choice falling this time on Ralph Neville, bishop of Chichester and chancellor of England. This election was quashed by Rome, so the monks offered the name of their prior, John of Sittingbourne, with the same result. Their third archbishop-elect, the Oxford master and pioneering teacher of Aristotelian science John Blund, was also turned down. Again the pope – this time Gregory IX (1227–41) – was able to provide an archbishop, Edmund of Abingdon, over the heads of the chapter, a pattern that occurred six times in the course of the thirteenth century. Again the monks had cause to regret this turn of events, for Edmund was a great advocate of monastic reform and so found himself more in sympathy with the Cistercians and the new orders of friars than with the Benedictines of Christ Church. Edmund was inclined to be litigious and quarrelled so fiercely with the community that he excommunicated them *en masse* in 1239. When he died in France in 1240, the monks had no desire to bury him in his cathedral and his body still remains in the abbey church at Pontigny. Edmund is a prime example of the axiom that saints do not always make the best archbishops.[25] In terms of appointment, Boniface of Savoy was the sole thirteenth-century case of an archbishop not imposed by Rome. The chapter elected Henry III's kinsman by marriage in 1241, but an eighteen-month vacancy between the death of Celestine IV and the election of Innocent IV (1243–54) caused papal confirmation to be delayed. Boniface did not reach England until 1244. It was a brief visit, but long enough to initiate financial reforms and consecrate the chapel at Lambeth. His enthronement at Canterbury did not take place until 1249, after which his aggressive attempt to undertake a metropolitan visitation aroused such resentment that he spent some years in Rome cooling his heels. Boniface's last visit to England was in 1265, five years before his death.

The Church in England, as elsewhere, made its final move from the desert to the city – and, indeed, to the new towns – in the high medieval period. The Lambeth connection was a neat reflection of this, for although the royal court continued to be peripatetic, nearby Westminster was ever more clearly the seat of power. Structural reform of the English Church, instituted by Lanfranc and continued by his Canterbury successors, was very much determined by urbanising and centralising impulses.

Lanfranc restructured the entire English Church in a manner that both corresponded to and complemented the imposition of new forms of secular government in the post-Conquest kingdom. In Anselm's phrase, Lanfranc was the ox who rebuilt the Church. His impact can be seen nowhere more graphically than on the map of his province. With further amendments soon after his death, it was a map that survived unchanged until the sixteenth century. The Sussex see, founded at Selsey by St Wilfrid during his exile from York in the 680s, was transferred to Chichester following the Council of London (1075), which sought to locate cathedrals in urban rather than rural centres. London and Rochester, respectively the most populous and the smallest of the suffragan sees, remained intact. In contrast to both earlier and later practice, no bishops of London were translated to Canterbury between Robert of Jumièges in 1052 and Simon Sudbury in 1375, but Rochester did provide an archbishop in the person of Ralph d'Escures, bishop from 1108 to 1114. In 1071 Bishop Herfast moved his East Anglian see from Elmham to

Thetford and in the mid-1090s, Bishop Herbert Losinga established the new see of Norwich with its magnificent new cathedral and chapter of Benedictine monks. Lincoln became a cathedral city in *c.* 1072–3 when Bishop Remigius, a monk of Fécamp, moved his see from Dorchester-on-Thames to the new site. Lincoln was the largest of the English dioceses, stretching from the Thames to the Humber and embracing the present Anglican dioceses of Oxford, Peterborough and Leicester, as well as modern Lincoln. By 1109 the diocese of Lincoln was considered too large and a new see was created in the south-east of the region, based on the Benedictine abbey at Ely. Like Norwich, Ely remained a monastic cathedral until the Dissolution. Richard le Grant was the only archbishop with direct experience of this region: the chancellorship of Lincoln was the highest office he held prior to his Canterbury appointment.

Wells had been established as a non-monastic cathedral for Somerset at the beginning of the tenth century and the see was moved to the monastic house at Bath in 1088–91. Bishop Savaric, who was abbot of Glastonbury, styled himself bishop of Bath and Glastonbury. Innocent IV confirmed the title 'Bath and Wells' in 1245 and until the Dissolution the Somerset bishopric had two cathedrals. So, for much of the period, had Lichfield, the Mercian see founded by St Chad (d. 672). The cathedral at Lichfield remained in use despite the bishop's removal to Chester in 1075, as a consequence of Lanfranc's London synod, and to Coventry in 1095. Chester's bishopric was short-lived, though it was revived in 1541, while Coventry's monastic cathedral all but disappeared at the Dissolution. Worcester, by contrast, presents a picture of stability, in spite of being claimed for the province of York in a bid to counter Lanfranc's high-handed approach to English Church government. Its bishop at the time of the Conquest was Wulfstan (d. 1095 and distinguishable by canonisation from Archbishop Wulfstan of York earlier in the century). He was a great builder and a rare survivor of the Anglo-Saxon tradition of saintly bishops. Lanfranc's initial suspicion of Wulfstan was unfounded and the bishop proved to be a useful ally during baronial revolts against the Crown. Like the cult of Gilbert of Sempringham, Wulfstan's was patriotically fostered by Archbishop Hubert Walter, Innocent III being persuaded to canonise him in 1203. Among Wulfstan's successors was Baldwin, who held the see for four years, prior to translation to Canterbury in 1184. It was seventy years since a suffragan bishop, Ralph d'Escures of Rochester, had been so promoted.

Together with the archdiocese of Rouen, Winchester was the richest see in pre-Reformation Christendom. Like Lichfield in the eighth century, it had metropolitan pretensions, at least during the magnificent episcopate of Henry of Blois (bishop 1129–71), grandson of William the Conqueror, brother of King Stephen (1135–54), and prolific builder of castles and churches. Unlike Lichfield, Winchester did not attain even fleeting metropolitan status. Salisbury emerged from the same nest as Winchester, St Birinus's foundation at Dorchester, from which also came Lincoln, Sherborne and Ramsbury. Herman, bishop of Ramsbury, united the dioceses of Ramsbury and Sherborne at Old Sarum in 1078. Here St Osmund (d. 1099) established Sarum's reputation as a model secular foundation and a centre of liturgical good practice. The Use of Sarum became established as the normative form of the liturgy for the province of Canterbury. Sarum loomed large in the eyes of the court whenever the king resided at nearby Clarendon, as Henry II did in 1164, when a council met there to determine the relationship between lay and ecclesiastical jurisdictions. The resulting Constitutions of Clarendon were presented to Archbishop Becket, who gave his verbal assent to them but pointedly refused to sign a document so favourable to the secular power. As Henry's chief justiciar, Hubert Walter was familiar with both Clarendon and Sarum before his appointment as bishop in 1189. His translation to Canterbury followed four years later. In 1219 the see was moved the short distance from Old to New Sarum, or Salisbury, and the magnificent Early English cathedral constructed between 1220 and 1266 (except for the spire, which is fourteenth-century). Salisbury's secular chapter was a nursery for pastoral bishops and an example of sound cathedral and liturgical administration. Edmund of Abingdon was appointed to it in 1222 and served as treasurer during the early phases of the construction process. Archbishop Langton's connection with Salisbury was comparatively slight: he consecrated three altars in the new cathedral in 1225.

Lanfranc sought to enhance the status of Canterbury to give it something like primacy over the whole of the British Isles. This brought conflict with York, a conflict which flared up during the archiepiscopates of Ralph d'Escures, William of Corbeil and Theobald, but it also brought bishops from Ireland coming to the archbishop for consecration and the foundation from Canterbury of the first Benedictine monastery in Scotland, at Dunfermline in c. 1070, under the patronage of the queen consort Margaret of Scotland (d. 1093, canonised 1249), granddaughter of King Edmund Ironside.

Margaret's church at Dunfermline may have been intended to provide an English-speaking royal chapel for her courtiers. In the twelfth century control over the Scottish Church was a four-sided contest between Canterbury, York, St Andrews and the papacy. Alexander III annulled York's rights over the Scottish Church in 1176 and Celestine III (1191–8), in 1192, began the process of bringing it directly under papal control. Looking westwards, Lanfranc and Anselm both cultivated the Irish Church and corresponded with its leaders. Before Anselm's death, six bishops-elect – four from Dublin, one each from Waterford and Limerick – had been consecrated at Canterbury and promised obedience to its archbishop as their primate. The episcopal structure in Ireland was Canterbury's primary concern, for there were too many bishops and a lack of territorial definition. It was not until the Council of Kells in 1152 that the Irish diocesan structure was reformed. Pope Eugenius III's legate presided over the council, which affirmed the primacy of Armagh (St Patrick's own see in the fifth century) and severed the Canterbury link. The council established four ecclesiastical provinces and thirty-eight dioceses, a scheme which remains more or less intact today and exists in parallel form in the Catholic and Church of Ireland hierarchies. The two senior metropolitans, Armagh and Dublin, were soon involved in a Canterbury/York type of dispute over primacy, which led eventually to Armagh being recognised as 'primate of all Ireland' and Dublin as 'primate of Ireland'.

English ecclesiastical involvement with Ireland did not end with the 1152 council. Henry II's sojourn there from October 1171 to April 1172 sowed the seeds for a permanent English royal administration. A national church council under Christian, the Irish Cistercian bishop of Lismore, was organised at Cashel in 1172. All the bishops present acknowledged Henry's lordship of Ireland and this was duly validated by Pope Alexander III. A process of steady anglicisation took place, which meant that, by the end of the thirteenth century, about half the Irish episcopate were of English origin, though Canterbury's claims to primacy did not emerge again. Alexander's immediate predecessor Adrian IV, the only English pope and a native of the Canterbury province, is said to have 'granted' Ireland to Henry II by the bull *Laudabiliter* (*c.* 1156), a document that came to prominence during the royal campaign of 1171–2. It had been alleged that *Laudabiliter* was part of a Canterbury plot to place the Irish Church under its control, but there is no firm evidence for this supposition.[26]

The Welsh Church was 'reformed' in a similar way to those of Scotland and Ireland in the twelfth century. St Davids, the site of a monastery since the sixth century, was the spiritual heart of the Welsh Church. Henry I forced the election of Bishop Bernard to St Davids in 1115 and thus acknowledgement of Canterbury's metropolitan status was acquired. Shortly afterwards an attempt by the chapter of St Davids to gain metropolitan status was unsuccessful, as was that by the imaginative historian Gerald of Wales, who was twice elected bishop of St Davids and twice failed to be consecrated on account of English suspicions that he would lead the Welsh Church into independence from Canterbury.

The archbishops of Canterbury reformed, centralised and urbanised the English Church on their own initiative, but they were, in turn, subject to and inspired by papal reform and Roman centralisation. Papal initiative and dominance in church reform was perhaps a little unexpected. In the tenth century the papacy had been at one of its lower ebbs, and it was only through the intervention of the German kings that the see of Peter was stirred from torpor. Pope Leo IX (1048–54), a kinsman of the German emperor Henry III, was the first of the great reforming popes who sought to use monasticism as the motor for church reform. Leo IX's new order coincided with the deepening stagnation of Stigand's Anglo-Saxon Church. It was only with the fiery Gregory VII (1073–85) that a full programme of papal reform was articulated, now combined with a thoroughly anti-German and anti-lay spirit. From 1078 the crux of the dispute between popes and emperors was over the investiture of bishops and abbots by secular rulers, with all that that implied for the relationship between *regnum* and *sacerdotium*.

Gregory VII saw Christendom as a seamless garment. He and his supporters used every means in their power to propagate papal centralisation and influence. The reformer's vision was to create a purified, monasticised clergy as agents of reform, looking towards the pope as 'universal ordinary'. The propagation of this reform ideology was enhanced by the dispatch of legates, who acquired greater significance in the eleventh century. By the early twelfth century legates came in three main types. *Legati missi*, 'sent legates', were the first to be sent to represent papal jurisdictional and personal interests. *Legati a latere*, 'legates from [the pope's] side', were entrusted with fuller authority and greater status; as the office of cardinal developed most of these legates were of cardinalitial rank. Legates were sent to England with increasing frequency, five of them in the years between 1125 and 1151.

Legati nati, 'born or native legates', were given a general jurisdictional role and were associated with particular historic sees, including Canterbury. Stephen Langton was England's first *legatus natus.* Another means of centralising the Church around the person of the pope was in the calling of general councils, which only he had the authority to do. The gathering of prelates in Rome was the most visible sign of papal centralisation and such councils were held at the Lateran, the cathedral church of Rome, in 1123, 1139, 1179 and 1215. The first of these confirmed the formal agreement which marked the end of the Investiture Controversy between popes and emperors; the second and third concluded periods of schism, when the remorseless drive to centralisation was temporarily curbed by anti-popes, rival claimants to the Holy See, of whom there was a total of fourteen between 1058 and 1179. Recognising the first of these, 'Benedict X', had been one of Archbishop Stigand's fundamental miscalculations.

The Third Lateran Council also formalised the process of papal elections by making the Sacred College of cardinals the sole electors to the papal office. Cardinals derived their status from Rome's larger churches and from neighbouring bishoprics, so were fitting electors of their own bishop. Prior to this council two cardinals had been appointed from among the ranks of the English clergy: Robert Pullen, a noted teacher in Paris, elevated *c.* 1144,[27] and Nicholas Breakspear of St Albans, cardinal from 1146, who duly became the only English pope, Adrian IV (1154–9).[28] The first archbishop of Canterbury to be a cardinal was Stephen Langton.[29] Permanent attendance upon the pope made it essential that cardinals resign any benefices they happened to hold and reside in Rome. Langton's case flew in the face of this practice, for Innocent III raised him to the cardinalate in 1205, in recognition of his reputation as a theologian in Paris, and then appointed him to Canterbury the following year in the wake of the disputed election. King John (1199–1216) refused to grant the cardinal permission to enter England, from which he was barred until 1213. Historians, especially those observing with Reformation hindsight, have used this episode to illustrate papal 'aggression' and unwarranted intervention in English affairs. More recent interpretations, following the lead of Sir Maurice Powicke in *Stephen Langton* (1928), have tended to regard things differently. Hardly had Langton returned than he was required to enact the reforming initiatives of the Fourth Lateran Council, summoned by Innocent in 1215. Thirty years later Innocent IV emulated his namesake by calling a council at Lyon, the first of two councils which met there in the thirteenth century. It was in the context of that council that Pope Innocent consecrated Boniface of Savoy as archbishop of Canterbury on 15 January 1245. One of the council's priorities was a renewal of crusading activity against the Saracens. This clearly struck a chord with Boniface, who set out for the Holy Land but died when he had got no further than Sainte-Hélène-des-Millières in Savoy.

Canon law, the law of the Church, reached a new maturity in the late eleventh and early twelfth centuries and was perhaps the strongest force in favour of increasing papal influence throughout the world beyond Rome. Collections of decretals, papal decrees – most notably Gratian's *Decretum* (*c.* 1140) – provided thorough and accessible case law. With reference to insular experience in these centuries, Charles Duggan described it as 'the one period in English history when the dominant trend in Anglo-papal relations was in favour of papal claims in a fullness which had not previously existed'.[30] The parallel growth of secular law and royal administration provided a potentially explosive conflict of jurisdictions. The emergence of canon law and the delegation of legates and other papal judges were made possible by the reform of the papal curia, which attracted a galaxy of teachers, thinkers and artists and thus played a part in the cultural phenomenon known as the twelfth-century renaissance. Diocesan chanceries were also restructured. More regular episcopal visitations also reflected a growing sense of an integrated Church and a clerical caste, though they were naturally met with suspicion at first.

Long before his Canterbury appointment, Lanfranc identified himself with the cause of ecclesiastical reform. In 1049 he attended Leo IX's council at Reims, which set out the papal reform agenda, and was supportive of papal aims: 'the abolition of simony and clerical marriage and, more generally, the spiritualization of the church'.[31] It should be remembered, though, that William I and Lanfranc made themselves masters of England and its Church before Gregory VII began to challenge the exercise of royal rights over ecclesiastical appointments. Indeed, it was crucial that Gregory's predecessor, Alexander II, was a former pupil of the archbishop and had no apparent objection to Lanfranc creating what was in effect an independent English Church. When Archbishop Thomas of York objected to Alexander about the threat to his own position, caused by Lanfranc's policy of centralising the English Church on Canterbury and asserting its primacy in an entirely new manner, the pope passed the buck to King William, who naturally favoured

Lanfranc and thereby created a centuries-long feud between the two archbishoprics.

Lanfranc's reforms can be regarded as a local manifestation of the reforming tide that swept through the eleventh-century Church, but where he certainly did not follow the lead of Gregory VII was in the exaltation of papal power at the expense of the English Crown, which may explain why he was not canonised. On the contrary, he regarded the lay investiture of bishops as perfectly normal and saw the collaboration of king and priest, *regnum* and *sacerdotium*, as the essential foundation of the State. Lanfranc's reformed *Ecclesia anglicana* was not so much a Gregorian Church as a royal Church of the traditional type. His excellent working relations with William I made this possible. Lanfranc's successors were generally less successful in maintaining a similar equilibrium, but the foundations he laid were strong.

Personal relations were poor between Anselm and William Rufus; the king showed no interest in religion, nor did he recognise Pope Urban II (1088–99), who gave Anselm his pallium. With custody of Canterbury's temporalities being sold to the highest bidder, the four-year vacancy which followed Lanfranc's death clearly suited William Rufus. It was only when he happened to be seriously ill in 1093 that he agreed to Anselm's appointment. After a sequence of disputes, Anselm retreated to Rome in 1098 and stayed there until the king's death in 1100. This gave Anselm first-hand experience of the Council of Rome (1099), which articulated papal opposition to lay investiture and set him on a collision course with the next king, Henry I, who invested bishops in Anselm's absence. Henry proved to be as intransigent as his brother, and Anselm experienced a second period of exile from 1103. Exile became a way of life for the high medieval archbishops and exile was a challenging place for any prospect of compromise; in exile one archbishop after another learned a sterner and more defined model of episcopal authority and sacerdotal superiority. Anselm's ultramontanism was more than nostalgia for the land of his birth. Peace was made between Anselm and the Crown in 1106/7 when Pope Paschal II (1099–1118) brokered a compromise whereby the Church invested bishops with their staff and ring – the issue at the very heart of the Investiture Controversy – but left the king responsible for their selection.

William of Corbeil's reforming tendencies showed themselves in the legatine councils of 1125, 1127 and 1129, which called for an end to simony and clerical concupiscence. His reputation as a reforming archbishop was then damaged by his coronation of Stephen as king of England in 1135, after his previous confirmation of Henry I's daughter Matilda as rightful heir in 1128. This led his contemporary, Henry of Huntingdon, to regard William as the only archbishop of Canterbury since the Norman Conquest to be unworthy of the post.[32] It took time for Archbishop Theobald to establish his authority, but he had a firm friend in Rome in the person of Cardinal Pullen and his own visits there in 1143 and 1144 confirmed Canterbury's primacy over all England and Wales. In 1149 Theobald's attendance at the Council of Reims caused Stephen to exile the archbishop and confiscate his property. Eugenius III responded by placing England under an interdict, but the crisis soon passed. Although Theobald had supported Stephen's claims against those of Matilda, he nevertheless refused to crown Stephen's son, Eustace, in 1152. Again he fled the country, returning when Matilda's son, Henry of Anjou, had secured his claim to the throne. It was Theobald who crowned Henry II.

From the start of his reign in 1154, Henry was confronted with a more coherent corpus of canon law and a formalised system of legations, ecclesiastical jurisdiction and appeals to Rome. He was also faced with reordering the State after the anarchy of Stephen's time, during which the Church had taken its opportunities. Theobald's men were in key positions in the royal administration, none more obviously than Thomas Becket, who doubled up as Theobald's archdeacon (from 1154) and royal chancellor (from 1155). On Theobald's death, Henry thought the appointment of his chancellor as archbishop would lead to a new era of co-operation between the Church and the secular power on the pattern of Rainald of Dassel, archbishop of Cologne and arch-chancellor of the Empire.

In all the contemporaneous *vitae*, Becket appears as a man of dignified appearance and high personal standards. He had an exalted sense of his office and, once consecrated, left behind the secular concerns of the royal chancery and took on the persona of a metropolitan. 'In his consecration,' wrote his biographer William FitzStephen, 'he was anointed with the visible unction of God's mercy. Putting off the secular man, he now put on Jesus Christ. He vacated the secular duties of his chancellorship, and was at pains to fulfil the functions of a good archbishop.'[33] Many of his fellow bishops had cause to resent this, for they included Henry of Blois, still at Winchester, and the Cluniac monk Gilbert Foliot (Becket's fiercest rival) at London, both of whom entertained metropolitan ambitions. Foliot was a reformer, but a skilled compromiser in what he believed was an essential *rencontre* between Church and kingdom. Bishops Hilary of Chichester and Bartholomew of Exeter were canonists and 'high Gregorians' who looked to the pope and to canon law for authoritative answers to all their legal questions. Another group of bishops, led by Nigel of Ely, were court officials who, in their personal life and attitudes, were out of sympathy with the reformers.[34]

David Knowles identified three stages in the struggle between Henry II and Becket, which had its dramatic denouement in the murder in the cathedral in 1170. At the outset, the controversy was about the forensic rights of the Church and the clerical order in a context which saw so many clerics operating at both a secular and spiritual level. At the Council of Woodstock (1163) the issue was the payment of customary dues and, in the same year, at the Council of Westminster, it was the question of criminous clerks and their protection by the Church. The attempted reconciliation of king and archbishop failed and Becket received letters from the pope and cardinals urging him to give in to the king's demands. When an attempt was made in the Constitutions of Clarendon (1164) to define the respective jurisdictions of Church and Crown, the object of the dispute became the freedom of the English Church as part of the Universal Church in its relationship to Rome. Finally, in Knowles' analysis, it became a question of God's rights as against Caesar's.

The Council of Northampton, in October 1164, led to a final rupture between king and archbishop. Becket was tried and condemned but managed to flee from Northampton on 13 October and cross the Channel on 2 November, proceeding first to the Cistercian monastery of Clair-Marais near Saint-Omer, and then to Saint-Bertin. At the end of November 1164 he had an audience with Alexander III, who lived in France for much of the seventeen-year schism that blighted his pontificate. At that meeting Becket formally resigned his archbishopric into the pope's hands. The pope considered the archbishop's case and immediately returned him to office on condition that he stayed for a while – in fact it was to be until 1166 – at the abbey of Pontigny. Altogether his exile lasted until 1170, the latter years being spent with the Benedictine monks of Sainte-Colombe at Sens. On Whit Sunday 1166, Henry II and his followers were excommunicated. The king was now concerned that this would be followed by an interdict, which would weaken his position inside his realm and in the eyes of neighbouring powers. Peace was almost reached between the feuding parties at Montmartre in November 1169, and an agreement finally made at Fréteval in July 1170.

Behind the drama and the histrionics, in which both main principals were great adepts, lay a complex problem of reconciling feudal discipline with the requirements of canon law and, in particular, the rights of unrestricted access to the papal court, those of the spiritual power to use fully the spiritual weapons, and those of the king and his courts to judge and sentence 'criminous' clerks. The king and the archbishop approached these legal conundrums from fundamentally distinct positions. Becket was not concerned, as the royal legislators were, with whether a particular law was an ancient custom. Echoing the language of Gregory VII, he stated bluntly: Christ said 'I am the truth', not 'I am the custom'. He had become the champion of the *sacerdotium* over the *regnum*, operating not only as an individual but with papal approval. His martyrdom set the seal on his championship; as Herbert of Bosham reflected to Thomas on his final return to Canterbury on 1 December 1170: 'My lord, it matters not to us now when you depart out of this world, since today in you Christ's spouse the Church has conquered; nay rather, Christ conquers, Christ reigns, Christ rules.'[35]

Thomas Becket, Henry II's turbulent priest but 'no traitor to the king', was murdered in Canterbury Cathedral about 5pm on Thursday 29 December 1070 in a singular act of sacriligious violence by four knights of the king's household – Reginald FitzUrse, William de Tracy, Hugh de Morville and Richard le Breton – who killed him without resistance. His split skull and brains were dashed to the floor. His last words were emblematic: 'For the Name of Jesus and the protection of the Church I am ready to embrace death.' While Becket's body still lay on the pavement, citizens of Canterbury attempted to take as relics some of his blood, either in bottles or on cloths dipped in it. The cathedral community was stunned and it was only the next morning that the body was stripped of its outer garments and adorned with pontifical vestments. The monks discovered that Becket not only wore a monastic habit under his robes but also that his body was clad in vermin-infested sackcloth. King Henry's reaction was to exchange his own royal robes for sackcloth and ashes, but his main problem was to make some sort of settlement with the pope. It was not until September 1172 that the king made his peace with the pontiff at Avranches in Normandy, and not until 12 July 1174 that he made his act of public penance at the archbishop's tomb. The latter included prayer and fasting and, of his own free will, a scourging by all the bishops and abbots who were present, as well as by all the monks of Christ Church. By then Thomas was already a saint, canonised by a bull of Pope Alexander III dated 12 March 1173.

William Rufus's failure to recognise Urban II had effectively spared England from involvement in the First Crusade, preached by that pope at the Council of Clermont in 1095. By 1100, the French knights had not merely freed Jerusalem from Muslim control but had established a Christian kingdom there. Another of the Latin states, the county of Edessa, fell in 1144, prompting the Second Crusade, which was preached by Bernard of Clairvaux. In 1187 Saladin captured Jerusalem and thereby gave King Richard I (1189–99) the cause for which he is best remembered: the Third Crusade ensued between 1189 and 1192. Richard showed little interest in ecclesiastical matters and, indeed, little interest in his English kingdom, but was strongly motivated by the crusading ideal. As the conflict widened into a cultural battle between Christendom and Islam, the concept of crusade broadened the meaning of what could be seen as a just war and 'crusade' itself became a theological as well as a military concept, a way to sanctification as well as a way to acquiring land and status. In common with many of his contemporaries, Archbishop Baldwin saw the crusading movement as the cutting edge of the Christian mission. He crowned Richard I and travelled with him to the Holy Land, the English contingent also including Bishop Hubert Walter of Salisbury. Baldwin died at Acre. Jerusalem was not recovered.

The next primate, Hubert Walter, had a worldly temperament, but he was an effective steward of his see. C.R. Cheney, his biographer, credits him

> with a genuine desire to use his talents and his ecclesiastical power for the furtherance of religion . . . he legislated wisely for the Church in legatine and provincial councils . . . his dealings with successive rulers of England showed strength of character and statesmanship. Few archbishops of Canterbury can have used their opportunities to greater advantage.[36]

For most of the last six years of Richard's reign, Hubert Walter held the office of chief justiciar, and was vicegerent during the king's absence overseas. From 1195 he was also Celestine III's legate in England: it was a unique combination of powers, but it must be acknowledged that he was an exemplary administrator. Relations between Church and State at the highest level could hardly have been more harmonious, but when Innocent III renewed the papal prohibition against clergy holding secular office, Hubert

resigned the chief justiciarship in 1198. Just as the rise of the universities at
the expense of the monasteries tended to centralise knowledge, so more
administrative documents were produced by the trained professionals they
produced. Charismatic monks had been considerably less bureaucratic.
Documents of all sorts proliferated in the twelfth and thirteenth centuries –
charters and cartularies, rolls and registers, writs and certificates, surveys
and rentals – reflecting acute consciousness of legal rights, particularly with
regard to land. Although the earliest surviving archiepiscopal register for
Canterbury does not begin until 1279, those for many of the other English
dioceses predate it. Michael Clanchy singles out the contribution Hubert
Walter in his capacity as chief justiciar and chancellor, under kings Richard
and John, to the development of efficient record-keeping at national level. The
principles of producing authenticated documents and transcriptions on rolls
date from his period in royal service between 1193 and 1205: 'The
proliferation of documents was a European and a continuing phenomenon
yet if it were to be associated in England with one man, he would be Hubert
Walter.'[37] Hubert Walter's work was the completion of a process which began
under Lanfranc, whose Latin record-keeping replaced the previous use of
Anglo-Saxon.

Richard I died on 6 April 1199, following a wound received at a siege, and
was buried alongside his parents, Henry II and Eleanor of Aquitaine, at
Fontevrault. He was the last English king to be buried in France. Richard had
not been in England for five years when John managed to secure the English
throne and to be crowned by the archbishop on Ascension Day, 27 May
1199. In spite of Innocent's injunction, Hubert resumed the chancellorship
and provided a measure of continuity in the secular administration until his
death in 1205.

From the point of view of relations between the king and the Church,
John's reign was deeply flawed. The manner of Cardinal Langton's
appointment to Canterbury was novel and the resulting exile of the Christ
Church community high in drama, but these were followed in 1208 by
Innocent III's interdict, according to which most of English sacramental life
was suspended. The king's response was to confiscate all church property. The
pope's response was to excommunicate the king. Threatened not only with
papal deposition but also with baronial revolt and French invasion, John
capitulated in May 1213 and consented to the kingdoms of England and
Ireland being held in fief from the pope. Innocent was not vindictive.

By means of Magna Carta (1215) Langton, who played a significant part in drafting the text, allied with the barons in questioning the king's authority. John responded by declaring it null and void and by suspending Langton from office. Honorius III (1216–27) duly restored him to the primatial dignity in 1218, and the last decade of his Canterbury pontificate was a period of notable ecclesiastical reform, inspired by the Fourth Lateran Council, the English echo of which was Langton's provincial council at Oxford in 1222. His *annus mirabilis*, though, was 1220, when he presided over the translation of Becket's body to its magnificent shrine, took a relic of his martyred predecessor to Rome, and was rewarded with the office of *legatus natus*, the papal representative in England, for himself and for the archbishops of Canterbury from that point onwards. Langton's achievements thus marked the end of a process, begun by Lanfranc in England and by Gregory VII for the rest of western Christendom, whereby 'the Church had put into effect her determination that the clerical order should manage its own affairs'.[38]

1270–1486: FROM MENDICANTS TO PRINCES

or two agonising years, Adam Chillenden was archbishop-elect of
Canterbury. The monks of Christ Church elected Chillenden, their
prior, in September 1270, when news reached them of the death of
Archbishop Boniface in his native Savoy. They did so in defiance of violent
royal demands that Bishop Robert Burnell of Bath and Wells be elected to
the primacy. The uncertainty of Chillenden's position resulted from the
vacancy happening to coincide with the longest interregnum in papal
history. Increasingly desperate attempts were made to induce the cardinals to
reach a decision, but not even the removal of the roof from the palace where
they were meeting in Viterbo could persuade them to compose their
differences and choose a pope. Teobaldo Visconti of Piacenza was elected *in
absentia* on 1 September 1271, but only after the cardinals had wrangled for
thirty-three months. Visconti duly took the name Gregory X (1271–76) and
made the regularising of future conclaves a priority of his pontificate.
In October 1272, Gregory imposed his authority over the English Church
by ignoring Chillenden and the Christ Church monks, and nominating
the noted Dominican theologian Robert Kilwardby to the throne of
St Augustine.[1] Hardly had a primate been provided than England found
itself without a king, for Henry III died in November that year and his
successor, Edward I (1272–1307), did not return from his crusading
expedition to the Holy Land until August 1274. While in Acre the Lord
Edward had made the acquaintance of the future Pope Gregory. By means of
the Second Council of Lyon (1274), Gregory attempted to harness the
crusading enthusiasm so recently championed by Louis IX of France and
placed the crusade under papal protection. What the new pope shared with
the new king of England was a direct personal experience of Latin
Christendom at its most extensive.

The fall of Acre in 1291 signalled the geographical contraction of Christendom; its economic and demographic contraction followed in the fourteenth century. Considered in the broadest of terms, the two centuries with which this chapter is concerned – from the appointment of Kilwardby in 1272 to the death of Archbishop Thomas Bourchier in 1486 – were characterised by a steady narrowing of vision and experience occasioned by the economic circumstances: popes retreated into the Papal States and into wars with their Italian neighbours; English kings retreated into their own domain and even married native noblewomen rather than foreign princesses. In this context the archbishops of Canterbury can each be introduced in relation to the twin successions of popes and kings with whom they had to deal, and the vexed question of clerical taxation provides a thread running through the saga.

The English Church was taxed from two directions – royal and papal – and, in ordinary circumstances, was wealthy enough to sustain both sets of demands. Papal taxation came in various forms, including the service taxes and annates paid by benefice-holders, chancery, penitential and jurisdictional fees, fines, compositions and indulgences. These were straightforward facts of ecclesiastical life. What posed more acute problems were extraordinary subsidies, levied to finance the popes' wars in Italy, and crusading taxes for campaigns that were highly unlikely to happen. In 1278 Pope Nicholas III (1277–80) removed Kilwardby from England by raising him to the cardinalate, and it is thought that he did so because the archbishop had resisted the collection of a papal tenth in England. Again Edward I tried to ensure the election of his efficient chancellor, the notoriously worldly Robert Burnell, but a papal commission declared him unsuitable. Kilwardby's eventual successor was, like Stephen Langton earlier in the century, a troubleshooting outsider: the Franciscan John Pecham. Pecham (or Peckham[2]) had all the austerity of a mendicant, was devoted to the Church and its mission, and found himself frequently in dispute with King Edward, though there was no serious breach between Church and Crown in his time. The king found Pecham useful, not least when the archbishop obliged Edward by excommunicating the Welsh during the king's conquest of the principality. As this action demonstrated, Pecham was far from neutral in that conflict, considering the Welsh a barbarous and lawless people whose Church – part of his own province – was in even greater need of reform than that in England. In spite of these convictions, Pecham nevertheless endeavoured to mediate between the two sides in 1282, thereby providing the Welsh with a unique opportunity to make formal protests against atrocities committed by English soldiers.

Pope Boniface VIII (1294–1303) fearlessly asserted the supremacy of papal power over secular princes. When he issued the bull *Clericis laicos* (1296), declaring that churchmen were not to pay subsidies to the secular power without papal approval, it was a direct attack on Edward I just as he demanded a hefty clerical subsidy to fund his French and Scottish wars. Edward had brought matters to a head by demanding not a twelfth or a tenth of clerical revenue but a moiety (half). Archbishop Robert Winchelsey had the unenviable task of implementing this bull in England. Other primates might have concluded that it was safer to capitulate to the king as the more immediate power, but Winchelsey risked his personal safety and stuck fast to the papal ruling. The king reacted by seizing the archbishop's temporal estates in 1297, forcing Winchelsey to stay in the rectory at Maidstone because he was not permitted to set foot in his own manor there. Even his horses were confiscated. By the end of 1297 all sides had modified their positions. When the English were defeated by the Scots at Stirling Bridge, hardline clerics accepted the case for a subsidy as necessary to the defence of the realm: the Scots were a direct threat whereas the French were not. For his part, Boniface issued the bull *Etsi de statu* (1297), permitting the collection of clerical subsidies in extreme circumstances. Pope Boniface and King Edward were the Scylla and Charibdis of Winchelsey's primatial career, but his posthumous reputation lay in the hands of contemporary chroniclers, such as the monk of St Augustine's, Canterbury, who condemned him as a man 'hateful to God and proud, who throughout the realm of England had by the pride of his lips, like a harlot, brought disgrace on the priesthood and the clergy, and exercised unheard of tyranny over the people'.[3] It should be remembered that Winchelsey was a secular priest, for the days of the monk-archbishops had largely passed, and that his Canterbury detractor belonged to a house with a long history of asserting its exemption from episcopal control.

The next pontiff to have a significant impact in England was Clement V (1305–14) who, as Archbishop Bertrand de Got of Bordeaux, had been a subject of Edward I and was keen to reach an accommodation with him. *Clericis laicos* was revoked and Winchelsey's Becket-like credentials were reinforced by his suspension from the archiepiscopal office in 1306. This was not his first experience of such misfortune, for he had previously suffered the indignity of being excommunicated over a disputed papal provision to a minor benefice, but had been absolved by Pope Boniface. The aged, battle-weary and paralysed archbishop was obliged to 'shadow' the papal court in France for the two years of his exile, before being recalled to England by Edward II (1307–27). Like his father, this king sought to impose his own archbishop on the monks of Christ Church, who made strong representations for their own candidate, the 'virtuous and learned' Thomas Cobham. In keeping with his weakness for favourites, Edward chose for Canterbury a prominent member of his own household, Walter Reynolds, bishop of Worcester. Cobham was appointed to Reynolds' Worcester diocese by way of consolation. Eight archbishops were elected during the half-century of Edward III's reign (1327–77), with turnover being particularly brisk during the Black Death of 1348–9. Among those eight, the position of John Offord (or Ufford) remains problematic, for he was papally provided to Canterbury on 24 September 1348 and received the temporalities of the see the following November, and thus appears on those lists of archbishops which are based on papal records. He died of plague on 20 May 1349, before the pallium arrived and without having been consecrated, and so is omitted from the list that makes Rowan Williams the 104th holder of the office. The appointments of Simon Mepham (or Meopham), John Stratford, Thomas Bradwardine, Simon Islip, Simon Langham and William Whittlesey were straightforward in comparison. Mepham was twice suspended from office, the first time for refusing to institute the archbishop of Naples to the church of Maidstone, as conferred by John XXII (1316–34), and later, in 1329, when he attempted to visit St Augustine's, Canterbury, which appealed to Rome in defence of its liberties. The abbey's claims were upheld and the ailing archbishop suffered excommunication in addition to suspension.[4]

Clement V's successors were Frenchmen who continued his practice of residing in the papal enclave of Avignon, and had no cause to be partial towards England in the era of Edward III's French wars. For the most part, the English kings cultivated the Canterbury archbishops as the guardians of ecclesiastical revenue to be plundered in time of war. Edward I and Edward III therefore had more need of them than most. By the winter of 1340/1, Edward III had been at war with France for three years when a funding crisis emerged. Archbishop Stratford was the chancellor of England, and Edward accused him of failing to supply funds for the war and thus of scuppering the English cause. Preaching in his cathedral on the feast of St Thomas of Canterbury, 29 December 1340, it was the archbishop who consciously identified himself as another Becket.[5] The war context goes a long way towards explaining the timing of the English statutes of Provisors and Praemunire, the first of each sequence dating from 1351 and 1353 respectively, for they were nationalistic measures designed to protect the rights of the Crown from encroachment by the French popes. According to these statutes, the king and his lords were to present clerics to English benefices, while legal cases were to be heard in English courts, not those of the pope. In addition to the anti-French dimension, the statutes were also the clearest English expression of a general assertion of authority by the secular powers at a time of relative papal weakness. Relations between England and Avignon were therefore not particularly good when Urban V (1362–70) raised Archbishop Langham to the Sacred College in 1368. This he did without reference to Edward III, who declared a *sede vacante* (vacant see) at Canterbury and appropriated its revenues. For good measure, Edward also delayed granting Langham permission to leave the country. Just three years later, Langham returned to England as part of his legation to the still-warring French and English kings. At William Whittlesey's death the Christ Church monks re-elected Langham, their Benedictine confrère, as archbishop, only to have their candidate rejected and Simon Sudbury imposed on them by the Crown. Sudbury duly achieved infamy as the archbishop executed by the mob at the height of the Peasants' Revolt in 1381. Appreciation of his character and capabilities has been coloured by the St Albans chronicler Thomas Walsingham, who condemned him as weak, lethargic and subservient to the anticlerical will of John of Gaunt, duke of Lancaster. It proved to be a persuasive image, perpetuated by many later commentators. A more recent examination of key episodes in Sudbury's career has revealed a wiser figure who endeavoured to stand above factional rivalries.[6]

The formidable Gregory XI (1370–8) was elected at Avignon, but heeded the appeals of Catherine of Siena and others by returning the papacy to Rome. At this Langham made a final attempt to return home, but died before he could travel to any earthly destination. Gregory's decision had a notable impact in England, where the pope's brother had been imprisoned since 1370. Matters came to a head because the Crown sought clerical revenue to support the continuing French war at the same time as Gregory demanded subsidies from the English Church, under pain of excommunication, so that he might impose order in the Papal States and pursue his military campaign against Bernabò Visconti of Milan. The longer the Hundred Years War continued, the greater was the Crown's need for revenue. Parliament therefore met ever more frequently in order to approve taxation of the laity, as did the convocations of Canterbury and York to approve taxation of the clergy. In 1283 Archbishop Pecham had determined the composition of the Canterbury convocation, which consisted of bishops, abbots, deans, archdeacons and representative clergy from each diocese and chapter, though a similar assembly had been summoned by Stephen Langton in 1225. With Whittlesey incapacitated in the early 1370s, Sudbury, as bishop of London and dean of the province of Canterbury, took the chair in convocation and led calls for a clerical subsidy to the Crown. Bishop Courtenay of Hereford led the opposition to royal demands, but Sudbury and the Crown generally achieved their goals. When Whittlesey finally died in 1374 and Langham's claim had been disregarded, Sudbury and Courtenay were the chief contenders for Canterbury. It was Sudbury's compliance with the Crown's objectives and his ability to control convocation that secured his appointment, though Pope Gregory also had cause to be grateful for Sudbury's part in the papally-mediated Anglo-French talks at Bruges in 1375 and the parallel Anglo-papal concordat by which his brother, Roger Beaufort, was released by the English and the raising of a papal subsidy in England was permitted.[7] Thus the English clergy found themselves doubly taxed by the time the Good Parliament met in 1376. Courtenay was translated to London and championed both the anti-subsidy cause and ecclesiastical liberties against anticlericalism on the part of the Crown. John of Gaunt personified the threat to the Church. In 1376 the duke found the former chancellor William of Wykeham, bishop of Winchester, guilty of acts of malversation committed some five years earlier. Even in 1373, Wykeham had been named by Gaunt as an executor of his will, suggesting that the his motives were now less than honourable. Wykeham was deprived of his (considerable) temporal income and banned from coming within 20 miles of the court. When convocation met in February 1377, Courtenay presented the duke's treatment of the bishop as injurious to the Church in general, and persuaded his fellow churchmen to refuse to consider inclusion of the clergy in Gaunt's proposed poll tax until Wykeham was free to join them. Sudbury was forced to adjourn proceedings.

The achievements of the Good Parliament – which was the longest to date – were soon reversed by the Gaunt-led government, and relations between the duke and the bishop of London remained extremely tense. In 1378 two of the duke's associates, Sir Alan Buxhill and Sir Ralph Ferrers, attempted to arrest a couple of fugitive squires who had taken sanctuary in Westminster Abbey. One of the fugitives was killed in the fracas, which also left a sacristan mortally wounded. Courtenay issued a sentence of excommunication against those responsible, either directly or indirectly, for the violation of sanctuary and bloodshed in the house of God. Although Gaunt was among those specifically excluded from the excommunication, the force of his reaction left the chronicler Walsingham in no doubt that he interpreted Courtenay's action as aimed at him. These incidents should not be taken in isolation, for they do not present the full picture of Courtenay's relationship with Gaunt, let alone that of the Church with the Crown. Indeed, upon Courtenay's election as archbishop the duke sent him a dozen does with which to restock his deer park, and at a meeting of the royal council at Westminster in 1385, Courtenay provoked the king's wrath by defending the aged Gaunt when some of Richard II's close associates – 'unsound counsel' – plotted to kill him. Later that day the subject was raised again when the king and the archbishop happened to meet on the river. Richard's famously short temper flared and he threatened to run Courtenay through with his sword, but was restrained by the attendants on his barge. Reconciliation took seven months to achieve. The archbishop risked his personal safety by seeking to defend that of the realm. Richard had closer associates on the episcopal bench, among them Robert Braybrooke of London. When Anne of Bohemia married Richard in 1382, Braybrooke claimed precedence over Courtenay because the latter's pallium had yet to arrive from Rome. A compromise was effected whereby Braybrooke officiated at the royal wedding and Courtenay at the queen's coronation.

The papacy was consistently weak *vis-à-vis* the secular powers in the fourteenth and fifteenth centuries, but never more so than after the election of Urban VI (1378–89), when western Christendom became divided between Urbanists, who acknowledged Pope Urban in Rome, and Clementines, who supported the anti-pope 'Clement VII' (1378–94) in Avignon. In 1378, when most of the cardinals left Rome and elected one of their number as an alternative to Urban, Sudbury voiced anti-French loyalty to the pope by preaching on the text *Unis erit pastor noster*, but was not rewarded with a cardinal's hat when Urban sought to recreate the Sacred College from virtually nothing after the mass defection to Avignon.[8] That honour went instead to Bishop Courtenay of London, who nevertheless refused to recognise it. Had he accepted Urban's offer, the beleaguered pontiff would have acquired the services of a most stout-hearted churchman. By the same token, Courtenay would have been obliged to resign his bishopric and reside in Rome, a course of events by no means unattractive to Sudbury and Gaunt.

In 1380 Archbishop Sudbury, as chancellor, opened yet another parliament with an appeal for war finance. The sums were huge and the means chosen by parliament to raise them was a flat-rate poll tax of three groats per head, which put a proportionally greater burden on people poorer than the parliamentary elite who determined it. Encouraged by the excommunicated priest John Ball to 'lay aside the yoke of serfdom', the commons of Kent and East Anglia did just that by rebelling in June 1381 and briefly taking control of the capital. For his part, the rebel leader Wat Tyler suggested Ball as a suitable replacement for Sudbury. As government broke down, the archbishop joined King Richard in the Tower on 11 June and counselled negotiation with the rebels, which resulted in Richard's encounter with them at Mile End. Apportioning blame for the misgovernment of Richard's reign became commonplace, but the rebels had no doubt that Gaunt, Sudbury and the treasurer Sir Robert Hales were the guilty parties at that stage. John Ball had been imprisoned in the archbishop's palace at Maidstone and thus had a personal animus against Sudbury, but was released by the rebels, who also attacked the archbishop's property in Canterbury. Lambeth Palace was pillaged by a group of rebels on 12 June, but fared better than Gaunt's London palace of the Savoy, which was burned to the ground. Gaunt himself was in Berwick and retreated into Scotland for good measure, but his known associates were hunted down and some of them were executed. In the Tower, Sudbury resigned the chancellorship, but it was not enough to save his life, for the Kentish men stormed the fortress on the 14th and found Sudbury and Hales hiding in the chapel of St John in the White Tower. Both were thereupon taken to Tower Hill and executed. Sudbury's inexperienced executioner allegedly delivered eight blows before the archbishop's head was finally severed from his body. Although William Courtenay had been Sudbury's adversary within the governing elite, he was still a member of that elite and, as archbishop, duly led the government's tough approach towards the rebel regions. The Peasants' Revolt of 1381 resulted in the shedding of archiepiscopal blood, but it was not the only popular rebellion with which fourteenth- and fifteenth-century primates were confronted. Walter Reynolds retreated into Kent when Bishop Stapeldon of Exeter was murdered by a London mob in 1326 as a symbol of Edward II's misgovernment, and John Kemp took a leading role in stamping out Jack Cade's revolt in 1450.

Courtenay's successor at Canterbury, Thomas Arundel, met with the favour of Thomas Walsingham, that maker and breaker of the posthumous reputations of primates, who described him as a 'most eminent bulwark of the English church and invincible champion', and a man who 'preferred justice to gold, and equity to pure gold'. A bishop from the age of twenty, Arundel was a force to be reckoned with on the episcopal bench from 1374 through to his death in 1414.[9] The most dramatic episodes in his long career were occasioned by dealings with his kinsmen Richard II and Henry IV (1399–1413). Arundel's father had been a close friend of Edward III, while John of Gaunt counted Bishop Arundel among his clerical allies. After the bishop's brother, another Earl Richard, succeeded their father in 1376 relations soured, for the younger earl was an abrasive character who antagonised both Gaunt and King Richard. It was this earl who made common cause with Thomas Beauchamp, earl of Warwick, and Edward III's son Thomas of Woodstock, duke of Gloucester (grandfather of Archbishop Bourchier), to become known as the Lords Appellant. The men against whom they appealed were some of the king's favourites and counsellors, putting them in the tradition established by Archbishop Courtenay. In the Merciless Parliament of 1388 the Appellants gained the upper hand and two of the appellees were executed. This was during Bishop Arundel's first stint as chancellor of England: he was not a disinterested bystander. Indeed, Arundel's intermittent exercise of the office (1386–9, 1391–6, 1399) can be taken as a useful measure of the fluctuations in the Appellants' cause, for he lost office whenever Richard managed to assert control over the government. In January 1397, the new archbishop attended a dinner at which a plot was hatched to seize and imprison for life the king and the dukes of York and Lancaster. Richard learned of this and had the duke of Gloucester arrested. He died in prison. It was July that year, while parliament met, when the earls of Arundel and Warwick had previous pardons revoked and were also arrested. By this means the king gained his revenge for the Merciless Parliament. The earl of Arundel appeared before parliament to answer the charges against him, at which the archbishop rose to defend his brother, only to be silenced by Richard and told not to appear in that place. The earl was executed for treason that same day and the archbishop exiled. The king's sometime secretary, Roger Walden, was shoehorned into the Canterbury vacancy. Walden appears as no more than a footnote curiosity in the list of papally recognised archbishops, but is one of the 104 acknowledged by the modern Church of England.

Of the original Appellants only the earl of Warwick survived, but the king's critics were not silenced, for Henry Bolingbroke, earl of Hereford, and Thomas Mowbray, earl of Nottingham and duke of Norfolk, had now become Appellants. When these two accused each other of treason and were both exiled in 1398, one of the terms of the exile was that Bolingbroke would not make contact with his cousin the banished archbishop, which is precisely what happened within months.[10] Bolingbroke lacked both statesmanship and experience of government, so had particular need of Arundel. Together they landed at Ravenspur in Yorkshire and made their way to North Wales to confront Richard upon his return from Ireland. Arundel was a key figure at every stage of the usurpation process, but achieved greatest prominence as the official voice of the new Lancastrian regime, addressing Henry IV's first parliament in his capacity as chancellor: King Richard, he announced, had been a child, but King Henry was a man.[11] No immediate reprisal was taken against Walden, though he was briefly imprisoned in the Tower in 1400 in connection with a plot against Henry, but compensated with the see of London at Braybrooke's death in 1405.[12]

Not even Archbishop Arundel was immune to deception by the king he helped to create. In 1405, Archbishop Richard Scrope of York made common cause with the Percy family against his erstwhile ally Henry and raised a small army with which to resist the king. Henry arrested Scrope as a traitor, prompting Archbishop Arundel to ride all day and all night on Whit Sunday to intercede with Henry at Bishopthorpe, near York. It was an act of heroic futility, for Arundel was advised to rest after his exertions; while he slept Scrope was beheaded. As coups go, it was clever, but it was also an act that came to haunt the usurper king and gave Arundel a subtle personal authority over him towards the ends of both their lives.

From 1409 the papal schism was further confused by the election of a third alternative pope by the Council of Pisa: Alexander V, followed in 1410 by 'John XXIII'. Arundel was enthusiastic about the council and the English delegation to Pisa was led by men of considerable talent: Bishops Robert Hallum of Salisbury, Henry Chichele of St Davids and Nicholas Bubwith of Bath and Wells, together with Prior Thomas Chillenden of Christ Church, Canterbury. Resolution of the papal schism duly involved the highly reluctant abdication of Gregory XII (1406–15), French rejection of the Avignonese anti-pope 'Benedict XIII', the undignified deposition of 'John XXIII', and four years of debate about the structure and reform of the Church at the Council of Constance (1414–18). Between the deposition of 'John XXIII' in May 1415 and election of Martin V in November 1417, England recognised no pope. This left Henry V (1413–22) as master of the English Church and allowed his archbishop of Canterbury, Henry Chichele, to confirm appointments to vacant sees without reference to any higher authority. Neither of them participated personally at Constance. The king's uncle, Henry Beaufort, bishop of Winchester, did so and took the credit for securing the election of Martin V (1417–31), the anti-conciliar Roman patrician who took the papacy back to his native city. Martin rapidly expressed his appreciation by making Beaufort both a cardinal and *legatus a latere* in England, complete with exemption from the archbishop of Canterbury's jurisdiction. The king invoked Praemunire and quashed the appointment. Beaufort was in a stronger position after Henry V's death in 1422 and the accession of the infant Henry VI (1422–61, 1470–1), being one of the dominant figures in the regency government. It was only in 1426, therefore, that Beaufort was able to accept the cardinalate. Hardly had Henry V died than Martin launched an investigation into the indulgence Chichele had granted for pilgrims to Canterbury in 1420, the second centenary of the translation of Becket's remains. It took potential custom away from Martin's Roman Jubilee of 1423. The pope was given to understand that Beaufort had assumed Becket's mantle, defending the rights of the Church against encroachments by the Crown, while Chichele was depicted to Martin as anti-papal because he appeared to take no action against the statutes of Provisors. Between 1427 and 1429 Chichele's legatine powers were revoked by way of punishment for this perceived weakness. Underlying these tensions was Martin's sympathy with Beaufort as a fellow noble; Chichele, their social inferior, he treated with contempt. As if to rub salt in the wound, Chichele was forced to accept Martin's nephew Prospero Colonna as archdeacon of Canterbury.[13]

Further disputes followed with Martin's successor, the Venetian Eugenius IV (1431–47). In 1439, Eugenius appealed to the universality of his conciliarist adversaries by appointing a large number of new cardinals from a wide geographical spectrum. Chichele was not among them, but Archbishop Kemp of York was, giving rise to a particularly heated dispute about precedence. In the fourteenth century Simon Mepham had revived the old dispute about the carrying of primatial crosses before the archbishops of Canterbury and York when they happened to be in each other's provinces, but that was a minor detail in comparison with the northern primate doubling up as a prince of the Church. Emphasising the superiority of the papacy and all that pertained to it, Eugenius decreed that 'even in his own province an archbishop should go after a cardinal'. It was galling enough for Chichele to have Cardinal Beaufort as his suffragan at Winchester and Cardinal Kemp generally resident south of the Humber, but further insult was added to his injury by another of Eugenius's 1439 appointments to the Sacred College, Louis de Luxembourg, archbishop of English-held Rouen and bishop of Ely *(in commendam)* from 1437. This last appointment Chichele considered 'an evil precedent, to the great detriment and loss of the English church'.[14]

The Lancastrian dynasty sought legitimacy by consciously tying its fortunes to those of the Church. This is well illustrated by the positive relationship between Henry V and Archbishop Chichele. In 1410–11, when Henry IV ailed and Prince Henry assumed the reins of government, Chichele joined the king's council and went on to become one of Henry V's most trusted servants, chosen as godfather to the king's heir. Chichele found no contradiction in serving both Church and Crown: 'an archbishop of Canterbury, both spiritual leader and secular councillor, was acting for the good of society as a whole'.[15] Much has been made of the parts played by Cardinal Beaufort and Duke Humphrey of Gloucester in the creation of the legend surrounding Henry V, but it should not be forgotten that Chichele was present at many of the defining moments of the king's career. He accompanied Henry to Southampton in 1415 and welcomed the victorious king to Canterbury after Agincourt.[16] It was Chichele who made a cheap but effective contribution to the war effort by raising St George's day to one of the principal feasts of the English liturgical calendar, and who ordered that the feast of the French martyrs Crispin and Crispinian (25 October, the day of the famous victory) be given greater honour.[17] In 1416 Chichele greeted the Emperor Sigismund at Canterbury and when the latter stayed at Westminster, Henry took up temporary residence at Lambeth. The archbishop was with Henry to negotiate peace terms in Calais the same year, at the surrender of Rouen in 1419 and the siege of Melun in 1420; he received the king's body at Dover two years later. At the opening of the first parliament of Henry VI's reign, Chichele preached a sermon that articulated the government line: the late king's policies were to be maintained during his son's minority. The archbishop supported those policies with clerical taxation until that was no longer a viable option. At his death in 1443, Henry VI lauded him as a kindest of fathers to his province, which he had ruled in a 'genial, calm, peaceable and friendly way'.

From 1443 John Stafford was the quiet man of Canterbury. His identification with the Lancastrian dynasty and, indeed, his political astuteness, were such that he could be regarded as a client of Cardinal Beaufort and an ally of Humphrey of Gloucester, even when relations between those two royal uncles were at their most hostile. The question of clerical taxation recurred: Stafford got into trouble with Eugenius IV by turning a papal demand for the immediate levying of a crusading tenth into a voluntary contribution to be collected after a year or so.

John Kemp's translation from one province to the other came in 1452, thanks to the support of Edmund Beaufort, duke of Somerset and nephew of the late cardinal. Kemp was a keen advocate of Henry VI's Angevin marriage and godfather to the one child it produced. In 1453 the king suffered his first period of mental incapacity. Kemp's incapacity was physical, but the simultaneous weakness of both king and archbishop reflected the decay in the body politic of mid-fifteenth-century England. It was during Kemp's brief tenure at Canterbury (1452–4) that the English were finally forced to withdraw from Normandy and, shortly after his death, that the ruling elite descended into the open conflict known as the Wars of the Roses. Thomas Bourchier's translation to Canterbury in 1454 occurred during the first protectorship of Richard, duke of York. Bourchier's long archiepiscopate spanned the reigns of Henry VI, Edward IV, Edward V, Richard III and Henry VII, and thereby witnessed the full scope of the Yorkist and Lancastrian claims and counter-claims for the crown. From 1467 Bourchier was also a non-curial cardinal, a distinction that caused no disturbance whatsoever to the English government or hierarchy.

An alternative and much briefer way of introducing some of the archbishops of this period is to refer to Shakespeare's history plays. Chichele is the archbishop whose lengthy explanation of Salic law and Henry V's claim to the French crown is terminated by the arrival of the dauphin's tennis balls. Bourchier's function is to persuade Elizabeth Woodville to release her son Richard, duke of York (grandson of the eponymous protector), from sanctuary in Westminster Abbey to join his brother Edward V in the Tower and thus facilitate Richard of Gloucester's usurpation in 1483. Also in *Richard III*, John Morton is the bishop of Ely arrested by Gloucester, who emerged as Henry VII's choice for Canterbury just three years later. Though of a later era, it may also be noted that Thomas Cranmer makes an appearance in Shakespeare and Fletcher's *Henry VIII*.

In reality, Archbishop Bourchier was so much a part of England's ruling elite that he could claim kinship with the young duke of York by a number of genealogical routes. Most significantly, his mother, Anne, was the daughter of Thomas of Woodstock, duke of Gloucester, the youngest son of Edward III. The House of York was descended from Edward's second and fourth sons, that of Lancaster from his third, John of Gaunt. Moreover, Bourchier's sister Eleanor married John Mowbray, third duke of Norfolk, and it was to Anne Mowbray, the Norfolk heiress, that the infant Richard, duke of York, was married in 1478. In the period under review, two other archbishops were of noble birth: William Courtenay, son of Hugh, earl of Devon, and Thomas Arundel, son of Richard Fitzalan, earl of Arundel. Again, their maternal kin were the more significant, for Archbishop Arundel's maternal grandfather was Edward III's trusted associate Henry, earl of Lancaster, and Archbishop Courtenay's was Humphrey Bohun, earl of Hereford, who married a daughter of Edward I. To underline the sense of the English nobility as a closed elite, dynastic connections can be made easily enough between Courtenay, Arundel, Courtenay's great adversary John of Gaunt, and Gaunt's son Henry IV. Through his mother, Courtenay was the second cousin of Mary Bohun, Bolingbroke's first wife and the mother of his illustrious sons Henry V, Thomas, duke of Clarence, John, duke of Bedford, and Humphrey, duke of Gloucester.[19] For his part, Arundel was the cousin of Blanche of Lancaster, Gaunt's first wife and Bolingbroke's mother. Through his sister Joan, Arundel was also uncle to Mary Bohun. Exalted birth doubtless contributed to the fearlessness of both these archbishops when dealing with kings and princes.

One of the archbishops in this group was descended from the knightly class, John Stafford being the illegitimate son of Sir Humphrey Stafford of Southwick Court, Wiltshire. The granting of dispensations to men born out of wedlock so that they might pursue clerical careers, was a standard piece of business for canon lawyers during this period. Stafford's mother, Emma, joined a religious house in Canterbury and died three years after her son became archbishop. Among the other primates, Chichele was a representative of urban wealth, for his father was a leading man of Higham Ferrers, Northamptonshire, his mother was of a prosperous City of London family and his brothers duly became wealthy London grocers. As immediate successor to two nobly born archbishops, Chichele's relative social inferiority helps to explain his acute consciousness of his archiepiscopal status. It was a consciousness he shared with his more distant predecessor Robert Winchelsey, whose social origins are entirely obscure. Obscurity was certainly held against Walter Reynolds, appointed to Canterbury at Winchelsey's death, for his critics maintained that he was the son of a Windsor baker. A prejudicial source alleged that Roger Walden was the son of a Saffron Walden butcher. With slight geographical variation the story resembles that of Cardinal Wolsey over a century later. In general terms, the social profile of the archbishops tended to rise, and rise quite markedly, from the later thirteenth to the later fifteenth century.

The overwhelming majority of these archbishops came from the wealthy and populous south-east of England, including three from Kent (Winchelsey, Mepham and Kemp) and three from Sussex (Pecham, Bradwardine and Arundel), where the archbishops retained numerous estates. It was not without significance that Thomas Arundel chose to visit his native diocese of Chichester first, after the traditional visitation of Canterbury at the beginning of his archiepiscopate. Likewise, Courtenay headed first for Exeter and his family's Devon power base at the beginning of his extensive metropolitical visitation. Courtenay apart, John Stratford of Stratford-upon-Avon and Simon Langham of Rutland, were born furthest from Canterbury. Some of the archbishops' family names have become obscured, though it is known that Sudbury's parents were Nigel and Sarah Theobald of Sudbury, Suffolk, making it reasonable to refer to their son as 'Simon of Sudbury'. In contrast to contemporary practice in Italy and France, the families of the archbishops reveal few clear cases of clerical dynasticism: William Whittlesey (archbishop 1368–74) was the nephew of Simon Islip (archbishop 1349–66); John Stratford was the brother of Robert Stratford, bishop of Chichester, and probably the uncle of Ralph Stratford, bishop of London. Among the nobles, only Courtenay might be identified as part of a clerical dynasty. His nephew Richard Courtenay was bishop of Norwich, and Richard's nephew Peter Courtenay was successively bishop of Exeter and Winchester.

Clerical careers continued to provide ample opportunities for travel, whether in order to receive a university education, to serve the Universal Church in Rome, Avignon or elsewhere, or to serve the English Church at diocesan or metropolitan level. Between the late thirteenth and late fifteenth century subtle changes can be detected in the pattern of the archbishops' travels, changes that reflect the economic and political contractions mentioned above. Only the first three of the archbishops under consideration – Kilwardby, Pecham and Winchelsey – gravitated along the intellectually-charged Oxford-Paris axis, after which the majority were educated exclusively at Oxford, paralleling a trend away from theological studies and towards law. The rise of the Oxford legists at the expense of the Parisian theologians may be interpreted as a footnote to the history of Anglo-French relations, particularly after Edward III launched his prolonged bid for the French crown.

John Pecham may well have attended the Parisian lectures of the Franciscan polymath Roger Bacon; Winchelsey was certainly influenced by those of Aquinas. Only Simon Sudbury appears to have been educated exclusively at Paris, and only William Whittlesey seems to have been a product of Cambridge, his local Fenland university.[20] There is no evidence that either Reynolds or Walden were graduates, let alone scholars of any distinction. Thus the overwhelming majority of the archbishops in this period received one or more of their degrees from Oxford, with Winchelsey, Courtenay and Bourchier each briefly holding the chancellorship of the university: their names alone reflect the beginning of the gradual shift whereby the office became associated with men of high standing in the realm, rather than active members of the university. A clear majority of the archbishops held doctorates, with theologians – Kilwardby, Winchelsey, Mepham and Bradwardine – giving way over time to lawyers, Stratford, Offord, Whittlesey, Sudbury, Courtenay, Chichele and Kemp. The see of Canterbury was occupied by lawyers for all but two decades between 1333 and 1454, a trend reflected among their contemporaries throughout the hierarchy of western Christendom. The Oxford career of the period's only Benedictine archbishop, Simon Langham of Westminster, was terminated before he could graduate by the Black Death of 1348–9. Thomas Arundel also left in a hurry, but that was because of his appointment to the see of Ely at the sub-canonical age of twenty. By the mid-fourteenth century, six colleges had emerged among the plethora of Oxford's halls and inns for students: Merton, Balliol and University College in the thirteenth century, Exeter, Oriel and Queen's in the fourteenth. Thomas Bradwardine began his distinguished Oxford career at Balliol, William Courtenay was associated with the hall founded by Bishop Stapeldon of Exeter – the future Exeter College – and Thomas Arundel was resident at Oriel in 1373, where his father paid for the college's first chapel. However, these foundations paled academically when compared to Merton. Bradwardine was a fellow of Merton in 1323 and stayed until 1335 when he joined the household of Richard of Bury, bishop of Durham. John Offord was also a fellow of Merton, as was John Kemp at the end of the century. It has been claimed that archbishops Mepham, Stratford and Islip were fellows of the college, but there is a lack of evidence to support this assertion.[21] All four orders of friars had houses in Oxford, with the Dominicans at Blackfriars and Franciscans at Greyfriars rivalling Merton in academic distinction. From 1291 Gloucester College was home to Benedictine monks from throughout the province of Canterbury, having been founded eight years earlier for those of St Peter's Abbey, Gloucester.

Bradwardine was the last and most influential of the Schoolmen to be appointed to the see of Canterbury. The brevity of his pontificate was in inverse proportion to his academic reputation. The early fourteenth century was the 'great Mertonian period' in the history of Oxford, and Bradwardine was among the most distinguished ornaments of the college, the university and of late medieval scholarship in general. Together with his fellow Mertonian 'calculators' he sought to understand physical phenomena through mathematical principles, seen most notably in his work on motion, *Tractatus de proportionibus velocitatum motuum* (1328). The Oxford Franciscan William of Ockham also wrote on motion, but it was in theological matters that he clashed with Bradwardine. In *De causa Dei contra Pelagium* (written by 1344), the future primate condemned Ockham's followers as latter-day Pelagians who argued that man could make some contribution towards his salvation and, therefore, not be entirely dependent on divine will.[22] A further facet of Bradwardine's mind is revealed in his work on logic, *De insolubilibus*, treating of such teasing problems as the statement 'I am telling a lie'. The esteem in which Bradwardine was held in the academic community is reflected in the epithet by which he became known: the *Doctor profundus*. Thus he can be appreciated alongside William of Ockham, who was *invincibilis* or *singularis*, Alexander of Hales *(Doctor irrefragabilis)*, Roger Bacon *(Doctor (ad)mirabilis)* and, more prosaically, Richard of Middleton *(Doctor solidus* or *copiosus)*. It may be noted that English Schoolmen did not rise to the angelic, ecstatic or seraphic heights of their continental counterparts, Aquinas, Jan van Ruysbroeck and Bonaventure.

Intellectual eminence among the archbishops was determined first by the choice of theological studies in preference to the utilitarianism of law and then, Bradwardine apart, by membership of the new mendicant orders. Robert Kilwardby was the only Dominican to be archbishop of Canterbury and John Pecham the only Franciscan. Each was English provincial of his order prior to the Canterbury appointment and both were scholars of renown. The first friars had arrived in England in 1224, the year after Honorius III approved the Franciscan Rule, but had passed their prime by 1300, with the Franciscans divided by the debate over Christ's poverty. Kilwardby and Pecham therefore represented the brief golden age of their respective orders: Kilwardby was the contemporary of Aquinas and Albertus Magnus among the Preachers, while Pecham followed the lead of Bonaventure, general of the Franciscans from 1257 to 1274. Pecham was the more forceful and authoritarian of the two, disputing with Aquinas in Paris in the 1270s, attacking his English counterpart Kilwardby on matters of recruitment *(Contra Kilwardby)*, and defending his friars from attack by secular priests. In true Franciscan style, his poverty was the more conspicuous, manifested in his *Tractatus de paupertate evangelica* as much as in the debts he incurred upon his appointment to Canterbury. He was even threatened with excommunication if he failed to repay the money he owed to his Italian bankers. In the academic realm, Pecham's energy was channelled into attacks on the study of canon law, into preventing the spread of Thomism and Averroism, and into the composition of scientific works on spheres and perspective. Kilwardby was even more committed to providing aids for students, including the 'masterly' *De ortu scientiarum* for those studying the arts syllabus. His works on grammar, logic and rhetoric neatly spanned the trivium and his *Tabula super originalis patrum* made the patristic corpus more manageable. His commentaries included one of the earliest on the *Sentences* of Peter Lombard. Although Robert Winchelsey brought the return of the seculars to Canterbury after the death of Pecham, he continued the Dominican tradition of Kilwardby through his outspoken defence of Thomism. Winchelsey's reputation is that of a distinguished theologian, but it is a reputation that can only be supported by fragments. This can be contrasted with Bradwardine's extensive *oeuvre*.

In the pre-Avignon period, Kilwardby, Pecham and Winchelsey all gained experience of the papal court in Rome. Kilwardy also attended the Second Council of Lyon in 1274, and Pecham, in his capacity as English provincial, went to Padua in 1276 for the Franciscan general chapter. The Avignon papacy represented geographical contraction because Provence was so much more accessible for English clerics. Among the consecrations that took place there were Stratford's to Winchester and those of Mepham and Bradwardine to Canterbury. Sudbury's Parisian education acted as the springboard for his curial career as a chaplain to Innocent VI (1352–62) and as an auditor (judge) of the Rota, the court which took its name from the round table at which it met in the Palais des Papes. Sudbury was the only papal curialist to become archbishop of Canterbury in this period. In effect he squeezed through a small window of opportunity, for Italians increasingly dominated the papal administration once the popes returned to Rome.[23] Thereafter, Arundel and Chichele were the only members of the group to have direct experience of the papal court. Arundel passed through Rome briefly during his period of exile, which also witnessed his discovery of an 'earthly paradise' near Florence. With Richard II deposed and Arundel restored to Canterbury, Chichele's experience as king's proctor in Rome in the first decade of the fifteenth century set a pattern for numerous English clerics in the following generations, but not for his Canterbury successors. He was already Henry IV's envoy to Gregory XII when the see of St Davids became vacant in 1407; consecration by Gregory duly followed at Siena on 17 June 1408. The proctorship made Chichele a natural choice for inclusion in the English delegation to the Council of Pisa in 1409, after which he took no further part in the conciliar experiments.

St Davids was the richest of the four Welsh bishoprics, but wealthier than only Carlisle, Rochester and Chichester when compared against those in England. It was arguably not the most obvious route to take to Canterbury. Even Archbishop Laud, in the seventeenth century, was not translated directly from St Davids to Canterbury, but reached it only by way of Bath and Wells, and London. As the examples of Arundel and Bourchier illustrate, noble birth provided a means of bypassing the lower rungs of the clerical ladder and even the less lucrative bishoprics. In this they bore a closer resemblance to papal *nipoti* and the noble clerics of France and Italy than they did to their fellow English bishops. Ely, the fourth wealthiest bishopric in England, after Winchester, Canterbury and York, was held by more future primates than any other in the fourteenth and fifteenth centuries: Langham, Arundel, Bourchier and Morton. A particularly full set of accounts survive for Arundel's years at Ely, facilitating reconstruction of his household and his diocesan itineraries. London's official wealth was equivalent to only two-fifths of that of Ely, but this was countered by the bishop's geographical proximity to the heart of secular government. Two successive fourteenth-century bishops of London, Sudbury and Courtenay, were translated to Canterbury, and Roger Walden received it as consolation. The mendicants Kilwardby and Pecham, together with Winchelsey, Mepham, Bradwardine and Islip were promoted to

Canterbury without episcopal experience. By way of contrast, the overt careerist John Kemp was translated from Rochester to Chichester, Chichester to London, London to York, and York to Canterbury, with a rapidity that matched his ascent of the parallel ladder of royal service. York being furthest from the centre of political power, he rarely visited it and gained a negative reputation there.

As their clerical careers progressed, many of the future archbishops were employed on foreign missions by the Crown, missions with no specific ecclesiastical dimension. Again, this tended to be the preserve of the non-nobles, men who worked their way to the top. Stratford, Offord, Islip and Sudbury fell into this category, as did Kemp. In 1415 Kemp was sent to Aragon to treat for a Spanish marriage for Henry V, 1424 saw him in Scotland, and 1435 at Arras, where he led the English embassy to the triangular English-French-Burgundian peace congress. Diplomatic missions were of short duration and easily alternated with posts in domestic government. Thus the ablest of the king's clerks gained a wide range of experience both at home and abroad. With the rise of the civil and canon lawyers in the fourteenth and fifteenth centuries, a distinct pattern of royal service seems to emerge in the pre-Canterbury careers of future archbishops, seen most notably in the fact that Offord, Islip, Stafford and Kemp were all keepers of the privy seal, and that Stratford, Offord, Arundel, Stafford and Kemp were chancellors of England at the time of their Canterbury appointments. Reynolds, Walden and Stafford had been treasurers of England; Reynolds a particularly irresponsible one, by all accounts.

The role in which the archbishops most conspicuously served their kings was as chancellor of England. Kilwardby, Pecham and Winchelsey were sufficiently distanced from the Crown not to be invited to fill this office by Edward I. Edward II appointed eight chancellors over the twenty years of his reign, of whom just one – Reynolds – was archbishop. The ratio not only increased to three archbishops (Stratford, Offord and Langham) out of eighteen chancellors in Edward III's reign, but the office was fairly monopolised by John Stratford in the 1330s, except for short periods when it was held by his brother Robert. In January 1380 Simon Sudbury offered himself as the first primate-chancellor of Richard II's reign, albeit with the reputation of being a political lightweight. His speech at the opening of parliament in November 1380 called for a grant to the Crown, a grant for which the assembly levied the infamous poll tax and thereby triggered the sequence of events that led to the archbishop's violent death six months later. It was perhaps natural that the vigorous Courtenay succeeded the decapitated Sudbury as chancellor, but he was not the most conciliatory of figures and was rapidly replaced. From 1386 to 1389 and again from 1391 to 1396, Thomas Arundel was the chancellor imposed upon Richard II by his powerful adversaries. Three times in Henry IV's reign Arundel doubled up as archbishop and chancellor, making him the king's principal counsellor until Henry Beaufort emerged as the pre-eminent political cleric. John Kemp was archbishop of York when he first served as chancellor of England, after an apprenticeship as chancellor of English Normandy, and was succeeded by John Stafford in 1432. The fact that Stafford was an effective administrator and held the office for eighteen years, may be set against the usual picture of Henry VI's reign as a period of steady disintegration in political life. Kemp was chancellor again from 1450 and Bourchier held the office briefly in 1455–6, resigning it when Richard of York resumed the protectorship of the realm, after which none of the Lancastrian or Yorkist kings considered him suitable for the office.

The rise of the canon lawyers was also reflected in the evolving administration of the diocese and province of Canterbury, though it may be noted that defining the composition of the Canterbury convocation was not the only administrative development associated with the theologian Archbishop Pecham. In 1279 he granted Roger Rothwell the right to exercise jurisdiction over the deanery of St Mary-le-Bow, the church from which the archbishop's thirteen London peculiars were administered. By the end of the century the Court of Arches had become the most important ecclesiastical court in the province, and in 1419 John Stafford succeeded John Kemp as its dean. Fittingly, the earliest extant archiepiscopal register also dates from Pecham's time. His register, together with those of Winchelesy, Langham, Chichele, Bourchier, Morton, Warham and Parker have been published. An early compilation of material from the archbishops' archive was William Lyndwood's *Provinciale* (completed 1430), which includes all the provincial constitutions from Langton to Chichele (1222–1416) and forms the most important work devoted to English canon law. Lyndwood was a close associate of Archbishop Chichele, acting as his chancellor, and holding the offices of auditor of causes in the Court of Audience, and official principal of the provincial court of Canterbury. From 1432 he was keeper of the privy seal and held the bishopric of St Davids, Chichele's former see, from 1442 until his death in 1446.

Chichele's absences abroad made him particularly dependent on reliable servants, agents and associates such as Lyndwood, but all the archbishops required a vicar-general to assist them in the Canterbury diocese. This duty fell to members of the Christ Church community, sometimes even to the prior himself, as was the case with Prior John Wodnesburgh, who was Chichele's vicar-general.[24] From the early fourteenth to the early sixteenth century there was also an irregular sequence of suffragen bishops of dioceses *in partibus* based in the Canterbury diocese. Many of these were members of the mendicant orders and included, in Bourchier's time, the Augustinian friars William Westkarre and Henry Cranebroke.

Most of the archbishops took their metropolitan responsibilities seriously and managed to visit selected dioceses, though some were exceptionally conscientious visitors. Courtenay's energies were poured into one of the most extensive metropolitical visitations ever undertaken in England. Beginning in Exeter, where the tactless Archbishop Mepham had been denied entry to the cathedral, and continuing through Bath and Wells, Worcester, Chichester, Rochester, Lincoln, Salisbury, Canterbury and Hereford, he made a thorough investigation of the English portion of his province between 1384 and 1396.[25] Not even Courtenay could match Pecham's achievement of conducting visitations in every diocese of the southern province, including the four in Wales, a feat completed over an eight-year period. Arundel and Chichele were also notable visitors, but Arundel wisely avoided visiting dioceses where Courtenay's thoroughness had provoked conflict with his suffragans, and Chichele took the precaution of visiting Lincoln during his own *sede vacante* administration of the see.

For the earlier archbishops in this group, and most particularly for the zealous Pecham, the suppression of clerical abuses was a major priority. Fired with the reforming enthusiasm engendered by the Second Council of Lyon, he held two important provincial synods. The decrees enacted by these councils of Reading (1279) and Lambeth (1281) sought to counter abuses such as pluralism, the perennial problem of clerks holding more than one benefice with cure of souls, and to ensure that the laity received sound instruction in the faith.[26] His reforming vigour made him a number of enemies within the English hierarchy, the most notable of whom was his former pupil Thomas Cantilupe, bishop of Hereford, who died excommunicate in 1282 but was nevertheless canonised in 1320, following the emergence of a spontaneous popular cult.

Priorities changed when England acquired its own native heresy through the works of John Wycliffe and the practices of his Lollard followers. Wycliffe was an Oxford theologian, one of whose earlier dealings with an archbishop of Canterbury came in 1367, when Archbishop Langham dismissed him as master of Canterbury College, Simon Islip's Oxford foundation for secular clergy and Christ Church monks. Langham need not be credited with supernatural foresight, for Wycliffe had not lapsed into heresy at that stage and the Benedictine archbishop's prevailing concern was to make Canterbury College an exclusively monastic institution. What attracted the interest of John of Gaunt was less Wycliffe's theological opinions than his sharp criticisms of clerical wealth, in which the duke perceived the potential for material gain by the Crown. Together with Gaunt and Sudbury, Wycliffe was a member of the English delegation at the Anglo-French negotiations in Bruges in 1375, shortly after which Sudbury let Wycliffe off with a caution instead of making a thorough investigation of his views and trying him for heresy, as demanded by Gregory XI. In Sudbury's defence, it has been pointed out that Wycliffe was not technically a heretic at that point and that caution may have been the wisest option.[27] It was in the already heightened atmosphere of the Good Parliament, immediately after Bishop Courtenay and the duke of Lancaster clashed over William of Wykeham and clerical taxation, that there occurred one of the most intensely dramatic incidents in the entire history of relations between the Church and the English Crown. Courtenay obeyed the papal demand that Wycliffe's opinions be tried and he duly appeared in St Paul's Cathedral on 19 February 1377. The theologian was escorted by a group headed by his royal patron, who protested against the arraignment in the strongest terms and tried to have Wycliffe's prosecutors arrested. Thomas Walsingham brings the scene to life:

> . . . the duke . . . and the bishop strove to outdo the other in hurling reproaches. When the duke saw that he was not prevailing, his face became inflamed and he assailed the bishop with repeated threats and swore that he would humble his pride and that of the entire English hierarchy as well. And he added: 'You trust in your parents, who will not be able to assist you, for they will have enough to do defending themselves.' . . . For the sake of the truth the bishop protested. 'I do not put my trust in my parents,' he replied, 'nor in you, nor in any man, but in God, who is not one "who trusts in himself".' Then the duke muttered

under his breath: 'Rather than endure this, I should take him by the hair
and drag him out of the church.'[28]

The version of this altercation which spread among the crowd was that
Gaunt, who retreated to his riverside palace of the Savoy, had threatened to
behead their bishop or had even done so, and they sought to kill him in
revenge. The mob had reached Fleet Street by the time Courtenay persuaded
them to turn back, while Gaunt took the precaution of fleeing across the
Thames to Kennington.

Archbishop Sudbury did not live to see the political elite turn on Wycliffe,
but the chronicler Henry Knighton caught Gaunt's change of heart when he
wrote: 'He believed them [the Lollards] to be holy, because of their appealing
speech and appearance, but he was deceived, as were many others.' On 21
May 1382, at London's Blackfriars, Archbishop Courtenay formally
condemned as heretical or erroneous twenty-four theses taken from Wycliffe's
writings. It was in his rejection of the Church's eucharistic teaching that he
was found to be most at fault. It is related that London was shaken by an
earthquake that day, thereby gaining the Blackfriars assembly the name of
the Earthquake Synod. Gaunt instructed two prominent Wycliffites, Philip
Repingdon and Nicholas Hereford, to submit themselves to Courtenay's
authority. Repingdon was an Augustinian canon and abbot of St Mary-de-
Pré, Leicester, where Gaunt had one of his principal power bases, and took his
patron's advice. It was a useful career move, for he became bishop of Lincoln
in 1404 and was considered worthy of a cardinal's hat four years later, but
refused to acknowledge the promotion. Hereford was not so compliant.
Thereafter interest in and enthusiasm for Wycliffe's views on the sacraments,
priesthood and hierarchy, faith and works was taken up by unlearned lay men
and women such as John Badby, a tailor burned for heresy in 1409. Both
Archbishop Arundel, who interviewed him personally, and Prince Henry, who
was present at his execution, tried to save Badby from himself and from the
flames, but still the tailor persisted in his belief that the eucharistic host was
never more than merely bread. This was one of the more notable episodes in
Arundel's determined quest to root out Lollardy, another being his ban on the
making of vernacular translations of the Bible without permission and, later,
that on the possession or reading of such scriptural translations. Arundel's
campaign culminated in the arrest for heresy of Sir John Oldcastle (Lord
Cobham) in 1413, the knight's escape from the Tower and his leadership of

the Lollard rising of 1414. Oldcastle was captured and executed in 1417. The future archbishop John Kemp's part in the Oldcastle trial was one of the more prominent incidents in his lengthy career as an ecclesiastical lawyer. A measure of Arundel's success in repressing Lollardy, depriving it of its political bite and forcing it into the more obscure provincial backwaters, can be seen in the fact that that the mid-fifteenth century's most celebrated English heresy case concerned the anti-Lollard Reginald Pecock, bishop of Chichester. In 1457 Pecock chose to recant his views on the status of Scripture, was deprived of his bishopric, confined briefly at Canterbury and Maidstone at Archbishop Bourchier's pleasure, and finally at Thorney Abbey in Cambridgeshire.

Wycliffe's translation of the Bible was part of a wider flourishing of English vernacular literacy that can be seen as clearly in the works of Geoffrey Chaucer, William Langland and the Gawain poet, as in those of the English mystics. It is by making connections between literature and the repression of Lollardy that conspiracy theorists have recently pointed accusing fingers at Archbishop Arundel as the force at work behind Chaucer's disappearance from the historical record in 1400.[29] The hypothesis may appear attractive, but the evidence against Arundel is nothing more than circumstantial. In reality, the archbishop was a friend and patron to men of letters, albeit those who tended to write in Latin. During his brief Italian exile he made the acquaintance of the Florentine chancellor and humanist scholar Coluccio Salutati. He also enjoyed the distinction of being celebrated by the poet John Gower, who dedicated his *Vox clamantis* to the archbishop, neatly summarising his career and attributes in the process:

> Hic Thomas natus comitis fuit intitulatus,
> Clericus aptatus, doctor de iure creatus,
> Legibus ornatus, facundus, morigeratus,
> Cum Christo gratus, in plebeque magnificatus.
> O quam prelatus! tam purus et immaculatus![30]

Compared to the impact of Becket on English literature it is a modest achievement, but a rare distinction for an archbishop of Arundel's era. One primate certainly named by Chaucer is the learned Thomas Bradwardine, bracketed with St Augustine of Hippo and Boethius in a reference to predestination and free will in the Nun's Priest's Tale:

I   St Luke from the Gospels of St Augustine (the Canterbury Gospels), a sixth-century Italian gospel book thought to have been among the 'very many manuscripts' brought to England by St Augustine. Donated by Archbishop Parker to Corpus Christi College, Cambridge: MS 286, f. 129v. It is on this volume that the archbishop makes his corporal oath to observe the statutes and customs of Canterbury Cathedral just before his enthronement. *(Master and Fellows of Corpus Christi College, Cambridge)*

II Metropolitical throne of St Augustine, Trinity Chapel, Canterbury Cathedral, probably dating from the thirteenth century. In the modern enthronement ceremony the archbishop is enthroned twice, first in the Quire throne as bishop of the see of Canterbury and then in this Purbeck marble chair as primate of all England. *(John Crook)*

III Coronation of Edward II by Archbishop Robert Winchelsey, with other clergy including the archbishop of York, the bishop of Rochester and the abbot of Westminster, in a manuscript from Matthew Parker's collection: Corpus Christi College, Cambridge, MS 20, f. 68r. The importance of the archbishop in the English coronation rite was established by Dunstan's *ordo* for the coronation of Edgar in 973. (*Master and Fellows of Corpus Christi College, Cambridge*)

IV St Dunstan at the feet of the Wisdom of God, probably a self-portrait. This image is from St Dunstan's 'Classbook', a work of Canterbury provenance that contains a collection of texts with script and decoration attributed to Dunstan. The archbishop is shown as a humble monk. *(Bodleian Library, Oxford, MS Auct. F. IV. 32)*

Right: V Martyrdom of
St Thomas Becket: a mid-
fourteenth-century boss in
the nave of Exeter
Cathedral. The archbishop
is hacked to death by the
knights Reginald FitzUrse,
William de Tracy, Hugh de
Morville and Richard le
Breton. John Grandisson,
bishop of Exeter from 1327
to 1369 and one of the
builders of the cathedral,
was also a biographer of
Becket. *(John Crook)*

Below: VI St Thomas
Becket enshrined, from a
stained glass window of
the late twelfth century,
Trinity Chapel, Canterbury
Cathedral. *(John Crook)*

VII Tomb of Archbishop William Courtenay, Trinity Chapel, Canterbury Cathedral. A fearless champion of ecclesiastical liberties. Courtenay originally desired to be buried in Exeter Cathedral, where his parents' chantry had recently been founded, but then declared a deathbed preference for burial in his even more recent collegiate foundation at Maidstone. In the event, Richard II intervened and Courtenay was interred and commemorated in alabaster in his own cathedral church. (*John Crook*)

THOMAS FITZALLENVS FILIVS
COMITIS ARVNDELLIÆ ARC
HIEPISCOPVS CANTVARIENSIS
CONSTABVLARIVS CASTRI DE
QVEENEBOVRGH 27 APR
LIS ANNO DECIMO REGNI
HENRICI QVARTI

VIII   A posthumous depiction of Archbishop Thomas Arundel, scourge of the Lollards. An archbishop in his own province has the right to be preceded by his cross-bearer with cross displayed. The cross generally consists of a simple crucifix or cross mounted upon a staff. Such crosses became generally used by the twelfth century and were the cause of much dispute between the two English provinces. (*Courtauld Institute*)

EFFIGIES VERE REVERENDISSIMI D. THOMÆ CRANMER ARCHIEPISCOPI CANTUARIENSIS

Natus July 2.
MCCCCLXXXIX.
Confecratus Mar.30.
MDXXXIII.

Martyrio Coronatus
Mar.21.MDLV.
Ætatis LXVII.

IX   Archbishop Thomas Cranmer commemorated as a Protestant martyr. Cranmer's first taste of imprisonment was in September 1553, shortly after Mary Tudor made good her claim to the throne, and led to his trial for treason in November that year, along with other players in the unsuccessful attempt to create a Protestant Queen Jane. In March 1554 he was transferred to the Bocardo prison in Oxford, and tried for heresy in the university church in September, before witnessing the deaths of Ridley and Latimer on 16 October. After a period of house arrest at Christ Church, Cranmer was degraded from his ministry and returned to Bocardo. He delivered his final defence in St Mary's on 21 March 1556, and was straightaway burned to death in front of Balliol College. (*J. Strype, Memorials, 1694*)

X   Archbishop Matthew Parker, historian of the primates. The extent of the sixteenth-century archbishops' Protestant convictions can almost be measured by their facial hair. As a convinced Calvinist Edmund Grindal opted for the look of an Old Testament prophet, John Whitgift trimmed both beard and convictions as order and authority demanded, and Parker is sometimes depicted with a moustache but no beard, a neat illustration of the uneasy compromise that was the Elizabethan Settlement. In this print his visage appears to embody continuity over innovation. *(Private collection)*

Above: XI   Paul Delaroche, *Strafford on his way to execution* (1837). By 1641 the royalist cause had failed and both Archbishop Laud and Thomas Wentworth, earl of Strafford, were prisoners in the Tower. On 12 May, as Strafford was led to execution, he passed the place where the archbishop was confined. The earl requested his ally's prayers and blessing. 'The archbishop lifted up his hands and bestowed both, but, overcome with grief, fell to the ground *in animi diliquio*' (quoted by H. Trevor-Roper, *Archbishop Laud*, p. 409). *(Private collection)*

Right: XII   Archbishop William Juxon on his deathbed: the last breath of the prelate who ministered to Charles I on the scaffold and did not forget. *(Lambeth Palace Library)*

XIII   The Seven Bishops: Archbishop William Sancroft and his nonjuring allies in an iconic representation of episcopal fidelity to the Church of England. *(Private collection)*

XIV *The Principal Arch of Lambeth Palace:* Archbishop John Moore, comfortable and confident despite Dissent at home and revolution across the Channel. This image may be said to represent the archbishop as state functionary. *(Private collection)*

XV   Archbishop Archibald Campbell Tait, his daughter Edith Davidson, and her husband, the future archbishop Thomas Randall Davidson, *c.* 1879: keeping the primacy in the family. Davidson was not only Tait's son-in-law, but his secretary, chaplain and biographer. The world-weary Tait poses in the distinctive Anglican prelatical dress of frock coat, apron and gaiters. *(R.T. Davidson and D. Benham,* Life of Archbishop Tait, *1891)*

XVI *Radicals v Religion:* Archbishop Edward White Benson on the defensive between Cardinals Newman and Manning and in support of other Christian leaders, protecting the Church against a host of radicals, from *St Stephen's Review,* 28 November 1885. In reality, Benson was somewhat upstaged by the two cardinals in the national imagination and rather relieved when they died. Newman in 1890, Manning in 1892. *(Lambeth Palace Library)*

XVII Archbishop Cosmo Gordon Lang, painted by Sir William Orpen during Lang's time as archbishop of York. When Hensley Henson, the bishop of Durham, heard that the image had been described as 'proud, prelatical and pompous' he required clarification: 'And may I ask Your Grace to which of these epithets Your Grace takes exception?' *(J.G. Lockhart,* Cosmo Gordon Lang, *p. 290).*

XVIII   The smiling face of Anglicanism: Archbishop Michael Ramsey, accompanied on a journey by his wife Joan. The archbishop's flights were paid for by the Church Commissioners, Mrs Ramsey's by her husband. Ramsey's choice of the cassock on most occasions, in place of the frock coat and gaiters worn by his predecessors, brought him into the ecumenical mainstream, though his taste in headgear, the Canterbury cap, has not been favoured by his successors. *(Press Association)*

> But I ne cannot boult it to the bren,
> As can the holy doctour S. Austin,
> Or Boece, or the Bishop Bradwirdyn.

In addition to receiving their intellectual formation at Oxford, Bradwardine and the other archbishops dealt with the university in two principal capacities, as visitors and as benefactors. Those two noble prelates, William Courtenay and Thomas Arundel, visited the university in 1382 and 1411 respectively. As Oxford produced both John Wycliffe and a considerable proportion of England's beneficed clergy, the archbishops would have been neglecting their duties had they not investigated the orthodoxy of the teaching at what Courtenay called 'the university of heresies'. Equally understandable was the resentment felt by the masters at any threat to their academic independence. During Arundel's visitation, a fellow of Oriel (the archbishop's own college) allegedly claimed that Richard II had exiled the primate because he attempted to visit the university on a previous occasion. Oxonians may have felt they had additional cause to be suspicious of Archbishop Arundel, the man who had left their university to become bishop of Ely without attaining a degree. During his fourteen years at Ely, Arundel had established a Cambridge connection, particularly at Peterhouse. When he was translated to York in 1388, the spiritual writer Walter Hilton was among the Cambridge scholars who accompanied him there. This connection alone makes Arundel the archbishop who can be most clearly associated with the late medieval English mystics, most but not all of whom wrote in the vernacular. The better to appreciate him as part of their world, it may be noted that the span of his life – 1353–1414 – was entirely enveloped by that of Julian of Norwich (c. 1342–after 1416), who began to write down her 'shewings' at about the same time as Arundel was elected to Ely and became an anchoress shortly before his translation to Canterbury.

Even as the mystical and eremitical impulse was felt in fourteenth- and fifteenth-century England, then also flourished the larger monastic houses, such as Christ Church, Canterbury, which maintained a healthy level of recruitment even in the century after the Black Death. It was in 1361 that Archbishop Islip founded Canterbury College, just to the north of St Frideswide's Priory in Oxford, for use by the monks of Christ Church and by secular clerks. As already mentioned, the Benedictine Simon Langham duly extruded the seculars, leaving it as an exclusively monastic community.

In 1384 Archbishop Courtenay made new statutes for the college and strengthened its foundation with revenue from the rectory of Pagham, one of the archiepiscopal manors in Sussex. After the short-lived phenomenon of Wolsey's Cardinal College, St Frideswide's and Canterbury College together emerged from the ecclesiastical revolution of the sixteenth century as Christ Church, though its earlier history is recalled in the buildings of Canterbury Quad. The collegiate foundations of other fourteenth- and fifteenth-century bishops and archbishops survived in more recognisable form because they were not monastic. William of Wykeham founded New College, Oxford, in 1379 in conjunction with his college in Winchester. Henry Chichele was among the earliest beneficiaries of Wykeham's munificence, for he attended the school in Winchester which preceded the building of Winchester College; in similar fashion, he had to reside in a rented hall in Oxford while New College was under construction. Wykeham's example loomed large over Chichele's career, for both were non-noble and both were significant educational patrons. Chichele began in 1417 with his first attempts to promote the career prospects of graduates. In 1432 he founded the Chichele Chest to provide funds for students. 1437 saw the acquisition of land in Oxford for the creation of a Cistercian college dedicated to St Bernard, on the site of what is now St John's College. His outstanding contribution to the university, however, was the foundation of All Souls, the 'College of the Souls of all the faithful departed', primarily those of Henry V, Thomas, duke of Clarence, and all the English dead in the French wars, together with those of the co-founders, Chichele himself and his godson Henry VI, whose statues were placed on the main gate. Like similar collegiate foundations, All Souls was conceived as a large chantry, in which Masses were offered for the founders and for the named and unnamed souls. Unlike most chantries, the university colleges survived the sixteenth-century reform. In the Founder's Statutes of 1443, dated just ten days before his death, Chichele specified that there were to be forty fellows, twenty-four of them in arts and sixteen in law, who were already instructed

> . . . adequately in grammar and composition and competently in plain-song; who, having received the first tonsure, were fit and disposed to take priest's orders, were of free condition and born in lawful wedlock, were advantaged by good circumstances and character, and showed an effective desire to make progress in study.[31]

Among Chichele's gifts and bequests were important pieces of Parisian plate, physical reminders of the English military presence in France and the cause in which Henry V and Clarence died. There was also a sizeable library. All succeeding archbishops of Canterbury have been visitors of All Souls.

As its statutes demonstrate, All Souls was quite clearly inspired by New College. Like Wykeham, Chichele also anticipated his Oxford foundation with a school, which he founded in his home town, Higham Ferrers. It was a tripartite foundation consisting of a college of priests, almshouses and a grammar school, the entire community to pray daily for the souls of Henry V, Queen Catherine, Chichele and all Christian people. This model was perpetuated in the grammar school and college of secular priests founded by John Kemp at Wye, his native place in Kent, where the original flint buildings, arranged around three sides of a quadrangle, remain intact, the core of what has become an agricultural college. Kemp decreed that the provost of this institution was to be a fellow of his own college, Merton. Other chantries associated with the archbishops included that founded by Thomas Arundel in the collegiate church at Maidstone and John Stratford's, for five priests, in Holy Trinity, Stratford-upon-Avon. The latter, in the chapel of St Thomas the Martyr, was established in 1331, two years before Stratford's translation from Winchester to Canterbury, and almost a decade before he identified himself with Becket during the crisis of 1340–1. Along with other chantries, it was suppressed in the sixteenth century. Simon Sudbury displayed loyalty to his home town by rebuilding the west end of the parish church of St Gregory and raising it to collegiate status, accommodation for the warden and five priests being built at the expense of the archbishop and his brother on the spot where their father's house had stood. Of all the archbishops in this period, Simon Langham came to the office with the greatest experience as a patron of building for, as abbot of Westminster, it was he who began the rebuilding of the western part of the nave. Langham's post-abbatial career was short – just twenty-eight months at Canterbury and eight years as a cardinal – but it was sufficient to amass a considerable fortune. As Stratford, Sudbury and Chichele remembered their home towns, so Langham remembered Westminster and its community as his home and family, for his bequest paid for the rebuilding of the abbot's house (now the deanery) together with the southern and western cloisters.

Westminster Abbey was visible from the archbishops' riverside manor at Lambeth, where important building projects were undertaken in the decades following the Peasants' Revolt. In the palace, Archbishop Arundel dedicated a chapel to the Virgin Mary in 1407. Detailed accounts survive for the building of the so-called Lollards' Tower in Chichele's time, and the pier or 'great bridge' was built in 1424–5, on the site of the present Lambeth Pier, a reminder that the archbishops were obliged to travel to and from London and Westminster by barge. No account of the Church in fifteenth-century England would be quite complete without reference to the *Book of Margery Kempe*, in the sixteenth chapter of which the eponymous 'creature' from Lynn relates that she met Archbishop Arundel in his garden at Lambeth. There he provided her with assurances that her lachrymose devotions were perfectly acceptable: this from the scourge of the Lollards to one suspected by her contemporaries of being heretically inclined. Margery also took the opportunity to rebuke Arundel about the behaviour of his household:

My lord, our Lord of all, Almighty God, has not given you your benefice and great worldly wealth in order to maintain those who are traitors to him, and those who slay him every day by the swearing of great oaths. You shall answer for them, unless you correct them, or else put them out of your service.[32]

As Tim Tatton-Brown has pointed out in his history of Lambeth Palace, the archbishop's household was a sizeable organisation by the early fourteenth century, consisting of ten main departments: the wardrobe, chapel, chamber, almonry, buttery, pantry, kitchen, stables, armoury and hall, the last being responsible for heating and lighting.[33] The archbishops' network of more rural manors supplied wood and foodstuffs for Lambeth, as well as forming a series of staging posts between London/Westminster and Canterbury itself.[34] The first of these was Croydon, where the great hall and two-storey porch were built for Archbishop Courtenay, and the great parlour is otherwise known as Arundel's hall, thereby dating it to some time between 1396 and 1414. Stafford rebuilt the great hall less than half a century later, as part of a major scheme continued by Kemp and Bourchier. Moving eastwards from Croydon, the next stop was at Otford, near Sevenoaks, where Archbishop Winchelsey died in 1313. Simon Islip demolished the palace at Wrotham on the grounds that it was too close to Otford, but Archbishop Bourchier nevertheless purchased nearby Knole from Lord Saye and Sele in 1456, enlarged it extensively, enjoyed it in a habitable state for over two decades and died there in 1486. Whether from Otford, Wrotham or Knole, all roads to Canterbury met at Maidstone, the hub of many of the household's activities and, as has been noted, John Ball's place of imprisonment. Archbishops Islip and Courtenay built private rooms here, but more architecturally significant was the latter's reconstruction of the parish church, probably under the direction of Henry Yevele, the king's master mason, for a new college of priests. Courtenay died at Maidstone and requested burial in his collegiate church, but this Richard II ignored, personally supervising the archbishop's burial next to the king's own father, the Black Prince, in the nave of Canterbury Cathedral. Between Maidstone and Canterbury the route lay through Charing, where the great hall of the palace was probably built in Robert Winchelsey's time.

Mayfield in Sussex appears to have been popular with the fourteenth-century archbishops, who built the spectacular great hall there, now preserved as a convent chapel. Mepham, Stratford and Islip all died at Mayfield. In Kent, to the north of Canterbury was Ford, to the east Wingham and Bekesbourne, and to the south Aldington and Saltwood, the last rebuilt by Courtenay and the archbishops' only castle. It was at the rectory of Hackington, close to Canterbury, that Thomas Arundel died in 1414. Some days before his death he lost the power of speech, which his detractors interpreted as singularly appropriate justice for one who stopped the mouths of preachers. He was buried in the chantry that had cost him 1,000 marks in 1400–1, but the 'godly' had their revenge at the Dissolution, when his tomb was targeted for complete destruction. Arundel was one of the most munificent of all the archbishops towards their cathedral, completing the nave in 1405, providing four bells to be hung in the central tower, and adding the spire to the north-west tower which gave the west front an asymmetrical appearance until its removal in 1831. So much was achieved in a short time because Arundel's largesse coincided with the enterprising regime of Thomas Chillenden (d. 1411), 'the greatest builder of a prior there ever was'. Archbishops Sudbury and Courtenay were also major benefactors of the cathedral, the former financing the rebuilding of the nave in the perpendicular style of Henry Yevele. Courtenay, Arundel and Chichele all bequeathed books to the cathedral and, from 1432, Prior Thomas Goldstone I supervised the construction of a purpose-built library with funds supplied by Archbishop Chichele.[35] Sudbury and Arundel also made significant contributions to the walls and gates of Canterbury, a city of some 4,000 people in the post-plague period.

The cult of Becket, as well as proximity to the Channel ports, continued to provide Canterbury with a transient population of pilgrims and other travellers. Archbishop Chichele greeted the Emperor Sigismund there in 1416, and English royal pilgrims included Edward III in 1364 and Richard II on the eve of his journey to Ireland in 1399. In common with many of his subjects, Richard was devoted to native saints, including the new cult of John of Bridlington (d. 1379). He visited St Winifred's well at Holywell in 1398, the same year as Roger Walden, the temporary primate, ordered celebrations for the feasts of Sts Winifred, David and Chad.[36] Other royal visitors to Canterbury included Edward I, whose marriage to Margaret of France was celebrated by Archbishop Winchelsey in 1299, one of the quieter moments in the turbulent relationship between the king and the primate. In 1376 Sudbury conducted the Black Prince's funeral in the cathedral, and Henry IV was buried there in 1413. With odd exceptions, all the archbishops were also buried in their cathedral, though Mepham's excommunicated body had to receive absolution before it could be admitted to the church. Relations between the austere Franciscan John Pecham and the wealthy Benedictines of Christ Church were always difficult, and Pecham sought to put a distance between them by requesting burial among his mendicant confrères at the London Greyfriars. Prior Henry of Eastry persuaded him to reverse this decision, but the archbishop nevertheless left his heart to the Franciscans.[37] Miracles were reported at Winchelsey's tomb and it was also Prior Henry who promoted his cause, but canonisation was not forthcoming and Winchelsey's cult failed to develop beyond a localised phenomenon. Of all the finely wrought, canopied and (originally) polychromed tombs grouped around the high altar and the saint's shrine, it is that of Henry Chichele which best encapsulates the transient earthly glory of the late medieval primates. Contemporary authors debated the relative merits of nobility of birth and nobility of character. Chichele may have lacked the former, but appears to have had the latter in abundance, here conveyed by the effigy in its gorgeous red and gold vestments. Yet beneath that figure lies the rotting cadaver, one of the best English examples of the *transi* tomb, with its all-too-graphic message for future archbishops: *Pauper eram natus: post primas hic relevatus. Iam sum prostratus: et vermibus esca paratus*; 'I was born a poor man: and was afterwards raised to be primate here. Now I am cast down: and turned into food for worms.'

1486–1660: CANTERBURY BETWEEN ROME AND GENEVA

Archbishop John Morton's ornate funerary monument in the crypt of Canterbury Cathedral demonstrates the harmony that Henry Chichele had sought to achieve between the Church and the English Crown, for its sculpted decoration includes Tudor roses and Beaufort portcullises alongside wide-brimmed cardinals' hats. Morton's own modest request had been for burial under a simple marble slab, but the roses and portcullises confirm that Henry VII and Lady Margaret Beaufort, the king's mother, refused to let their loyal servant rest in relative obscurity. Aside from the tomb, the esteem in which Morton was held by his contemporaries is possibly best reflected in the nostalgic recollection of Thomas More who, as a youth, had spent some time in the archbishop's household:

> He was a man . . . as much respected for his wisdom and virtue as for his authority. He was of medium height, not bent over despite his age; his looks inspired respect, not fear. In conversation, he was not forbidding, though serious and grave. . . . His speech was polished and pointed, his knowledge of the law was great, he had an incomparable understanding and a prodigious memory, for he had improved excellent natural abilities by study and practice.[1]

The princely tomb and the extract from *Utopia* are equally posthumous celebrations of the archbishop; they illustrate the physical and literary elements of which historical reputations happen to be made. In view of the abundance of scholarly literature on the lives and ecclesiastically turbulent times of the Tudor and early Stuart archbishops of Canterbury, a brief survey of their reputations and of the material inheritance they bequeathed, provides a convenient means of introducing the eleven primates from Morton to Laud.

For a guide to Morton's political reputation as Henry VII's lord chancellor, we can again turn to More: 'The king depended greatly on his advice, and he seemed the mainspring of all public affairs.'[2] In 1493 Henry showed his appreciation by ensuring that Alexander VI created Morton a cardinal. Morton exercised cultural and educational patronage in keeping with this princely status, but nevertheless failed to match the reputations of his episcopal contemporaries Thomas Rotherham of York and John Alcock of Ely.[3] By the time of his death in 1500, Morton was chancellor of both universities and bequeathed enough money to provide exhibitions for at least twenty poor scholars at Oxford and ten at Cambridge. At Oxford, his own university, he also funded repairs to the canon law school and contributed to the rebuilding of St Mary's, the church in which his successor Thomas Cranmer was tried in 1555. Even before he became primate and a prince of the Church, Morton acquired credentials as a builder, his projects as bishop of Ely having included repairs to his palace at Hatfield and to his castle at Wisbech. As archbishop he undertook building work at all his main residences and completely rebuilt the house at Ford, near Canterbury, but he is most closely associated with the severe red brick gatehouse which still stands at the corner of Lambeth Palace nearest to the Thames. This originally contained a prison, as well as lodgings for eight senior members of the archbishop's household and the registry for his prerogative court, thereby providing a useful illustration of Morton's commitment to the practical business of administration in Church and State. At the opposite end of the patronage scale, in terms of material remains, Morton was a collector of manuscripts and printed books and, in 1500, commissioned the London printer Richard Pynson to print a Sarum rite missal which is now regarded as a 'landmark of English printing'. In this he was following the example of Margaret Beaufort, to whom he had been chaplain in the 1480s, the time when she had herself been a patron of William Caxton, England's first printer.

Henry Deane has the least conspicuous reputation of the sixteenth-century archbishops, in spite of being the primate who celebrated the ill-fated marriage of Prince Arthur and Catherine of Aragon in November 1502. That he was the only Augustinian canon to become archbishop of Canterbury and the last member of any religious order to do so, presumably accounted for his relative poverty and that, in turn, limited his capacity to leave much of a material inheritance. The brevity of his Canterbury tenure was of no less significance in this regard. As a long-serving prior of Llanthony at Gloucester,

Deane had made his architectural mark by building the gateway on which his arms can still be seen, and as bishop of Bangor he rebuilt the choir of his cathedral a century after it had been burned by the followers of Owain Glyn Dŵr.[4] After six years at Bangor, Deane was briefly bishop of Salisbury, before being translated to Canterbury in 1501. During his twenty-two months as primate, he rebuilt the manor at Otford and repaired the bridge at Rochester, but followed Morton's example in choosing a simple funerary monument, in contrast to the elaborate tombs of their predecessors. Of his 'flat stone of marble' near Archbishop Stafford's tomb, there is no longer any trace. Deane's resting place was in the north-west transept at Canterbury, near the site of Becket's martyrdom, where the tomb of his successor, William Warham, does survive. In life Warham had a reputation for personal frugality, but he was also the last archbishop of Canterbury to build on a princely scale. Before 1518 he effectively limited appreciation of Archbishop Deane yet further by demolishing the house at Otford and building a 'prodigy' of a palace that was alleged to have cost him £33,000. Fragments are all that survive of this earthly glory.

In contrast to his predecessors, Archbishop Thomas Cranmer's reputation has been determined less by physical remains than literary ones, chief among them the Book of Common Prayer (1549 and 1552), though, apart from the collects, it is impossible to be sure about precisely how much of it he personally composed. This is appropriate for the primate who presided over the Henrician and Edwardian reformations, phenomena characterised first by Erasmian philology and then by an emphasis on the written word of Scripture, to the exclusion of other forms of piety. Whatever Cranmer's precise contributions, the Book of Common Prayer remains the most significant vernacular literary achievement attributable to any archbishop of Canterbury. Like the Authorised Version of the Bible, it has permeated English thought and speech for many generations, though it is ironic that a work which began as an expression of religious radicalism has been rejected by latter-day radicals and championed by more traditionalist Anglicans. It may be noted that Cranmer was not an important educational patron and, in marked contrast to other sixteenth-century primates, was not a benefactor of his former college. For its part, Jesus College, Cambridge, has been unsure how to remember him. From 1534, as a footnote to the financial and juridical break with Rome, he was granted authority to award degrees in divinity, arts, law, medicine and music, a power which had previously belonged to the archbishops as *legati nati*. These Lambeth degrees continue to be awarded in the twenty-first century.

From 1537, at the height of the campaign to dissolve England's monasteries, Henry VIII led by example in depriving the Church of its landed wealth. Among the archiepiscopal estates Otford, Maidstone and Knole were the first to be claimed by the Crown, followed by Aldington, Saltwood and Lyminge in 1540, Charing and Mayfield in 1545. Cranmer and his family were left with the use of the palaces at Canterbury, Lambeth, Croydon, Ford and Bekesbourne, the last of which had been part of the Christ Church estates until the Dissolution. The palace at Bekesbourne, to the east of the church of St Peter, is now much reduced in circumstances, although a red brick cottage has a reset stone with the initials of both Cranmer and his successor Matthew Parker. Christ Church itself stood at the eye of the Reformation storm. Becket was declared a traitor and, in 1538, his shrine was completely destroyed.[5] This was not the only violent act sanctioned by Cranmer in his cathedral church, for in 1540 the tombs of Archbishop Arundel and Bishop John Buckingham of Lincoln were destroyed because they had been instrumental in suppressing Lollardy, in which the sixteenth-century reformers perceived the origins of their own crusade. The monastery was dissolved in 1540 and a 'new foundation' created in 1541; the chapter house became a 'sermon house' and Six Preachers were appointed to deliver anti-papal homilies.[6] In 1543 the nearby archbishop's palace was destroyed by fire and Cranmer's brother-in-law was among those who perished in the flames, a fate not altogether dissimilar to that of the deposed archbishop himself, burned at the stake in Oxford in 1556.

The lives of Cranmer and his Canterbury successor, Cardinal Reginald Pole, have each been told in considerable depth by their most recent biographers, but each acquires an extra dimension when told in parallel to the other.[7] They are like figures representing contrasting weather conditions which cannot both appear at the same time. If one was in favour with the monarch, the other most assuredly was not, as Pole discovered in the immediate aftermath of Henry VIII's break with Rome, when he produced his damning critique of royal policies, *Pro ecclesiasticae unitatis defensione* (1534–6). The tables were turned when the Catholic Mary succeeded the Protestant Edward VI in 1553 and Pole emerged as archbishop from the ashes of Cranmer's martyrdom. Even in the architectural sphere, Cranmer and Pole have proved curiously difficult to separate, with some confusion over the precise dating of the mid-sixteenth-century additions to Lambeth Palace. Tim Tatton-Brown is not convinced by the arguments advanced for Pole's patronage, though Thomas Mayer finds the Italianate influences appropriate for a patron who spent most of his adult life in Italy and remained conspicuously loyal to the Church of Rome.[8] Pole was not only the last of the archbishops to remain in communion with Rome; he was also the last of the pre-modern primates to receive burial in his cathedral, his severely classical tomb in the corona at Canterbury neatly illustrating England's brief Catholic – or Counter – Reformation.

Archbishop Matthew Parker was of too practical a cast of mind to be much preoccupied by 'Italianate influences' and contributed to Lambeth Palace the underground sewer emptying into the Thames. He helped to fill the philanthropic void created at the Dissolution by building almshouses in his native Norwich, and restored the fire-damaged palace at Canterbury, which remained in use until Archbishop Laud's time. However, his reputation has been determined more by his literary than either his architectural or sanitary bequests. Cranmer's library had been noted for its size and range of subject matter, but Parker's collection was all the more remarkable on account of the priceless medieval manuscripts acquired in the wake of the monastic Dissolution.[9] Like those of other sixteenth-century antiquarians, it was designed to preserve and disseminate the learning of centuries, to which end he bequeathed the collection to his former college, Corpus Christi, Cambridge, with the result that the college's Parker Library now boasts the third largest collection of Anglo-Saxon manuscripts after those of the British Library and the Bodleian Library, Oxford.[10] Parker's scholarly enthusiasms were essentially historical and these he turned to the service of the fledgling Church of England in *De antiquitate Britannicae ecclesiae* (1572), a history of the archbishops of Canterbury designed to emphasise continuity between the pre- and post-Reformation English Church, most particularly between the uncorrupted Church of the Anglo-Saxon period and the reformed Church over which he found himself a pastor. *De antiquitate* was largely the work of the archbishop's secretary John Josselyn, but it was made possible by Parker's extensive manuscript collection. Neither this, nor the pioneering Anglo-Saxon studies facilitated by the library, impressed Parker's Puritan critics, who had launched full-scale attacks on the 'pope of Lambeth' by the end of his life in 1575.

The next archbishop, Edmund Grindal, was much more to the taste of hotter Protestants. Unlike Parker, Grindal was not essentially a man of letters, his published *Remains* consisting largely of occasional pieces, visitation articles and correspondence.[11] Architectural remains associated with this primate are, if anything, even less substantial than literary ones, for he was bishop of London when St Paul's was devastated by fire in June 1561 and led the rebuilding campaign, but his work survived little more than a century, until the Great Fire of 1666. At Croydon parish church, adjacent to his palace, he was celebrated with an elaborate tomb, but fire destroyed much of the building in 1867 and only two of the original half-dozen archiepiscopal tombs remain. A charred inscription is all that survives of Grindal's memorial. At Canterbury he made still less impact, for he was enthroned by proxy and failed to visit his cathedral during the seven years of his primacy. More conventionally, he did remember his birthplace, St Bees, by the foundation of a grammar school and the funding of scholarships for its pupils at Pembroke Hall and Magdalene College, Cambridge, and at Queen's College, Oxford.[12]

John Whitgift succeeded Grindal in 1583. Looking at the entire history of the archbishops, it might be argued that the strength of Whitgift's posthumous association with Croydon runs a close second to the cult of Becket in Canterbury. He presided over further refurbishment of the palace, and the polychromed confection that is his tomb was one of the memorials that survived the fire of 1867. As Parker remembered Norwich and Grindal St Bees, so Whitgift demonstrated that Croydon was his adopted home by founding a school – now succeeded by the Whitgift School and the Trinity School of John Whitgift – together with the hospital of the Holy Trinity. The latter was built between 1595 and 1599 'to be an hospitall and abiding-place for the finding, sustenation and relief of certain maymed poore, needie or impotent people, to have continuence for ever'. Whitgift also undertook refurbishment at Bekesbourne, but his lavish hospitality caused more comment than his building works, for he lived as a nobleman, surrounded by a large number of retainers. This was done, he maintained, not out of personal ambition, but to increase the dignity of the Church: a distinction lost on his Puritan critics.

The next archbishop, Richard Bancroft, had a clear vision of his intended inheritance to the Church of England, for he sought to make a lasting contribution to its intellectual underpinning through the foundation at Chelsea of a college of controversial divinity. With the Established Church under attack from both Catholic gunpowder plotters and anti-episcopal Puritans, this was designed to be a twin-pronged initiative for 'answering popish books . . . [and] the errors of those that struck at hierarchy'. Leading by example, he was 'a greate gatherer together of bookes of Divinities, & of many other sortes of learning'. Some of the books and manuscripts he gathered in his study over the cloisters at Lambeth came from the library of his friend the antiquarian William Camden; a few can be traced to Archbishop Deane's priory at Llanthony. According to Bancroft's will, the library was to remain at Lambeth, providing that his successors could keep it in safety. If not, the books were to go to the Chelsea college or to Cambridge, in the tradition of Parker's major donation of manuscripts to Corpus Christi and Whitgift's to his Cambridge colleges, Trinity and Pembroke Hall. The Chelsea project foundered; the books, supplemented by Archbishop Abbot's library, went to Cambridge after Laud's death, but were returned to Lambeth by Archbishop Sheldon after the Restoration.[13] What Bancroft did not do was to remember his birthplace, Bold, in the vast Lancashire parish of Prescot, with either philanthropic or educational bequests: there was already a grammar school at nearby Farnworth, which Bancroft himself had attended.[14]

Appreciation of the early seventeenth-century archbishops has become distorted by the heightened emotions, historiographical and otherwise, issuing from the Civil War and the debate about its origins. In the opinion of the staunchly Royalist and Anglican Edward Hyde, earl of Clarendon, Bancroft set a standard that his successor, George Abbot, failed to meet: '[Bancroft] disposed the clergy to a more solid course of study than they had been accustomed to; and if he had lived would quickly have extinguished all that fire in England which had been kindled at Geneva, or if he had been succeeded by bishop Andrewes, bishop Overall, or any man who understood and loved the Church.'[15] Abbot was a committed Calvinist at a time when the anti-Calvinism associated with the likes of Lancelot Andrewes was in the ascendant in the Church of England, and what he understood was Scripture. The Old Testament book of Jonah contains just forty-eight verses, yet Abbot managed the prodigious feat of writing thirty sermons on it between 1594 and 1599. No less pedantic is his *Brief Description of the Whole World, Wherein is particularly Described all the Monarchies, Empires, and Kingdoms of the Same* (1599), written for the benefit of his Oxford students and somewhat similar in concept to the cabinets of curiosities assembled by his contemporaries. Like Grindal, Abbot was enthroned by proxy and did not continue his predecessors' practice of spending the summer at Canterbury, but he did leave a conspicuous material legacy in the distinguished shape of the hospital of the Blessed Trinity in his native Guildford. Founded in 1619, this was designed to house a master, twelve men and eight women; a suite of rooms was provided for the archbishop's use. Some of the building materials are thought to have come from the nearby Dominican friary, which was demolished at this time. In the same anti-monastic vein, Abbot took a keen interest in the re-foundation of the London Charterhouse as a school and hospital.

William Laud contributed a Corinthian portico to St Paul's Cathedral when he was bishop of London and a stone gallery to Lambeth Palace after he became resident there in 1633, neither of which survives. More controversial was his rearrangement of the chapel at Lambeth, with the communion table placed altarwise behind rails and the Crucifixion depicted in stained glass. Herein may be found characteristic Laudian concern with the beauty of holiness, which was readily misinterpreted as 'popery'. Laudian Lambeth has been lost, but Laudian Oxford remains triumphantly visible. In the 1630s the archbishop was a highly interventionist chancellor of the university, requesting a weekly report from the vice-chancellor. Through the statutes promulgated in 1636, he endeavoured to recreate the university in his own orderly image: 'the University accepted the impress of Laud's character, and exchanged the doubtful prospect of disorderly originality for the staid antiquarian learning of a rich clerical foundation.'[16] The riches came in the form of generous donations by Laud himself, whether of oriental manuscripts to the Bodleian or the foundation of a chair in Arabic, or from the wealthy benefactors whose largesse he directed towards the university. Most conspicuously of all, Laud commissioned the building of that stunning example of 'Albion's classicism', Canterbury Quad at St John's, the college of which he had been president. It was completed in 1636.

No archbishop of Canterbury has proved to be more controversial than William Laud: to contemporaries he was 'the little urchin', 'the little meddling hocus-pocus'; to historian Patrick Collinson he was nothing less than 'the greatest calamity ever visited upon the Church of England'.[17] Aristocrats regarded him with contempt, ardent Calvinists condemned his apparent abandonment of Reformation principles and alleged 'innovation' in religious practice, and Charles I's parliamentary opponents saw in him one of the leading players in the king's 'tyrannical' government. Laud was executed by order of the Long Parliament in 1645; Charles went to the scaffold four years later: both were hailed as martyrs. To his former chaplain Peter Heylyn, Laud was *Cyprianus Anglicus*, in reference to the third-century bishop of Carthage who took a strict stand against heresy, schism and apostasy, and met a martyr's end. From 1660 Laud was the inspiration for Restoration Anglicanism and something of a hero to High Churchmen thereafter. In the later nineteenth century, for example, he featured in that curiously influential work of romantic High Church fiction, *John Inglesant*. He is celebrated as a martyr on 10 January, the anniversary of his execution, in the American Book of Common Prayer, complete with apposite lessons from Hebrews 12 on the importance of discipline and from Matthew 10 on Christ coming to bring not peace, but a sword.

His opinion unclouded by civil war and martyrdom, James I did not rate Laud highly and complained that 'He hath a restless spirit and cannot see when matters are well, but loves to toss and change and bring things to a pitch of reformation floating in his own brain.'[18] It was a perceptive comment, which can be borne out by reading Laud's meticulously kept diary. His conscience may have been no more or less troubled than those of other primates, but the difference lies in the fact that we can read of his nightmares and gain some impression of the inner turmoil behind his outbursts of temper at court. Some commentators have chosen to emphasise the homosexual leanings suggested by his diary as the source of his disquiet.[19] What certainly troubled him was an error of judgement made in 1603, a decision that stalled his career for decades. He was then chaplain to Charles Blount, Lord Mountjoy, who had a liaison with and three children by Penelope Devereux, Lady Rich, the woman immortalised as 'Stella' by her former lover Philip Sidney. The court of High Commission granted a divorce to Lord and Lady Rich, thereby giving Laud the opportunity to marry her to Mountjoy on 26 December that year. Doubts arose about the validity of this marriage, doubts which were not forgotten after Mountjoy died in 1606. Laud's contrition was marked by prayer and fasting on each anniversary of the marriage and by the self-abasement of his prayer for St Stephen's Day: 'I am become a reproach to thy Holy name by serving my ambition and the sins of others.' There could be no second lapse, and the Laud known to posterity was a man of personal austerity, integrity and devotion to business, who set the highest standards for himself and expected no less of others.

Charles I's court was an uncongenial milieu for Laud, dominated as it was by the queen, Henrietta Maria, and her Catholic associates, who effectively undermined the Established Church at the highest level, but his difficulty was compounded by his relatively humble birth. As the English court became steadily more courtly in the first post-Reformation century, so the bench of bishops became markedly less noble. James I lamented the lack of nobly born bishops, and the indefatigable Puritan writer William Prynne poured scorn on 'lordly prelates raised from the dunghill'.[20] Of the eleven archbishops of Canterbury from Morton to Laud, only Pole was of noble birth, so much so that he had a stronger claim than the Tudors to succeed the Yorkist kings. Like Archbishops Courtenay, Arundel and Bourchier, Pole's maternal descent was the more exalted, for his mother was the daughter of George, duke of Clarence, and thus the niece of Edward IV and Richard III. Reginald, her third son by Sir Richard Pole, was born at Stourton Castle in Staffordshire in 1500. He embodied the old order, both socially and ecclesiastically. Against this may be set Cranmer's family connections among the East Midlands gentry, the very people whose economic rise was facilitated by the overthrow of that order. Cranmer's family conveniently illustrates the sixteenth-century religious divide in microcosm. When it came to the final crisis of his life in Oxford in 1556 – the agonising over his six recantations of Protestantism, his eleventh-hour renunciation of the recantations, and the serenity with which he accepted death – his soul was being fought over by two of his sisters, one Catholic, the other Protestant.[21] In terms of their geographical origins, this set of archbishops was more diverse than their predecessors, coming from Dorset (Morton) and Hampshire (Warham) in the south, Lancashire (Bancroft) and Cumberland (Grindal) in the north, the Forest of Dean (Deane) in the west, Norwich (Parker) and Grimsby (Whitgift) in the east. Whenever possible, well-placed kinsmen assisted the future archbishops' early careers. Whitgift's uncle and mentor was abbot of the Augustinian house at Wellow in Nottinghamshire, and Bancroft's great-uncle was Hugh Curwen, second bishop of Oxford and archbishop of Dublin. What is not known is whether, or how, Archbishop Grindal was related to Queen Elizabeth's tutor William Grindal. In their turn, the archbishops furthered the clerical careers of their kinsmen. Robert Morton became bishop of Worcester in the same year that his uncle was translated to the primacy, and Warham's eponymous nephew served as his uncle's archdeacon at Canterbury.[22] Laud's half-brother was a prebend of St Davids and archdeacon of Nottingham. At the same time, the overtly Protestant Abbots were a humble family of natural distinction, for George Abbot's eldest brother Robert was master of Balliol College, Oxford, Regius professor of theology and bishop of Salisbury; another brother, Maurice, served as lord mayor of London in 1639.

Where we have information about the pre-university education of these eleven primates, it generally assures us that they attended schools close to home, the exception being Whitgift, who was sent to St Anthony's school in London and lodged with an aunt whose husband was a verger of St Paul's. It was an arrangement that ended acrimoniously when the aunt discovered the extent of her nephew's commitment to the reformed religion. In the previous century Warham had been educated at Winchester and New College, making him the second of the three Wykehamists to have been archbishop of Canterbury. Pole can also be distinguished by his early scholarly and spiritual formation which was either at Christ Church, Canterbury, or at Sheen Charterhouse. Thereafter, the financial support of his kinsman Henry VIII saw him through Magdalen College, Oxford, and into the humanist circles of Padua. Those firmly pre-Reformation figures John Morton and William Warham were doctors of laws in what had become the traditional mould, but Cranmer, Parker, Grindal, Whitgift and Bancroft were all Cambridge doctors of divinity. By the end of the period, the Oxford men – Abbot and Laud – were also DDs. With regard to the academic record of the archbishops, therefore, the English Reformation can be characterised as the rise of the Cambridge theologians at the expense of the Oxford legists, though this fails to take into account the diversity of opinion to be found in each of the universities. All of which leaves only Henry Deane, who has been claimed for Cambridge, but traced in Oxford on various occasions between 1457 and 1488, and was admitted to Lincoln's Inn in 1489.

Whether they were Oxford or Cambridge men, Catholics or Protestants, Calvinists or anti-Calvinists, all eleven primates were inevitably leading players in English political and ecclesiastical history; most of them featured no less highly in its intellectual history as well. The remainder of this chapter is therefore devoted to a chronological account of their activities in both Church and State in a time of rapid religious change.

One of fifteenth-century England's natural Lancastrians, John Morton had been imprisoned in the Tower of London after the battle of Towton in 1461, but escaped and joined Margaret of Anjou in exile. He became reconciled to the Yorkist Edward IV in the 1470s and resumed his legal career, becoming master of the rolls in 1472. Appointment to the bishopric of Ely followed in 1479. His arrest by Richard of Gloucester on 13 June 1483 sparked the train of events that led him into alliance with Henry Tudor, earl of Richmond. In 1485 Richmond became England's second usurper king in little over two years. Archbishop Bourchier died in January 1486, just five months after the battle of Bosworth, leaving Morton as the new king's clear choice for Canterbury. Nothing in his fifteen years at Canterbury offered as much drama as the means by which he reached that position, but they were characterised by a strongly interventionist leadership style, as he endeavoured to extend his powers over the sees and monasteries of his province.

After Morton's death in September 1500, Henry VII's choice for the archbishopric fell on Thomas Langton, whose career exemplified many characteristics of the late fifteenth-century episcopal bench, whether in terms of diplomatic missions, multiplicity of benefices, or rapid translations (St Davids in 1483, Salisbury in 1485 and Winchester in 1493). Langton died of plague on 27 January 1501, just five days after his election to Canterbury, and was buried in his cathedral at Winchester: he was the last of the archbishops-elect who failed to make it to consecration. Bishop Deane of Salisbury was therefore the king's second choice.[23] During his time at Bangor, Deane had doubled up as chancellor of Ireland, the idea being that Bangor and Dublin were sufficiently close for him to combine both positions. Henry required some of his most trusted servants in Ireland, for the earl of Kildare had given support to the Yorkist pretenders Lambert Simnel and Perkin Warbeck and consequently had been deprived of the lord-deputyship. When Sir Edward Poynings was recalled to England in 1496, Deane, as deputy-governor, was left in charge of Irish government for some months. Thereafter, as bishop of Salisbury, he became keeper of the great seal in succession to Morton. Once installed at Canterbury, one of his principal services for the king was negotiation the Anglo-Scottish peace of January 1502.

With William Warham the practice of combining the primacy and the chancellorship was revived, as was the assertion of the primate's jurisdictional rights. The latter met with sustained resistance from bishops and abbots, not least from the eminent and scholarly Richard Fox of Winchester.[24] Like Morton, Warham was well travelled and gained considerable diplomatic experience, particularly in the Low Countries. In the later years of his reign, Henry VII was much engaged in inter-state diplomacy, his sons' Spanish marriages and his own frustrated quest for a second wife being but the clearest examples of this. That diplomatic activity provided the context in which Warham rose to prominence. It was a prominence that endured for about a decade, until he was eclipsed by his own (and Deane's) chaplain, Thomas Wolsey, whose brilliance more obviously matched that of the young king Henry VIII and his dynamic court. It has often been suggested that Wolsey, as the chief beneficiary, engineered Warham's resignation as lord chancellor in December 1515, though Peter Gwyn has countered this by arguing that the ageing Warham positively wanted to retire to his diocese.[25] The archbishop evidently had no particular objection to Wolsey being made a cardinal in 1515, with all the implications for precedence that had so frustrated Archbishop Chichele, for he sang the Mass celebrated to mark the arrival of Wosley's red hat. What did cut Warham to the quick was Wolsey's acquisition of legatine powers from 1518. He complained to Wolsey that he 'should be as a shadow and image of an archbishop and legate [legatus natus], void of authority and jurisdiction, which should be to my perpetual reproach, and to my Church [Canterbury] a perpetual prejudice.'[26]

Warham was chancellor of Oxford from 1506 and a patron of the great Dutch humanist Erasmus, but his record was eclipsed by Margaret Beaufort's patronage of the universities, whether through her readerships (later professorships) in divinity or through the foundations of Christ's and St John's Colleges (1505 and 1511, respectively) in Cambridge. Christ's now claims to have produced more archbishops of Canterbury than any other Cambridge college: Grindal, Bancroft, Hutton, Cornwallis and Williams. John Whitgift was one of the earlier Lady Margaret professors at Cambridge and Rowan Williams one of the most recent at Oxford. As a founder of colleges, Margaret Beaufort followed the example of John Alcock who, in 1496, suppressed the Cambridge convent of St Radegund and founded Jesus College in its buildings. Thomas Cranmer was sent to this fledgling college just seven years later. With Erasmus initially attracted to Cambridge in 1506 and wooed back as Lady Margaret professor between 1511 and 1514, one can easily imagine an atmosphere of intellectual excitement in the early sixteenth-century university, and it seems that Cranmer appreciated both the traditional 'scholastic' and the 'new' humanist learning.[27]

Meanwhile, scholarship in Oxford was by no means stagnant, with William Grocyn lecturing on Greek from 1500 and Bishop Richard Fox encouraging the study of Latin, Greek and divinity through his foundation of Corpus Christi College in 1517. If anything, Oxford provided greater intellectual excitement for Reginald Pole during his time at Magdalen than Cambridge could for Cranmer. Pole's Oxford contacts read like a Who's Who of English humanism: he was taught by Thomas Linacre and William Latimer, he made the acquaintance of Thomas More, and came under the influence of John

Colet, the learned dean of St Paul's.[28] Through these friends of Erasmus, Pole entered the pan-European republic of letters, the society he cultivated throughout his long years in Italy, particularly in the university city of Padua. While Pole led the seemingly charmed life of the social elite, Cranmer had managed to lose his college fellowship on account of entering into a marriage with a woman called Joan, who died in childbirth some time between 1515 and 1519. After that uncharacteristically incautious episode he was readmitted to his fellowship, proceeded to holy orders in 1520 and became a doctor of divinity in 1526. It had been an unlikely detour on the road to future eminence.

Buildings of contrasting size and reputation illustrate the diverging paths taken by Oxford and Cambridge in the 1520s. At Oxford, Thomas Wolsey had ambitious plans for Cardinal College, which incorporated St Frideswide's Priory and the neighbouring Canterbury College. So keen was the university to cultivate Wolsey that Archbishop Warham, its chancellor, tended to be overlooked. At Cambridge, Erasmus's criticisms of clerical abuses and clericalism in general took root and merged with news of the religious ferment in Germany inspired by Martin Luther. Cambridge soon emerged as the intellectual home of English Protestant reform, but the initial meeting place of those members of the university attracted to Luther's works was the White Horse tavern, consequently known as 'Little Germany'. Thomas Cranmer, Hugh Latimer and Miles Coverdale were among the men already frequenting the tavern by 1520. In 1522 Matthew Parker entered Corpus Christi College and soon gravitated into the White Horse circle. Their activities had to be covert, for ecclesiastical revolution was thought to be but a short step from secular revolution, the overthrow of the clerical hierarchy a prelude to rejecting rule by the king. The English government seized copies of Luther's writings at the Channel ports and, in 1521, Henry VIII brought out his defence of the seven Sacraments, most of which Luther had rejected. Wolsey endeavoured to eradicate the Cambridge Lutherans, but they were so adept at concealing themselves that even Parker was headhunted for Cardinal College. He declined the invitation.

Later in the decade, Cranmer emerged from academic obscurity because Henry VIII had become embroiled in theological and legal contortions in order to lose the wife whom Warham had helped to bring to England in the first place.[29] Cranmer gained his own second wife in the process, enabling him to make history as the first married archbishop of Canterbury. His first diplomatic mission was to the imperial court in Spain in 1527, the year that Henry told Queen Catherine that they were living in sin and must separate. When Cardinals Lorenzo Campeggi and Wolsey examined the validity of Henry's marriage in their legatine court at Blackfriars, London, and were forced to abandon proceedings in July 1529, the king found himself in need of both new ideas and new agents in order to realise his objective. At the beginning of August that year, Cranmer suggested to his fellow diplomats Stephen Gardiner and Edward Foxe that Henry might gain his annulment by consulting Europe's universities rather than by lobbying the beleaguered pope Clement VII, whose independence of action was thwarted by the emperor Charles V's military dominance in Italy. Cranmer was soon installed in the household of Thomas Boleyn, Henry's would-be father-in-law, and told to produce the arguments that would clinch the king's case. There followed for Cranmer a flurry of continental travel to the same end, first as an unaccredited member of Boleyn's embassy to Clement and Charles at Bologna in 1530. For much of 1532 Cranmer was himself accredited to the imperial court in Germany and Italy. His mission bore no diplomatic fruit, but it did bring him into direct contact with Lutheran theologians in Nuremberg, where he conformed to local clerical practice by taking a wife, Margarete, niece of the leading Lutheran Andreas Osiander.[30] Margarete appears to have remained in Nuremberg for the time being. Cranmer was at Mantua when word reached him that Henry had appointed him to Canterbury upon the death of Archbishop Warham. Among the existing bishops, Gardiner of Winchester was the most obvious candidate for the primacy, and his resentment at being passed over in favour of his former protégé provides a useful perspective on their later disputes.[31] Although Cranmer owed his promotion to Boleyn patronage and it has long been assumed that he performed the marriage of Henry and Anne upon his return to England in January 1533, it seems that a wedding ceremony had already taken place in November 1532.[32] That detail notwithstanding, rarely has an archbishop of Canterbury been so completely the king's creature. In 1534 the relationship between Church and State in England was revolutionised by the Act of Supremacy, by which Henry became 'supreme head' of the Church in England and severed all links with the papacy.

In 1535 Matthew Parker became chaplain to Anne Boleyn and dean of the collegiate church at Stoke-by-Clare in Suffolk. Anne was executed a little over twelve months later, but the deanery continued to provide Parker with time to study and opportunities to hone his administrative skills. Cranmer's fortunes had been so much tied to those of the disgraced queen that his career might have been more difficult to salvage. In the event, it freed him from the moderate – essentially French – humanistic religious reform that Anne had espoused and allowed him to cultivate his friends among the more radical German reformers. The 'bare ruin'd choirs' of the monasteries dissolved by Thomas Cromwell may suggest that the English Reformation was a *fait accompli* by 1540 but, in reality, the fight for the soul of the English Church continued.[33] Cranmer could not impose his will on an episcopal bench that included his erstwhile diplomatic colleague, the intransigent Stephen Gardiner of Winchester, or the more quietly Catholic Cuthbert Tunstall of Durham. Though Cranmer never entirely lost favour with the king, Henry tended towards caution and towards these more conservative bishops. The archbishop felt frustrated by the Ten Articles of faith issued by the Crown in 1536, because they compromised the Lutheran programme and retained too many essentially Catholic beliefs and practices. Another reversal came with the Act for Abolishing Diversity of Opinions or, more popularly, the Act of Six Articles (1539). The approved 'opinions' it contained were decidedly Catholic in character, upholding clerical celibacy, transubstantiation and auricular confession. Cranmer and his ally Cromwell, who was effectively the king's minister for ecclesiastical affairs, tried another approach with the Great Bible, Coverdale's Protestant translation of the *Byble in Englysshe* (1539), complete with pictures of themselves on the title page. Among the bishops, only William Barlow and Thomas Goodrich supported it, while Gardiner led a campaign in favour of the Latin Vulgate. Cromwell's execution in 1540, in the wake of the disastrous Cleves marriage, deprived Cranmer of his greatest ally, but the archbishop's position was never more seriously threatened than in 1543, when Henry heard of the complaints made by some of the Canterbury prebendaries against Cranmer's support for radical preachers and fostering of religious division in his own diocese. In a scene vaguely reminiscent of Richard II's encounter with Archbishop Courtenay, Henry summoned Cranmer into his barge on the Thames and taunted him: 'Ah, my chaplain, I have news for you. I know now who is the greatest heretic in Kent.' Cranmer could so easily have been arrested and attainted, but the king chose merely to give him a fright.

England was on the fringes of the debates about Christian doctrine and ecclesiastical reform which convulsed Europe in the mid-sixteenth century; Reginald Pole and his friends were closer to their centre. Pole was so notable an advocate of papally-led reform that Pope Paul III made him a cardinal in 1536 and appointed him in 1542 as legate to the impending Council of Trent. The closer his association with the papacy, the more he became a target for Henry's assassins. When he proved to be beyond their reach, members of his family were arrested instead. In 1541 his mother, Margaret, countess of Salisbury, was executed for treason after displaying conspicuous loyalty to Catherine of Aragon and to Rome. There had been speculation that Pole might marry Queen Catherine's daughter, Princess Mary, in order to secure an indisputably English and unequivocally Catholic succession. Among Pole's friends and correspondents was the Venetian cardinal Gasparo Contarini, whose mission to Regensburg in 1541 offered a last opportunity for conciliation with the Lutherans. Contarini, Pole and many of their *spirituali* friends managed to combine 'advanced' ideas on the central Lutheran tenet of justification by faith with loyalty to the structure of the Church of Rome, but others could not.[33] Pietro Martire Vermigli and Bernardino Ochino were among those who declared themselves Protestants, fled from the Italian states and entered the orbit of the Cambridge reformers. They arrived in England in 1547 under Cranmer's patronage, bringing with them a text of St John Chrysostom which they used to counter traditional teaching about the real presence of the Body and Blood of Christ in the Eucharist. While he was still a Cambridge theologian Cranmer had been conventional in his eucharistic belief, but that belief evolved, briefly passing through a Lutheran phase in which he seems to have advocated some form of consubstantiation, before settling for complete rejection of the real presence by the summer of 1548.[34] The first version of the Book of Common Prayer appeared the following year. It replaced the Mass with a totally new communion rite, but the more advanced reformers nevertheless came to regard it as unacceptably 'Roman'. This debate is therefore emblematic of Cranmer's position in the maelstrom of sixteenth-century Christian thought.

Another refugee was the Strassburg reformer and former Dominican, Martin Bucer. As Regius professor of divinity at Cambridge from 1549 until his death in 1551, Bucer made a great impact on the young Edmund Grindal. By 1550 John Whitgift had also begun his long Cambridge career, first at Queens' College and then Pembroke Hall. Elsewhere in the university, Matthew Parker was master of Corpus Christi from 1544. In 1545 Parker was elected vice-chancellor and had to answer to the chancellor, Stephen Gardiner, for the behaviour of students and the doubtful orthodoxy of some of the fellows. This was a temporary inconvenience for Parker, as Gardiner fell foul of the unambiguously Protestant government of Edward VI, suffered two periods of imprisonment and was deprived of his Winchester bishopric in 1548. Tunstall of Durham and Edmund Bonner of London were likewise deprived during Edward's reign, while a new breed of bishops sympathetic to Cranmer included Miles Coverdale at Exeter and John Hooper at Gloucester. The latter fired the first shot in what became known as the Vestiarian Controversy by refusing to wear the prescribed vestments for his consecration. England's radical reformation had arrived and a wave of iconoclasm swept through the country, encouraged by the duke of Somerset as the young king's protector and by Cranmer as his archbishop. It was in this reign that Cranmer came closest to creating a thoroughly reformed Protestant Church in England, with fresh inspiration coming from Calvin's theocracy in Geneva. Luther's death in 1546 had been followed by divisions among Lutherans on most of his doctrines, but Calvinism offered a new certainty. Calvin's eucharistic theology was somewhere between that of Luther's consubstantiation and the total symbolism of Ulrich Zwingli, but his most distinctive teaching concerned double predestination, that of the elect to salvation and the reprobate to damnation (as opposed to the *single* predestination of Archbishop Bradwardine). Where Lutheranism was moderate, Calvinism, as presented in its founder's *Institutio religionis Christianae* (1539), was radical, whether in its emphasis on both the Old and New Testaments, its preaching ministry or its strict sabbatarianism. The impact of Calvinism was first felt in England in Edward's reign, the king, his chaplain Edmund Grindal and Protector Somerset corresponding with Calvin in Geneva, and over subsequent generations it became pervasive, especially in urban centres. Calvinism was the theological norm of later sixteenth-century England, but it was a curious sort of Calvinism that could accommodate itself to episcopal government of the Church. The more fervent Protestants emerged as the Puritans of Elizabeth's and later reigns, pointedly rejecting any outward religious signs that might smack of popery and siding with their Scottish brethren in their rejection of episcopacy. In his later years Cranmer embraced predestinarianism and the Forty-two Articles of belief, which he framed in 1552, were fully Protestant in nature, but he showed no sign of rejecting episcopacy and this caused some of his continental friends to regret the apparent half-heartedness of English reform. The hybrid nature of the English Church was therefore evident well before the Elizabethan Settlement of 1559.

The short-lived King Edward was not required to appoint an archbishop of Canterbury. Cranmer remained in office for two decades altogether and had advanced so far in his reforming ideas by *c.* 1550 that the execution of the Crown's equally advanced ecclesiastical policies was highly congenial to him. By 1549 religious radicals and traditionalists were dismantling the visible signs of England's Catholic culture – altars, rood screens, images and so forth – with greater or lesser enthusiasm. As they did so the English cardinal, Reginald Pole, came close to being elected pope in a protracted and tenaciously contested conclave of 1549–50, fought out between French and imperial parties. Pole was a highly reluctant imperialist candidate, but the eventual victor was Cardinal del Monte, who took the name Julius III. At Edward VI's death, it was with some reluctance that Cranmer recognised the claim of the Protestant Lady Jane Grey – Edward's own choice of heir – against the Catholic Princess Mary, but it was enough to condemn him as a traitor when Mary successfully claimed her inheritance in 1553. She was not inclined to treat the old man leniently, for she could not forget that he had pronounced the nullity of her parents' marriage and her own illegitimacy. A jubilant Pope Julius sent Pole as legate to England, though Charles V hindered his travel for some months as a means of ensuring that Pole would not scupper plans for a marriage between the English queen and the emperor's son. It was the end of November 1554 when Pole was finally permitted to cross the Channel; the attainder against him was lifted and he formally reconciled his homeland to Rome. Again Gardiner was overlooked for Canterbury, receiving compensation in the form of the chancellorship. Pole was Mary's archbishop from December 1555 although he was, strictly speaking, only administrator of the see until Cranmer's execution three months later.[35] The two men exchanged correspondence but did not meet during the difficult transitional period of the latter's confinement and painful recantations. When Cranmer's fate was sealed, Pole was ordained priest at the revived Observant Franciscan church in Greenwich on 20 March 1556. The following day Pole celebrated his first Mass and Cranmer was burned to death in Oxford, famously rejecting his recantations with the words: 'And forasmuch as my hand offended, writing contrary to my heart, my hand shall first be punished therefor; for, may I come to the fire, it shall be first burned.' With Canterbury finally and unequivocally vacant, Pole was consecrated as archbishop on Sunday 22nd, again at Greenwich. There followed just thirty-two months before the deaths of Queen Mary and her archbishop, twelve hours apart, on 17 November 1558. It was long enough for Pole to persuade Mary to renounce the Crown's income from the clerical taxes of first fruits and tenths, but it was not long enough to win over the hearts and minds of convinced Protestants.

One such was Edmund Grindal, who chose exile rather than martyrdom in Marian England. The fact that Grindal attended the Strassburg lectures of Pietro Martire Vermigli, Pole's former associate, is a reminder that Pole only appears as a reactionary figure when viewed through the prism of Protestant historiography: to Pope Paul IV (1555–9), Pole was a dangerous heretic. The tradition of Protestant historiography was founded on the exile John Foxe's *Acts and Monuments of Matters Happening in the Church* (or *Book of Martyrs*), a work that Grindal helped to launch and with which his *Fruitful Dialogue between Custom and Verity* was originally published. Back in Cambridge, John Whitgift was learning valuable lessons in the art of compromise. His Pembroke Hall tutor, John Bradford, was burned for heresy at Smithfield in London in 1555 and thus became one of the most notable of the Protestant martyrs celebrated by Foxe. However, when Pole's representatives undertook a visitation of the university in 1557, the master of Peterhouse, Andrew Perne, a man of flexible opinions, deliberately failed to bring Whitgift's Protestantism to their attention. Meanwhile in Oxford, 1555 saw the foundation of St John's College by Sir Thomas White, complete with two scholarships for boys from his native town of Reading. St John's retained the flavour of the Catholic revival during which it was founded and this duly shaped the anti-Calvinism of its own archbishops, Laud and Juxon. By such small steps both the universities inched towards the practice – and theory – of the post-1559 Church of England, at once Catholic and reformed.

William Cecil and Nicholas Bacon, ministers of that much-celebrated Protestant heroine Elizabeth I, first presided over the Settlement in religion – episcopal in government but reformed in theology – and then set about finding a suitably conciliatory figure to become archbishop of Canterbury. Bacon received a character sketch of the ideal primate:

God grant it chanceth neither on arrogant man, neither on fainthearted man, nor on covetous man. The first shall both sit in his own light, and shall discourage his fellows to join with him in unity of doctrine, which must be their whole strength; for if any heart-burning be betwixt them, if private quarrels stirred abroad be brought him, and so shall shiver them asunder, it may chance to have that success which I fear in the conclusion will follow. The second man should be too weak to commune with the adversaries, who would be the stouter upon his pusillanimity. The third man not worth his bread, profitable for no estate in any Christian commonwealth, to serve it rightly.[36]

The writer was Matthew Parker, who declared himself content to live quietly 'amongst the simple strayed sheep of God's fold', but was considered by Cecil and Bacon to be ideally suited to the primacy. Parker met the job specifications as much by his renowned administrative ability as by his lack of religious extremism. He had been neither a leader of the more radical Edwardian reformation, nor one of the notoriously factious Marian exiles in Germany. Thirteen months after Pole's death and with considerable reluctance, Parker became the first archbishop of Canterbury to be appointed without reference to Rome. Catholics subsequently alleged that the apostolic succession was lost because Parker was invalidly consecrated in the Nag's Head in London's Cheapside; in reality his consecration was performed by four of the Edwardian bishops at Lambeth on 17 December 1559. Much as she could respect him for his intellectual and administrative abilities, Elizabeth had no genuine affection for Parker and had a particular problem with the fact that he was the second married archbishop of Canterbury. He had had a seven-year 'understanding' with Margaret Harlstòn, from his home town of Norwich, and married her as soon as the Act of Six Articles (1539), which had forbidden clerical marriage, was repealed in 1547. It was an extremely happy marriage and Parker accepted it as the price to be paid for his career stalling in Mary's reign. Elizabeth was hardly more accommodating than her Catholic sister and there was an awkward moment when she was obliged to express her thanks for Mrs Parker's hospitality at Lambeth: 'Madam I may not call you: mistress I am ashamed to call you: so I know not what to call you: but yet I thank you.'[37] The Parkers had four sons, of whom two died in infancy; another, John, married the daughter of Bishop Richard Cox of Ely.

The 1560s saw Perne's faith in Whitgift justified as the younger man became successively master of Pembroke Hall and of Trinity. Another future archbishop entered the university in this decade: Richard Bancroft began his studies at Christ's, but migrated to Jesus after his BA on account of the Puritan 'novellism' then flourishing at his first college. It was the beginning of a lifelong antipathy to Puritanism. Meanwhile, Archbishop Parker had to deal with the problem of diversity in religious worship on a national scale:

Some say the service and prayers in the chancel, others in the body of the church . . . some say in a surplice, others without a surplice; the table standeth in the body of the church in some places, in others it standeth in the chancel . . . administration of the Communion is done by some with surplice and cope, some with surplice alone, others with none; some with unleavened bread, others with leavened; some receive kneeling, others standing, others sitting; some baptise in a font, others in a basin; some sign with the sign of the cross, others do not . . .[38]

From 1563 Puritans also expressed dissatisfaction at the deliberate theological vagueness of the Church of England's Thirty-nine Articles of belief (revised down from Cranmer's forty-two by Parker himself), but the principal issue upon which Puritan ministers took their stand was the wearing of vestments, which in practice meant the cope for communion services and the surplice at other times. As they saw it, among a priesthood of all believers no such distinction was necessary, while any distraction from the word of God was a potential lapse into popery. Parker, who was described by the Church of England's early apologist John Jewel as a 'holy anchor', held fast and saw numerous Puritan clergy deprived of their livings in the mid-1560s for refusing to wear the surplice. It was a high-risk strategy in the face of overwhelming opposition from convocation and precious little support from his fellow bishops, but Parker was convinced that firm leadership and a principled stand were required if the Church of England was to command respect and social order was to be upheld. His position was summarised in his last letter to William Cecil: 'Does your lordship think that I care for either cap, tippet, surplice, or wafer-bread, or any such? But for the laws so established I esteem them, and not more for exercise of contempt against law and authority, which I see will be the end of it.'[39] Parker's chief literary endeavour in the 1560s was the Bishops' Bible, produced under his editorial direction and published in 1568. It was the official translation which churchwardens were ordered to obtain for their churches, but it could not dent the popularity of the Calvinist Geneva (or 'breeches') Bible.

Support from among Parker's fellow bishops was conspicuously lacking. Edmund Grindal, a correspondent of Calvin and as suspicious of Lutherans as he was of papists, was bishop of the Puritan stronghold of London from 1559 to 1570, where Parker considered him 'not resolute and severe enough' in dealing with the Church of England's Puritan critics. He opposed their presbyterianism but, on the key issue of surplice-wearing, was distinctly lukewarm. Though Parker lacked support among the bishops, he was not without allies in the universities, as the Cambridge career of John Whitgift, his Canterbury successor-but-one, amply demonstrates. In 1569 the thoroughly Calvinist divine, Thomas Cartwright, was appointed to the Lady Margaret professorship of divinity at Cambridge and used that position to advocate presbyterian reform of church government. Whitgift was master of Cartwright's college, Trinity, but was elected vice-chancellor in November 1570 and, in that capacity, had Cartwright removed from the professorship in order to prevent the next generation of clergy from listening to his subversive notions. Cartwright briefly retreated to Geneva to recharge his Calvinist batteries, but his cause was taken up by two Puritan clerics, Thomas Wilcox and John Field, who anonymously published *An Admonition to the Parliament* (1572), warning of the 'popish abuses' which were said to be corrupting the English Church. To this Whitgift responded with an *Answer* that demonstrated the 'great absurdity' of practising biblical fundamentalism as advocated by the *Admonition*. Cartwright responded rapidly and venomously with a *Reply to an Answer Made of Mr Dr Whitgift* (1573). The duel continued: Whitgift parried with a *Defence of the Answer* (1574); from exile Cartwright made a *Second Reply* (1575). Cartwright then lost his Trinity fellowship: Whitgift did not need to make any further response. Richard Cox, though a former Marian exile, rejoiced: 'Our Puritan brethren are now lying in concealment, partly terrified by the authority of our Queen, and partly silenced by a most able treatise written by a most learned man'.[40] From 1574 the Lady Margaret professor at Cambridge was the Frenchman known in England as Peter Baro, who had spent some time with Calvin in Geneva but evolved an anti-Calvinist theology that influenced such Cambridge men as John Overall and Lancelot Andrewes, bishops in the Jacobean Church.[41]

Archbishop Parker was not required to fight a battle on two fronts in the 1560s, for English Catholicism was then all but extinguished. Popery only became a threat to the English Crown after the Northern Rising of 1569, which was so severely put down by the government that Pius V responded by excommunicating Elizabeth the following year. As part of the government's crackdown Grindal was translated from London to York, in the accurate expectation that rooting out northern Catholics would be congenial to what Parker called his 'Germanical spirit'. Tension was increased by Catholic plotters attracted to the imprisoned figure of Mary, queen of Scots, and by the arrival in England of Jesuit missionaries and William Allen's first seminary priests in the 1570s. After Parker's death in 1575, Cecil's patronage brought Grindal's translation from York to Canterbury: he was the first primate since Warham to have had prior episcopal experience. Elizabeth and her ministers soon had cause to regret this appointment, for the archbishop was so devoted to the cause of thoroughgoing religious reform, that he failed to appreciate that the Church of England was in essence the religious arm of the State. Parker had occasionally despaired of the government's want of principle, but Grindal went much further. His fate was sealed on 20 December 1576 with a letter to the queen, in which he emphasised the rights of bishops in spiritual matters and how these were quite distinct from the responsibilities of the secular power. He acted according to his conscience and not as befitted an instrument of the Crown. Grindal's resolution most notably concerned 'prophesyings', which were meetings of clergy to discuss Scripture and not nearly as remarkable as their name might suggest. He considered prophesyings to be legitimate gatherings for ministers of religion, but Elizabeth was suspicious of such unauthorised associations and preferred ministers to confine themselves to the delivery of officially approved homilies. The following June he was suspended from his temporal duties and threatened with deprivation. Cecil urged him to make peace with the queen, and convocation appealed to her on his behalf in 1581, but the impasse continued: Grindal still refused to yield on the key points he had raised in his letter and the queen yielded to no one. A martyr to the 'stone' and blinded by cataracts, the sequestered archbishop made a pitiful figure, whose resignation Elizabeth was prepared to accept. Terms were drawn up and a pension negotiated, but he was restored to office late in 1582 and allowed to die with dignity as archbishop in name and in deed, which he did at Croydon on 6 July 1583.

For her third archbishop of Canterbury, Elizabeth needed a prelate who could impose order and authority on the more ardent Protestants favoured by Grindal, but who recognised the importance of pastoral ministry and was committed to improving the education of ministers. John Whitgift was that complete Elizabethan primate: a fearless vice-chancellor of Cambridge in theologically fraught times, a conscientious bishop of Worcester, and even a Crown servant as vice-president of the council of the Welsh marches. Elizabeth entirely trusted Whitgift, her 'little black husband', and appointed him to the Privy Council, a distinction which had not been accorded to Parker or Grindal. She even offered him the post of lord chancellor in 1587, but this he declined. His loyalty was confirmed in 1601 when his armed retainers helped to put down the earl of Essex's rebellion and secured the rebel lord's arrest.

With exceptions made for church government and biblical fundamentalism, Archbishop Whitgift breathed the same Calvinist air as most of his English clerical contemporaries and, like them, held it as a matter of course that the pope was the Antichrist. Whitgift's Calvinism was most evident in the 1595 Lambeth Articles, which were designed in part to refute Baro's anti-Calvinist teaching, but these failed to meet with Elizabeth's approval and they were not adopted as the official Church of England position on predestination and other matters. In spite of the *Admonition* exchange, Whitgift's strength lay more in administration than in theological debate, and he set about using all the legal and administrative means at his disposal to enforce uniformity and stifle the Church of England's Puritan critics. He operated with a thoroughness of which even Archbishop Laud and the earl of Strafford might only have imagined, but to those who were being repressed Whitgift's style of repression was no more palatable than that of any other authoritarian figure. The break with Rome had left holes in the operation of canon law in England, holes that Matthew Parker attempted to fill with reform of the archbishop's courts. Whitgift enhanced the powers of the court of High Commission, which dealt with heresy cases and enforced officially sanctioned forms of public worship, and used all available means to root out Puritans. Most notoriously, he employed the *ex officio* oath: suspected persons were brought before the High Commission and forced to swear that they would answer certain questions without knowing the nature of the questions in advance. The enquiries were extremely searching and designed to root out any ministers who refused to accept any aspect of the Church of England's beliefs and practices: 'The meshes in the net were so small that no convinced Puritan could hope to escape.'[42] Whitgift's old adversary Thomas Cartwright went to prison rather than take the oath.

Between October 1588 and September 1589, seven scurrilous satires appeared in defiance of Whitgift's licensing system, under the pseudonym of Martin Marprelate. Their anonymous authors styled Whitgift as 'John Cant' and libellously condemned him 'as more ambitious than Wolsey, prouder than Gardiner and more tyrannical than Bonner', 'past shame and a notorious liar', and made heavy accusations about the nature of his relationship with Andrew Perne. Cartwright and other serious-minded Puritans denounced the tracts. On 9 February 1589, at the height of Marprelate mania, Richard Bancroft preached on 1 John 4:1 at St Paul's Cross in London, warning his hearers to test the spirits and beware of false prophets; most tellingly, he made a powerful defence of the divine origin of episcopacy. It was mainly through Bancroft's agency that the Marprelate printers were detected, though the authors were never identified. At that stage Bancroft had already compiled an unpublished *Discourse Upon the Bill and Book Exhibited in Parliament by the Puritans for a Further Reformation of the Church Principles* (c. 1585), and went on to publish other works in the same resolutely anti-Puritan vein. Of greater lasting impact, though, were the eight books of Richard Hooker's *Laws of Ecclesiastical Polity*, which began to appear in 1593. Generations of editors, commentators and readers – not least John Keble and Rowan Williams – have found in Hooker the most comprehensive justification of the Church of England's hierarchy, liturgy and inclusive mission to the English people.[43] Although the word was not coined until the nineteenth century, it was Hooker who effectively put the 'Anglicanism' into the Church of England. In 1585 he was appointed master of the Temple in London, where Walter Travers, an ally of Cartwright, was already employed. As Hooker was an anti-Calvinist who considered Calvin's teaching on double predestination 'novel and perilous', for a short while it was said that 'the pulpit spake pure Canterbury in the morning and Geneva in the afternoon'.[44] Whitgift ensured that Travers was removed.

In 1589 the sixteen-year-old William Laud went up to St John's College, Oxford, on one of the founder's scholarships for Reading boys. It remained his home – 'the place where I was bred up' – for the next thirty-two years, culminating in a decade as president of the college. Oxford in general and St John's in particular were not just the making of Laud; they were the love of his life and he never tired of expressing his devotion. On 30 August 1625, for example, when visiting his diocese of St Davids, he recorded in his diary: 'I consecrated the Chapel or Oratory which I had built at my own charge in my house called Abergwili House. I named it the chapel of St John Baptist in grateful remembrance of St John Baptist College, Oxford, of which I had been first fellow, and afterwards president.'[45]

By 1600 Archbishop Whitgift was aged and infirm. As in the pre-Reformation period, it fell to the bishop of London as dean of the province to act as the primate's understudy, a role performed by Richard Bancroft from 1597. In 1603 Whitgift attended the dying Elizabeth, but it was Bancroft who rode out to meet King James on his southward progress from Scotland. At the same time, the king's experience of Scottish presbyterianism gave hope to English Puritans, who also made their appeal to him before he reached London. This was in the form of the Millenary Petition, so called because it claimed to represent the views of a thousand ministers. The petition summarised most Puritan grievances against the Church of England, including objections to the sign of the cross at baptism, the rite of confirmation, the surplice as distinctive clerical garb, wedding rings and bowing at the name of Jesus. The petitioners diplomatically made no reference to episcopacy, but might have been able to anticipate the king's motto 'No bishop, no king', for he had recently tried to reintroduce bishops in Scotland on the grounds that they were more compatible with his concept of divinely ordained monarchy. Never one to pass over an opportunity for theological debate, James duly presided over the Hampton Court conference of bishops – led by the hot-tempered Bancroft – and Puritan leaders in January 1604. The Puritans went away largely disappointed, but with the promise of a new, authoritative English translation of the Bible as a temporising measure. This task was assigned to fifty-four scholars divided into six teams, two each in Oxford, Cambridge and Westminster. Among the Oxford men allocated the four gospels and the books of Acts and Revelation was the dean of Winchester, George Abbot. Abbot had entered Balliol College in 1579, duly became a fellow there, and migrated to University College as its master in 1597. He served as vice-chancellor of the university three times, in 1600, 1603 and 1605, and made his mark by imprisoning 140 undergraduates who sat in St Mary's with their hats on in his presence.[46] In his *Treatise of the Perpetual Visibility and the Succession of the True Church in All Ages* (written 1603, published 1624), Abbot felt bound to articulate the Protestant's response to the question 'Where was your Church before Luther?' With the bishop of Rome as the Antichrist, the 'true Church' was that of such Christian worthies as Wycliffe and Hus, Luther and Calvin. Clarification was evidently required on this matter, because young Mr Laud of St John's had lectured on the perpetual visibility of Christ's Church and implied that even popery had 'served a useful purpose'.[47] Work on the Bible provided timely relief from what developed into a lifelong feud between the two future primates. The Authorised Version was completed in 1611.

As if there had been any doubt about it, Archbishop Whitgift's last words explained his life's work: 'Pro ecclesia Dei'. He then caused confusion for anyone wishing to remember the event more frequently than every fourth year by dying on 29 February 1604. The first parliament of the new reign opened in March, paralleled by the first meeting of convocation. Richard Bancroft had yet to move from Fulham to Lambeth, but was nevertheless the driving force in convocation, and sought to deliver a final, decisive blow against the Puritans with his book of 141 canons, a comprehensive legal framework for the Church of England. These were accepted by convocation, but rejected by the common lawyers in parliament, causing Bancroft to respond with the 1605 articles of abuses *(Articuli cleri)*. There was a stand-off between the two legal systems. James sided with his bishops. The opening of the second session of James's first parliament is still remembered for the exploits of the Catholic gunpowder plotters and provides a convenient key to Bancroft's policy with regard to the English Catholics, who experienced renewed persecution in the first decade of the seventeenth century. Bancroft also tried to break them by more subtle means, encouraging divisions between the Jesuit and non-Jesuit priests held in custody.

At Bancroft's death in 1610, there was strong speculation that Lancelot Andrewes, the palpably holy bishop of Ely, would be promoted to Canterbury on account of the king's high regard for his erudite and eloquent preaching. In the event, favouritism of a different hue determined the outcome, as James selected George Abbot, the 48-year-old bishop of London, who had been a client of the late earl of Dunbar, and had helped Dunbar to execute the king's policy of promoting episcopacy in Scotland. 'By a strong north wind coming out of Scotland,' Abbot was said to have been 'blown over the Thames to Lambeth.' His rapid promotion did not pass without comment, for he had been at London only twelve months, after less than a year as bishop of Lichfield and Coventry. With hindsight, it did not prove to be the wisest of choices, suggesting to some that James may have been motivated by nothing more than caprice. Alternatively, it is argued that the canny monarch consciously balanced the appointments of Calvinists and anti-Calvinists, just as he sought to balance the Protestant and Catholic powers of Europe, and that what England happened to need in 1610–11 was a committed advocate for the cause of international Protestantism.[48] Abbot was not just the writer of a geographical treatise; he maintained contacts throughout the Protestant and potentially Protestant world. This brought him into the sphere of the Servite friar Paolo Sarpi, who was the propagandist for and public face of Venice's anti-papal policies from the time that the republic was placed under a papal interdict in 1606–7. In the case of Venice, what Abbot and other English observers failed to appreciate was the distinction between anti-papalism and anti-Catholicism. Some seventeenth-century Anglicans looked further east and identified Orthodoxy as an alternative tradition to that presented by Rome and as a purer form of Christianity than Roman Catholicism.[49] James I and Abbot tapped into that line of thought with their innovative support for Greek students in Oxford, where Laud later had unrealised ambitions for the establishment of a Greek printing press.[50] Calvinists of Abbot's generation could also define themselves against the anti-Calvinism emanating from the Low Countries in the works of the Dutch theologians Jacobus Arminius, Conradus Vorstius and Hugo Grotius, who modified the difficult Calvinist line on predestination. In 1618–19 debate came to a head at the Synod of Dort, an assembly of Calvinist theologians heavily weighted against these 'Arminians'. James and Abbot sought to assert themselves as potential leaders of international Protestantism and sent a delegation to Dort to help defeat the Arminian heresy. As the king appreciated more than his archbishop, this was a diplomatic move and not designed to have implications for domestic policy.

In terms of foreign policy, the distance between James and Abbot was brought to the fore in marriage plans for the royal children, for here the archbishop's anti-Catholicism came into conflict with the king's basic need for money. Prince Henry, that Protestant prodigy, died in 1612, so fell out of the calculations. In 1611–12 James wanted his daughter Elizabeth to marry into the House of Savoy, but Abbot was hostile to this; not only was the duke of Savoy a Catholic, he was also brother-in-law to that most Catholic of monarchs, the king of Spain. Abbot cultivated a useful relationship with the Protestant elector palatine of the Rhine, and managed to secure the princess's marriage to him in 1613. When the elector accepted the throne of Bohemia and championed the cause of the Bohemian Protestants against the Catholic Habsburgs, Abbot caught the populist mood in England by wishing to send practical support to fellow Protestants, but the king's fear of expenditure prevailed. It was Abbot's turn to despair when Prince Charles and the duke of Buckingham quixotically journeyed to Spain in search of an infanta and a dowry in 1623. He shared the widely held sense of relief when they returned empty-handed from that extraordinary escapade.

In spite of his overt Protestantism, Abbot was regarded quite highly by Queen Anne of Denmark, a discreet convert to Catholicism, and his relationship with King James began positively, though it soon disintegrated in the mire of court factionalism. James tended to favour the aristocratic Howard faction, who were themselves friendly with Spain and with English Catholics, while Abbot allied himself with William Herbert, earl of Pembroke, and others who favoured an anti-Spanish, thoroughly Protestant agenda. In 1613 it happened that Frances Howard, daughter of the earl of Suffolk, wished to divorce her husband Robert Devereux, earl of Essex, in order to marry James's current favourite, Robert Carr, earl of Rochester. The Essex marriage had not been consummated. Non-consummation had been the countess's choice, but that was no reason in law to nullify the marriage. A commission met at Lambeth to consider the matter: most members accepted the king's arguments in favour of the divorce, Abbot was resolutely opposed and Lancelot Andrewes maintained a studied silence. Abbot was present for the celebration of the countess's second marriage, but it was not enough to heal the breach between the archbishop and the king, who resolved not to involve Abbot in any further temporal matters.[51] Undaunted, Abbot and Pembroke continued to play courtly politics by introducing to the king to the young and exceedingly handsome George Villiers, in the hope of distracting James's attention from Carr and the Howards. James was charmed and Villiers was rapidly promoted through the ranks of the nobility to become duke of Buckingham. Carr and his wife, earl and countess of Somerset, were soundly defeated when they were found guilty in 1616 of the murder of Sir Thomas Overbury, and languished in the Tower until James pardoned them in 1624. At another level, though, Abbot's plot backfired when William Laud, already a thorn in the archbishop's side, emerged as Buckingham's chaplain and confidant.

At Abbot's appointment to Canterbury, the Venetian ambassador Marcantonio Correr reported that 'the Catholics complain bitterly as he is held to be their bitterest persecutor.' On 6 August 1614 one of them went so far as to attempt to assassinate the archbishop in his study.[52] The hotter Protestants soon had their own cause for disappointment as the government took action against the more extreme manifestations of Puritanism. An example of this was the issuing of the Book of Sports, first in Lancashire in 1617 and then in the rest of the country in 1618. This was designed to counter sabbatarianism by listing those activities, such as archery and dancing, which were permissible on Sundays. More moderate Churchmen watched their archbishop defend the rights of the Church of England and of High Commission against the common lawyers, but without the zeal of his predecessor. All this left him with no natural supporters when fate dealt him the cruellest blow of all. In July 1621 the archbishop went hunting at Bramshill, Lord Zouch's estate in Hampshire, and accidentally shot dead one of the gamekeepers. At a personal level Abbot was devastated. However generous the financial compensation he paid to the keeper's widow and children, it could not ease his conscience. At that point the archbishop ought to have been suspended from all his ecclesiastical functions, but James understood that it had been a most unfortunate accident and was prepared to overlook the matter. Legal commentators extracted much mileage from the case: Was it legal for clerics to hunt? Did the canon *De clero venatore* apply in post-Reformation England? Could bishops own deer parks and yet not hunt in them?[53] Churchmen had no hesitation in condemning Abbot as a 'man of blood': John Williams and William Laud refused to accept consecration from him as bishops of Lincoln and St Davids respectively, but it was thought that Williams was himself ambitious for Canterbury and keen to see Abbot's downfall. Lancelot Andrewes, by then bishop of Winchester, was one of the few to offer the archbishop true Christian friendship. This surprised Abbot, since the two of them represented opposing groups within the Anglican hierarchy.

By the 1620s Andrewes's saintly restraint was being replaced by more strident voices on the anti-Calvinist wing of the Church. Chief among these was Richard Montagu who, in 1624, brought out a controversial book called *A New Gag for an Old Goose*. King James had no particular problem with the piece, but the keener Protestants were incited to fever pitch by it and condemned Montagu as an Arminian, a papist and a traitor. He responded with an *Appello Caesarem*, which was also condemned by the Puritan majority in parliament. Charles I raised the stakes still higher by appointing Montagu to the see of Chichester in 1628, with translation to Norwich following a decade later. Charles had succeeded his father in 1625 and consistently put conviction before prudence in his ecclesiastical policies. For the first nine years of the reign, Abbot remained in office, but was not invited to play any part in government. This was the period in which Charles antagonised his early parliaments by collecting tonnage and poundage without their consent and used his prerogative powers to collect the forced loan of 1627. As the archbishop's health deteriorated, further appointments of the Montagu type demonstrated that the new king was determined to advance anti-Calvinists regardless of the resentment it caused. None advanced more conspicuously than Bishop Laud of St Davids (1621–6), Bath and Wells (1626–8) and London (1628–33), initially through the good offices of the duke of Buckingham and then, after the duke's assassination in 1628, through the favour of the king himself. Meanwhile, Abbot's relationship with Charles reached its nadir over a sermon by Dr Robert Sibthorpe supporting the doctrine of the divine right of kings. No subject was dearer to the king's heart or more likely to inflame his critics. As with the Essex divorce case thirteen years earlier, Abbot was guided by his conscience and refused to license the sermon. On 5 July 1626 Charles ordered the archbishop to withdraw to his diocese, leaving his temporal jurisdiction to be exercised by the bishops of London, Durham, Rochester, Oxford and Bath and Wells. Thus was salt poured in Abbot's wounds, for the bishop of Durham was Richard Neile, who became archbishop of York in 1632 and was more or less the Laud of the north, the bishop of Rochester was John Buckeridge, Laud's sometime tutor at St John's and co-editor with him of Andrewes's sermons (1629), and the bishop of Bath and Wells was none other than Laud himself. In the event it proved to be a much briefer reversal than that suffered by Archbishop Grindal, for Abbot was restored to favour in 1628. He remained archbishop throughout the first four of the eleven years of Charles I's personal rule, though it was abundantly evident that Laud, as bishop of London, was the king's most trusted prelate. It was through cases such as that of the iconoclast Henry Sherfield, recorder of Salisbury, that Laud became popularly identified as an intransigent opponent of Puritanism. Sherfield smashed a window in St Edmund's church in Salisbury because it depicted God the Father and he duly appeared before the court of Star Chamber in February 1633. Among the judges, Laud and Neile favoured a heavy fine of £1,000, though in the end they had to settle for £500.[54]

At almost sixty, Laud was relatively advanced in years by the time of his promotion to Canterbury in September 1633. His religious opinions had been formed some decades earlier among the anti-Calvinists of late sixteenth- and early seventeenth-century Oxford. He was clearly repelled by Calvin's teaching on reprobation: 'My very soul abominates this doctrine, for it makes God, the God of all mercies, to be the most fierce and unreasonable tyrant in the whole world.'[55] The word 'Arminian' was readily bandied about as a term of abuse, and William Prynne did not hesitate to use it against Laud, who embodied all that the Puritan polemicist opposed in the Church of England. One of the most curious features of the Caroline Church was Nicholas

Ferrar's community, established at Little Gidding in 1625 and condemned as *The Arminian Nunnery* in a pamphlet of 1641. Although Ferrar acted with the support of his bishop, John Williams, it was Laud who ordained him deacon in 1626. Significantly, Arminianism was not listed among the charges brought against Laud by the Long Parliament in 1641, presumably because of the lack of evidence to support it.[56] A charge that appealed more directly to the popular imagination was that of popery, though the parliamentarian John Seldon was honest enough to admit that 'We charge the prelatical clergy with popery to make them odious, though we know they are guilty of no such thing.'[57] Even the pope suspected that Charles I and Archbishop Laud might be crypto-Catholics. In the 1630s, Urban VIII sent his emissaries Gregorio Panzani and George Con to reconcile England with Rome, complete with offers of a bust by Bernini for Charles and a cardinal's hat for Laud. The real gift in this was for Prynne and Laud's other critics, who maintained that the archbishop really did entertain such ambitions. While it is true that Catholicism flourished at court and that royal reprieves saved Catholics condemned to death, recusancy fines were collected more assiduously than they had been under King James. Charles and his archbishop shared a profound commitment to the Church of England, and Laud declared himself resolutely opposed to such characteristics of Catholic belief and practice as transubstantiation, communion in one kind, religious images and saintly intercession. He conceived of the Church of Rome and the Church of England as equally valid branches of one universal Church. Rome was 'a true church', not *the* true Church: his opponents chose to ignore the nuance.

Even more obviously than Whitgift, Laud was less of a theologian and more of an administrator, whether at Oxford or at Lambeth. He had a keen appreciation of the sources of weakness in the Church of England, and identified as a particular problem the diversity in public worship that had effectively been encouraged by Abbot's inadequate leadership and Puritan sympathies. This he articulated in debate with an English Catholic convert known as Fisher the Jesuit: 'No one thing hath made conscientious men more wavering in their own minds, or more apt and easy to be drawn aside from the sincerity of religion professed in the church of England than the want of uniform and decent order in too many churches of the kingdom.'[58] Independent Puritan preachers, supported by lay patrons, undermined the Church of England organisationally and financially by separating themselves from it, but lay encroachment on the wealth and independence of the Church was far too strong a tide for even a king and a small number of determined prelates to reverse. As early as 1504, Bishop Richard Nix of Norwich lamented to Archbishop Warham that 'lay men be much bolder against the Church than ever they were'.[59] That boldness was positively encouraged by the government of Henry VIII and his successors, as the wealth of the Church was allowed to pass into private hands. Clerical wealth had been a standard target for stinging Erasmian criticism, but the alternative – clerical poverty – encouraged the laity to treat the Church with disrespect. Archbishop Whitgift expressed this succinctly: 'The temporality seek to make the clergy beggars, that we may depend on them.'[60] He doubted the motives of his Puritan adversaries, who sought 'the spoil of the church . . . under pretence of zeal'[61], and estimated that only 600 out of the Church of England's 9,000 livings were financially capable of supporting a minister. When Charles and Laud sought to free the clergy from financial dependence on the laity, they were building on the concerns and initiatives of Whitgift, Bancroft and even Abbot, all of whom had been conscious of the need to put the Church on a firmer financial footing. This brought the king and his primate into further conflict with the same section of English society that sat in parliament and took up the Puritan cause with varying degrees of conviction and opportunism.

In response to Puritan undermining of the parochial system, Laud sought to reinforce the position of parishes and parish churches as the basic components of a unified Church of England. He actively encouraged the repair of church buildings, which had been neglected amid the ecclesiastical uncertainty of the later sixteenth century and, more recently, on account of 'the remissness of Abbot and of other bishops by his example': the words are Clarendon's and not intended to be impartial. What sparked intense debate were changes to the internal arrangement of churches, particularly the positioning of communion tables and, to a lesser extent, the placing of rails around them. As dean of Gloucester in 1617, Laud had excited the enmity of local Puritans by moving the communion table from the nave to the chancel, where it looked suspiciously like a Catholic altar. Contrary to popular perception, it did not follow that he sought to make this uniform Anglican practice. His visitation articles in London and Canterbury enquired merely whether the table was 'placed in such convenient sort within the chancel or church as that the minister may best be heard in his prayer and administration and that the greater number may communicate'. It was the king who favoured tables being placed in the east end of churches and who issued order to that effect in 1633–4.[62] As Kevin Sharpe has argued, because historians have been too ready to believe the version of events written by Laud's enemies, the archbishop has been thought of as the architect and originator of the Crown's ecclesiastical policies in the 1630s, rather than as their sometimes reluctant executor. The altar controversy provides a case in point.

As archbishop of Canterbury, Laud was in a position to further the fortunes of the Church of England at governmental as well as parochial level. In some quarters there was highly exaggerated talk of Laud as 'England's Richelieu', or at least of encouraging him to believe that he might be, but the archbishop had no reason to imagine himself as an all-powerful minister operating above factions rather than among them. Laud's correspondence with Sir Thomas Wentworth (later the earl of Strafford), Charles I's lord-deputy in Ireland, reveals the depth of his suspicion of rival court factions and their leaders, particularly Sir Francis (later Baron) Cottington and the lord high treasurer Sir Richard Weston, first earl of Portland. He feared such rivals, some of whom were Catholics or crypto-Catholics, and sought to counter their influence through the promotion of Anglican clerics to important positions in government. His most notable victory was the appointment of the future primate William Juxon to the treasurership in 1636, though this was celebrated with such ostentation as to arouse long-remembered anticlerical resentment. Juxon was Laud's Oxford protégé and entirely devoted to him, but there remained a more senior bishop – a Cambridge man – who was a constant thorn in the side of the busy little primate. Bishop Williams had been his rival since the days of Buckingham's dominance. He was lord keeper in the last years of James I's reign and attended the king on his deathbed. In the 1630s he smarted when his Canterbury ambitions were thwarted by Laud's promotion. A man more noted for his wealth than for his principles, he intrigued with whichever court faction happened to be opposed to the archbishop, and compounded the latter's discomfort over the positioning of communion tables with his anonymously published *Holy Table: Name and Thing* (1637). For a decade he stood accused of protecting Puritans and was finally found guilty in Star Chamber in July 1637, fined £10,000, suspended from his Lincoln bishopric, and imprisoned in Tower of London. A more subtle primate might have sought conciliation with a bishop of Williams's wealth and skill, but Laud was temperamentally unsuited to such an approach. Still less subtle was Charles I that same year, when he sought to impose a new prayer book in

Scotland and only succeeded in uniting his northern kingdom against him in a rebellion which created a precedent for war in England in the following decade.

Laud was certainly party to this Scottish débâcle, but continued in his mission to impose order and obedience on the English Church until Charles was forced by the Scottish Bishops' Wars to call the Short Parliament in April–May 1640. Feelings reached fever pitch when Laud introduced new canons for the Church of England, laws designed to be accepted with the taking of an oath against altering 'the government of this Church by archbishops, deans, and archdeacons etc'. This 'et cetera' oath was the final straw for his parliamentary enemies, who sought vengeance after (what became) the Long Parliament was called in November the same year. As the hated instruments of the king's secular and ecclesiastical policies respectively, Strafford and Laud were both arrested for high treason. The common lawyers got their revenge by abolishing the court of High Commission, regarded as one of the means by which Charles had exercised his eleven years' 'tyranny'. Its 'arbitrary proceedings, biased judges, numerous suspensions and harsh fines' were condemned; the pent-up frustrations of genuine Puritans were released, but so were the less honourable ambitions of anticlerical laymen. As king and parliament took up arms against each other, the archbishop languished in the Tower for three years. It was 1644 before he was finally tried and the thoughts recorded in his private diary became twisted for public consumption. The Commons were determined to be rid of the man who personified all that they detested about the king's religious policies. There was talk of him being hanged, castrated and disembowelled, but the Lords prevented so ignoble an ending for one of their own and he was given forty-eight hours in which to prepare for execution on Tower Hill on 10 January 1645. The Puritans had triumphed over the bishops; the laymen had humbled the prelates.

Laud was the only bishop executed by the Long Parliament, but all the others were deprived of their sees. Exacerbating Laud's misfortunes, Williams had been translated to York in 1641, but subsequently retired to his native Wales. Juxon devoted himself to the rural life and to his pack of hounds. Writing six years after Laud's execution, John Milton rejoiced that England was no longer troubled by bishops:

Most certain it is (as all our Stories bear witness) that ever since their coming to the See of Canterbury for near twelve hundred years, to speak of them in general, they have been in England to our Souls a sad and doleful succession of illiterate and blind guides: to our purses, and goods a wasteful band of robbers, a perpetual havoc, and rapine: to our state a continual Hydra of mischief, and molestation, the forge of discord and Rebellion: This is the Trophy of their Antiquity, and boasted Succession through so many Ages. And for those Prelate-Martyrs they glory of, they are to be judged what they were by the Gospel, and not the Gospel to be tried by them.[63]

What Milton reckoned without was not Juxon's pack of hounds but Laud's tortoise, which outlived its master by over a century until being accidentally killed by a Lambeth Palace gardener. For all the controversy he excited, Laud was one of the shorter-serving primates of the early modern period, but his long-lived tortoise can be regarded as symbolic of his lasting influence beyond the Commonwealth period and beyond what turned out to be the temporary abolition of the see of Canterbury.

1660–1848: Ecclesia Anglicana Instaurata

I have, alas, only one illusion left, and that is the Archbishop of Canterbury

Sydney Smith[1]

The history of the Church of England between the Restoration of 1660 and the mid nineteenth century, is less readily told through the lives of the archbishops of Canterbury than it is through the alternating tides of parliamentary legislation, one defending the Church from Dissent in its various forms, the other effectively undermining it by encouraging freedom to worship outside the national Church. First came the four acts collectively known as the Clarendon Code, from the name of Charles II's principal minister in the early 1660s, Edward Hyde, earl of Clarendon. The Corporation Act (1661) was designed to ensure loyalty to both the Crown and the Church of England by members of municipal corporations, who were required to abjure rebellion and receive communion according to the rite of the Church. The 1662 Act of Uniformity decreed that Christian worship be according to the Book of Common Prayer, the revision of which was completed that year. The Act also effectively countered Charles II's first Declaration of Indulgence (1662), by which he sought to honour a promise to mitigate laws against Dissenters. Although this piece of legislation has been modified a number of times, it remains on the statute book, just as the 1662 edition of the Prayer Book remains in use, albeit for a small minority of services in the twenty-first-century Church of England. In 1664 the Conventicles Act outlawed private assemblies for non-Prayer Book worship. Again, it was designed to strike at the root of Dissenting practices. In contrast to the Act of Uniformity, it was repealed in the nineteenth century, though amendments had been made as early as 1670. The fourth measure in the Clarendon Code was the Five Mile Act (1665), which barred Dissenting ministers from coming within 5 miles of any city or incorporated town, and unintentionally led to the spread of nonconformity in rural areas. By these measures some 1,200 ministers were ejected from their livings.

All of which was countered by Charles II's second Declaration of Indulgence (1672), an act of toleration of benefit to both Dissenters and to the Catholics to whom he quite literally owed his life, but one which lacked the force of legislation. Parliament's unequivocal response was the Test Act of 1673, which not only required public office holders to swear oaths of supremacy and allegiance to the Crown, but also required them to declare their rejection of the doctrine of Transubstantiation, which effectively barred Catholics from civil office, from James, duke of York, downwards. This bar notwithstanding, and after the furore of the fictional Popish Plot of 1678, James duly ascended the throne in 1685 and proceeded to issue his own Declarations of Indulgence in April 1687 and April 1688, to the intended advantage of not only his co-religionists but also of Protestant Dissenters. Within nine months of the second measure he had been deposed, replaced by his daughter Mary and her Calvinist husband William of Orange. James's declarations were superseded by the Toleration Act of 1689, the purpose of which was to tolerate Protestant Dissenters while demonstrating official intolerance of Catholics. With Queen Anne the balance briefly tilted away from Dissent, for she was a strong advocate of the Occasional Conformity Act (1711), which sought to end the anomaly of Dissenters occasionally receiving communion in their parish churches in order to qualify for public office. In 1714 the Schism Act prevented Dissenters from teaching or running schools, in the hope of keeping the young within the Established Church. This measure was repealed just four years later: with the Hanoverian succession the pendulum had swung again. Though recusancy laws were more enthusiastically enforced in the wake of the Jacobite rising of 1715, the eighteenth century was a comparatively fallow time for new legislation relating to the Church of England and its rivals. Towards the end of the century the Roman Catholic Relief Acts of 1778 and 1791, which permitted Catholic worship and Catholic schools, provided a sign of things to come. Another burst of parliamentary interest between 1828 and 1836 loosened the ties that bound Church and State, as the Clarendon Code had enforced them. In 1828 the Corporation Act of 1661 was repealed. The following year the most important of the Catholic Emancipation Acts was passed, removing almost all the disabilities against Catholics. Although the Reform Act of 1832 dealt with purely secular matters, extending the franchise and recognising the size and importance of Britain's industrial cities, churchmen of a conservative disposition felt threatened by such radical change and the probability of more. They were even more directly affected by the Ecclesiastical Commissioners Act (1836), which removed Church estates and revenues from the hands of individual prelates and entrusted them to the commissioners.[2] Thus it was, for example, that the prince-bishops of Durham ceased with William van Mildert: he preferred to donate his episcopal endowments to the newly founded University of Durham rather than let them go to the Ecclesiastical Commissioners. In the southern province, William Howley (pronounced 'Hooley') was the last of the 'prince-archbishops' of Canterbury: at his death he did not deny the commissioners the right to manage the archiepiscopal estates. Thus was 1848 a year of revolution even in the Church of England.

Fourteen archbishops of Canterbury promoted and defended, or feared and opposed, those various pieces of legislation between 1660 and 1848. So rarely are their personal histories projected on to the ecclesiastical history of Britain that three of them – Matthew Hutton, Frederick Cornwallis and John Moore – do not even merit entries in the *Oxford Dictionary of the Christian Church*. In the century of John Wesley and even of the well-*connected* Selina, countess of Huntingdon, the primates were in danger of being eclipsed. Their careers nevertheless shed useful light on England's *ancien régime*, in which the Church of England was populated by High and Low Churchmen, the ruling elite adopted the labels of Whig and Tory, and public life of any kind was activated by the exercise of patronage, although there was nothing new about that last feature.

In terms of their geographical origins the archbishops were, if anything, atypical of their age. Their long eighteenth century was characterised by a dramatic increase in the urban population of England, especially in the latter part of the period, that of Birmingham expanding from 3,500 in 1650 to 144,000 in 1831, Manchester's growing from 4,500 to 223,000 over the same period. Towns and cities cultivated manufacturing, commercial or leisure economies, while a diminishing proportion of the population remained in the agriculturally revolutionised countryside, although even in 1850 some 50 per cent of the population was still rural. The archbishops, meanwhile, tended to come from villages or small towns, eleven of them from the southern province, including William Sancroft from Fressingfield in Suffolk,

William Wake from Blandford in Dorset, and Thomas Herring from Walsoken in Norfolk. There were, however, three Yorkshiremen: John Tillotson of Sowerby, John Potter from Wakefield, and Matthew Hutton from Marske, near Richmond. For the most part the primates' backgrounds were solid rather than grand. Tillotson and Potter were from mercantile families. It was said that Archbishop John Moore's father was a Gloucester butcher, but an alternative interpretation has him as a gentleman. The countryman Sancroft was the son of a yeoman farmer but comfortably settled, with good connections at Cambridge; he spelt the family name 'Sandcroft'; the archbishop was the first to drop the 'd'. Thomas Secker was born at Sibthorpe, in Nottinghamshire, and his family were said to be 'small' people.[3] Gilbert Sheldon was born in Derbyshire to a family of humble status, but his forebears were a Staffordshire family, the antiquity of whose line is emphasised on the archbishop's thoroughly classical tomb in Croydon parish church. Sheldon's immediate predecessor, William Juxon, the earliest of the primates in this section, was born into the Church in the sense that his father, Richard, was receiver-general of the estates of the see of Chichester. Providing that one discounts archbishop-elect Reginald FitzJocelin and possibly Baldwin of Forde in the twelfth century, the Cambridgeshire-born Thomas Tenison's distinction lay in being the first archbishop to be the son and, indeed, grandson of a cleric. Herring and Howley followed in that tradition, while Hutton was descended from Archbishop Matthew Hutton of York (d. 1606). The Wakes claimed descent from the celebrated Hereward and Archbishop Wake was the grandson and nephew of clerics, Colonel William Wake, had served the Royalist cause in the Civil War. Frederick Cornwallis was the first high-born prelate since Reginald Pole. Born in 1713, he was a younger son of Charles, fourth Lord Cornwallis of Eye, Suffolk. It was during the archiepiscopate of Archbishop Cornwallis that his kinsman, the first Marquis Cornwallis, surrendered Yorktown and thus precipitated the loss of the North American colonies. The last aristocrat to occupy the see of Canterbury was Charles Manners Sutton, grandson of John Manners, third duke of Rutland. The 'Sutton' was assumed by the archbishop's father on account of estates acquired by marriage.

Most of these archbishops received their early education at grammar schools in towns close to their family homes, including Sancroft at Bury St Edmunds, Tillotson at Colne and Halifax, Tenison at Norwich, Herring at Wisbech, and Moore at Gloucester. The exceptions tended to come at either end of the period. Juxon reinforced a family connection with the Merchant Taylors' Company by attending their school in London in the 1590s. Cornwallis was an Etonian, Manners Sutton a Carthusian, in the Charterhouse School sense of the term, and the Hampshire-born Howley a Wykehamist, continuing the tradition of Archbishops Chichele and Warham. Only Secker received his education outside the Church of England, for his family were Dissenters and he attended the Dissenting academies at Attercliffe, Gloucester and Tewkesbury. His non-Anglican background barred him from the universities of Oxford and Cambridge and he pursued medical studies in London and Paris, gaining his MD at Leyden in 1721. Friends regretted that a man of his talent was lost to the Church of England and persuaded him to renounce Dissent. This he did, entering Exeter College, Oxford, as a gentleman-commoner, and immersing himself in theological studies. In consequence of that career change, all fourteen of the archbishops were graduates of the two English universities, seven from each. In addition to Secker, the Oxonians were Juxon who, like his mentor Laud, spent his entire academic career at St John's and succeeded Laud as its president, Sheldon (of Trinity College), Wake (Christ Church), Potter (University College, later a fellow of Lincoln), Moore (Pembroke), and Howley (New College). Sheldon was a significant figure in Laudian Oxford and was elected warden of All Souls in 1626. In 1648 he was ousted from the wardenship and briefly imprisoned in Oxford for his allegiance to the Royalist cause. Together with Laud and Juxon, he remained deeply wedded to the university throughout his career and was its chancellor from 1667 to 1669. The principal expression of Sheldon's devotion came in the shape of the Sheldonian Theatre, which was opened in 1669 to the design of Christopher Wren. Its architectural exuberance and ceremonial acts epitomised the primate's vision of the restoration of both king and Church. The showmanship suggested by the Sheldonian, and by his reclining effigy at Croydon, should not obscure the fact that Sheldon himself demonstrated strong pastoral care for his clergy, or at least for those who conformed to his version of orthodoxy and, unlike the court, he did not retreat to Oxford during the plague of 1665, remaining in residence at Lambeth.

Among the Cambridge colleges, Emmanuel and Jesus each produced two archbishops in this period. William Sancroft's uncle, also William, was master of Emmanuel from 1628 to 1637, at the end of which the future archbishop graduated BA. His MA followed in 1641, after which he became a college tutor and gained his BD in 1648. While the more venerable Juxon, deposed from his London bishopric, lived as quietly as his pack of hounds would let him at Little Compton in Warwickshire and the no less distinguished Sheldon worked for the Royalist cause at Snelston in Derbyshire, Sancroft retreated first to Fressingfield and then, from 1657, emulated his king by going on 'travels'. Fittingly, these took him to both Geneva and Rome, and included a stint as a student at Padua. In 1678 Sancroft became the first archbishop of Canterbury since Pole to have spent time in Rome and also the first Cambridge graduate to be appointed to the primacy since Richard Bancroft in 1604. As Sancroft's subsequent career demonstrated, By the 1640s Emmanuel was losing its reputation as a Puritan college. Manners Sutton was also a graduate of Emmanuel (MA 1780, DD 1792), but otherwise had no need of an academic career to further his promotion. The Jesus men were Herring and Hutton, though each of them migrated to other colleges to become fellows, Herring to Corpus Christi, of which Thomas Tenison (inheriting Matthew Parker's Norfolk mantle) had also been a fellow, and Hutton to Christ's. It was during his undergraduate career at Christ's that Frederick Cornwallis suffered the stroke which left him partially paralysed throughout his life and forced him to write with his left hand. Tillotson's Cambridge career was confined to Clare Hall. In marked contrast to Sancroft, Tillotson not only espoused nonconformity in the 1650s but married the niece of Oliver Cromwell.

Archbishop Potter was arguably the most scholarly primate of the eighteenth century. A precocious talent, he published on Plutarch at the age of twenty, following this with the two-volume *Archaeologia Graeca* (1697–9) while still in his twenties. He went on to edit the works of the patristic writer Clement of Alexandria. Potter and Howley crowned their Oxford careers by becoming Regius professors of divinity, in 1707 and 1809 respectively. It may be noted that Regius professorships increased at both universities in the early eighteenth century as a way of reconciling them to the Hanoverian dynasty and its Whig administration. The inspiration behind this bold scheme was Edmund Gibson, bishop of London (d. 1749). As a crucial figure in the *rapprochement* between the bishops and the Whig political establishment, Gibson has been depicted as the 'lost leader' of the Georgian Church.[4]

As a means to the top of the Anglican tree, academic distinction came second to royal or aristocratic patronage in the long eighteenth century. The first post-Cromwellian archbishop of Canterbury, William Juxon, was emblematic of the Restoration of the monarchy, for he had attended Charles I on the scaffold at Whitehall on 30 January 1649. It was to Juxon that the king addressed his final word – 'remember' – and it was also Juxon who conducted the royal martyr's funeral service at Windsor eight days later, during a blinding snow storm. To those who remembered, Laud was no less of a martyr, but fifteen years separated his execution in 1645 from Juxon's final elevation to Canterbury in 1660, by which time the latter was old and ailing. Indeed, the average age of the new bishops at the Restoration was sixty-five; the 1650s had witnessed the distinct possibility of a break in the episcopal succession. Juxon's long years of retirement concluded, he was able to take part in the coronation of Charles II on St George's day, 23 April 1661. Just two years later, Gilbert Sheldon became the fifth successive bishop of London to be translated to Canterbury. He had effectively understudied Juxon as Bancroft had assisted Whitgift at the very beginning of the century. Like Juxon, Sheldon was dedicated to the memory of Laud and held fast to 'the true orthodox profession of the Catholique faith of Christ . . . being a true member of this Catholique church within the communion of a living part thereof, the present church of England.' Like Bancroft, he was a strong anti-Puritan; after his experiences during the republican period, he was an even stronger royalist. Clarendon rightly regarded Sheldon as one of his closest friends and allies. At the Restoration he came into his own, being made bishop of London, a privy councillor and master of the Savoy (the hospital built on the site of John of Gaunt's palace) by the end of 1660. In the last of these capacities he hosted and was a principal player in the Savoy Conference of 1661, which was called to consider the revision of the Book of Common Prayer in such a way as to retain the more numerous of the Dissenting sects within the Establishment. It proved to be a reassertion of episcopal rights and 'Catholic' principles, which were given official sanction by the Cavalier Parliament of May 1661 and the Clarendon Code. Sheldon was to prove an implacable enemy to Dissent.

William Sancroft was a less combative character than Sheldon. As a fellow of Emmanuel he had established himself as an apologist of anti-Calvinism. After the Restoration, of which he heard during his visit to Rome, he was soon on the ecclesiastical fast track, becoming in quick succession a canon of Durham, master of Emmanuel, a royal chaplain and dean of York. In 1664 he became dean of St Paul's and was much engaged in the rebuilding of the cathedral following the great fire in 1666. It was from the deanery, rather than any bishopric, that he was elected to Canterbury in 1668, a fact which not only highlights his personal contribution to the city of London in its time of crisis, but also provides a reminder that three of his archiepiscopal successors in the period covered by this chapter (Tillotson, Secker and Cornwallis) also served as deans of the capital's cathedral. It is less surprising that Sancroft's successor, John Tillotson, came to Canterbury without prior episcopal experience, for the Protector's kinsman-by-marriage had made his name as a Presbyterian and took part in the Savoy Conference as a nonconformist observer. Ever a shameless networker, he accommodated himself with ease to the restored Church of England. He became a noted preacher and polemicist with important pulpits in London, at Lincoln's Inn and St Lawrence Jewry. He subsequently became dean of Canterbury and of St Paul's and clerk of the king's closet. He could perhaps be caricatured as a placeman or an opportunist, but William III declared that he had never known a more honest man and Bishop Burnet, who presided at his funeral, saw him as having 'had the brightest thoughts and the most correct style of all our divines, and was esteemed the best preacher of his age'.[5] His pious prolixity meant that when his complete works were published they ran to some fourteen volumes. In fairness, it should be stressed that Tillotson came to the primacy as a consequence of Sancroft's suspension in 1689 and deprivation in 1690 and accepted it only with reluctance.

Thomas Tenison, Tillotson's successor, also excelled as a preacher, especially of funeral orations, which were much appreciated by his contemporaries. He came to prominence at St-Martin-in-the-Fields, to which living he was appointed in 1680. In July 1685 he attended the rebellious duke of Monmouth in prison and on the scaffold, and was a frequent preacher against the evils of popery and a fervent supporter of the anti-Jacobite Protestant succession. Tenison was very pastorally minded: he established a free school and a free library in his London parish and was said to have distributed some £300 of his own money to his parishioners during the 'great frost' of 1683. His election as bishop of Lincoln in 1691 offended some people, who felt that he had lavished too much praise in his funeral sermon for Nell Gwynne. 'I have heard as much,' Queen Mary is said to have reflected, 'and it convinces me that the unhappy creature died penitent, otherwise the good doctor would not have spoken of her so charitably.'[6] As archbishop he attended Mary on her deathbed in December 1694, provided the sermon that accompanied Purcell's musical contribution to her funeral, and also witnessed the passing of King William in March 1702. He crowned both Queen Anne in April that year and George I in October 1714.

Tenison's later years were much clouded by the 'patrician' disease that afflicted not a few eighteenth-century prelates: gout. He died on 14 December 1715. With his successor William Wake the Oxonians returned to Lambeth. In his contacts and interests, Wake was probably the most wide-ranging of the Georgian archbishops. In 1682, he went to the French court as chaplain to Richard Graham, Viscount Preston, Charles II's ambassador to Louis XIV. There he began a lifetime's fascination with the French Church, then at its most magnificent zenith. It was Gallicanism, a strong sense of national French identity in the French Church, which attracted Wake's interest. His biographer Norman Sykes writes: 'The eirenic disposition and catholic sympathies thus implanted in Wake by his residence in Paris from 1682 to 1685 was to bear abundant fruit in his ecumenical correspondence in the cause of ecclesiastical unity during his primacy a generation later.'[7] He came to Canterbury by way of the deanery of Exeter and the bishopric of Lincoln, and gained a reputation as a devoted pastor:

> Alike in the large and unwieldy diocese of Lincoln and in the smaller territory of that of Canterbury, he was a model of industry, diligence, and zeal. In discharge of the official duties of ordination, confirmation, and visitation he was regular, careful, and indefatigable; in pastoral counsel he was fatherly, considerate, and where possible merciful; as judge, when judicial process and sentence could not be avoided, he was learned, judicious, and as impartial as his concern for the honour and credit of the church and clergy allowed; in private correspondence and communication with his clergy he was painstaking and patient; and in close co-operation with his archdeacons he did as much as his own physical strength, the extent of his diocese, and the obligations of other avocations of the episcopal office, made practicable for the good estate and sound government of ministers and people under his care.[8]

The cultivation of patrons was not Wake's strong suit, but it was an art mastered by John Potter, who found it necessary to compensate for his humble birth. Consigned for a brief time to a series of country livings, he came to prominence as domestic chaplain to Archbishop Tenison and resided at Lambeth, but owed the Regius professorship to the patronage of John

Churchill, duke of Marlborough, that dominant presence in the reign of Queen Anne. In 1715 Potter became bishop of Oxford, his diocese including the Marlborough pile at Blenheim. It was Potter, still bishop of Oxford, who preached at the coronation of George II in 1727, though Archbishop Wake was the Zadok-figure who did the anointing. On Wake's death, a decade later, the intervention of Queen Caroline was instrumental in securing the primacy for Potter.

Like so many prelates of his generation Thomas Herring gained a reputation for scholarship, pulpit oratory and patronage. Dean of Rochester by 1732 and bishop of Bangor by 1738, he was translated to York in 1742. He made himself comfortable in Bishopthorpe, the residence of the northern primate, and conducted a visitation of his diocese. Herring was at York for only four years, but this brief period included the heightened tension of the 1745 Jacobite rebellion. In contrast to his early fifteenth-century predecessor Archbishop Scrope, who had raised arms against his king, Herring acquired notability as the last bishop to raise arms in defence of the government. His strong anti-Jacobite sympathies and the eagerness with which he welcomed the duke of Cumberland to York after the rout of Culloden, were said to provide the key to his Canterbury preferment in 1747. There was little in his ability to recommend him. If it had not been for his less-than-grand origins, he might have exemplified the career closed to talent. Dean Swift had not encountered 'so stupid, so injudicious, and so prostitute a divine'.[9] Herring's ill health led to periods of somnolence, spent mainly at Croydon. Matthew Hutton's episcopal career exactly shadowed that of Herring, whose successor he was at Bangor, York and Canterbury. Like his predecessors, Hutton was adept in the ways of patronage, for he was chaplain to Charles Seymour, duke of Somerset, and to the king, with whom he travelled to Hanover in 1736. He was also a friend of Thomas Pelham-Holles, the powerful duke of Newcastle, who took a keen interest in the exercise of ecclesiastical patronage.

It was the exercise of patronage by an ecclesiastic that set the former Dissenter Thomas Secker on the lower rungs of the clerical ladder: William Talbot, successively bishop of Salisbury and Durham, provided him to the parish of Houghton-le-Spring in the prince-bishopric. Secker's ability to cure the body as well as the soul was particularly appreciated by his poor parishioners. Queen Caroline was among his later patrons: he obtained the see of Bristol in 1735 and succeeded Potter at Oxford in 1737, where he followed Potter's example in befriending the widowed Sarah, duchess of

Marlborough, who made him executor of her will. From 1750 he was also dean of St Paul's, the holding of deaneries and bishoprics in plurality being a fairly common occurrence in this period. Secker preached at Queen Caroline's funeral in 1737 and retained a close association with the Hanoverian dynasty. He was the bishop who baptised and confirmed the earnestly devout young man who became King George III in 1760, after which he also conducted George's coronation and marriage. While aristocratic patronage was the heart that powered the eighteenth-century Church of England, aristocratic vocations were rare phenomena, that of Frederick Cornwallis being something of an exception that proved the rule. Unsurprisingly, his first rectory was presented by his brother. Promotion came easily: the see of Lichfield in 1750, the deanery of St Paul's *(in commendam)* in 1766, and the archbishopric in 1768. It was whispered that advantages of birth rather than more formal qualifications got him the primacy, but he was a pleasant and convivial bishop. Indeed, some considered him too convivial. With John Moore the standard patronage pattern resumed, for he was a tutor to Lords Charles and Robert Spencer at Blenheim. Marlborough patronage secured for him a prebend at Durham, a canonry at Christ Church, Oxford, and the deanery of Canterbury in 1771. In 1775 he became bishop of Bangor. Welsh bishoprics were poorly endowed and many were held by absentee bishops awaiting better things in England or holding them in plurality with English benefices. Eight years later Moore was said to have been the third choice for Canterbury, the preferred candidates having declined the office on grounds of age.

With Archbishop Charles Manners Sutton the pattern established by Cornwallis was revived. He held a number of family livings and family connections helped him to higher office, as dean of Peterborough (1791), bishop of Norwich (1792), and dean of Windsor (1794, again *in commendam*). At Norwich, Manners Sutton lived famously well and got into debt; the Windsor deanery brought him greater income than the bishopric and he preferred to live there. Canterbury came to him through a particularly direct intervention on the part of the increasingly eccentric George III. At Moore's death 1805, Bishop George Pretyman Tomline of Lincoln was expected to succeed, but the king himself sent to the deanery and, taking Manners Sutton away from a dinner party, addressed him thus: 'My Lord Archbishop of Canterbury, I wish you joy. No, not a word, go back to your friends.' William Pitt, who had been a pupil of Tomline at Cambridge, came to Windsor the following morning, urging his former tutor's case. It was too late. The king announced: 'I have already wished Manners Sutton joy, and he must go to Canterbury.'[10] Manners Sutton duly enjoyed his high office for twenty-three years, longer than any archbishop of Canterbury since Warham in the early sixteenth century. By the time of his death in 1828, patronage was still crucial to ecclesiastical appointments – as Mr Collins had been reminding readers of Jane Austen since 1813 – but the cast of characters on the national stage was now quite different. George IV had reigned briefly but spectacularly and died in 1830, leaving his considerably duller brother William to occupy the throne. Even more briefly was the duke of Wellington prime minister (1828–30), but it was he who influenced the appointment to Canterbury of William Howley, bishop of London. Wellington did not share Howley's antipathy to Catholic emancipation, one of the key issues of the day, but he did regard him as a safe pair of hands.

In appearance and style Howley embodied the old order: he was not only the last archbishop of Canterbury to enjoy the revenues of an ecclesiastical prince; he was also the last to wear a wig. He is perhaps best remembered for telling the young Victoria of her accession to the throne on the death of William IV in 1837 and it was he who crowned her and presided at her wedding to Prince Albert. A 'safe pair of hands' was precisely what Victoria did not consider Howley to be at her coronation when, by putting the ring on the wrong finger, he caused a delay of over an hour. 'Pray tell me what I am to do,' the teenage monarch pleaded, 'for they [the officiating clergy] don't know.' Howley's hesitant personality showed itself in his lack of facility with words. He began a speech at a girls' school with repetitive circumlocution: 'My dear young friends – my dear girls – my dear young catechumens – my dear Christian friends – my dear young female women.' *The Times* obituarist put it succinctly, if bluntly: 'It can scarcely be said that what fell from his lips ever deserved to be called a speech.' Yet he retained respect, affection and even influence.[11]

If the early careers of the archbishops provide an object lesson in the receipt of patronage, so their own exercise of it is no less instructive about the workings of England's *ancien régime*. As Jeremy Gregory has explained, the archbishops' patronage is particularly evident in the composition of the Canterbury chapter, to which Tenison, Wake, Potter, Moore and Manners Sutton appointed kinsmen or former chaplains.[12] Archbishop Potter's son, also called John Potter, was appointed to the chapter in 1745 and became dean in 1766, as did James Cornwallis in 1775 and Manners Sutton's son-in-law Hugh Percy in 1825. James Cornwallis duly followed his uncle's example by becoming bishop of Lichfield (1781–1824), and Hugh Percy was promoted to the sees of Rochester (1827) and Carlisle (1827–56) shortly before his father-in-law's death. What had previously been accepted as conventional practice, did not pass without censure by the time Archbishop Moore appointed his two sons to stalls at Canterbury and Manners Sutton set his son-in-law's career on a sound footing.

'Convention' had not been long practised, for John Tillotson was the first married archbishop since the death of Matthew Parker's wife in 1570. In the days when members of Oxbridge colleges resigned their fellowships upon marriage, Archbishops Juxon and Sheldon remained firmly wedded to their university. In like manner, William Sancroft was as wedded to the Church as any primate had ever been. Thomas Herring was also a bachelor, but the other ten archbishops between 1660 and 1848 were married, John Moore twice. Some wives had more impact than others on their husbands' careers and reputations. The Dissenter Thomas Secker married Catherine Benson, whose brother Martin was an Anglican cleric and among those who persuaded Secker to abandon Dissent. Martin Benson was bishop of Gloucester from 1735 to 1752. Before his appointment to Oxford, Secker's household also included the widowed daughter-in-law and granddaughter of Bishop Talbot of Durham; the granddaughter, Catherine Talbot, gained a reputation as a poet and essayist. Caroline Cornwallis was a conspicuous hostess and her salon the most fashionable to have been seen at Lambeth Palace. Entertainments and balls were flamboyant enough to receive a reprimand from George III:

> I hold these levities and vain dissipations as utterly inexpedient, if not unlawful, to pass in a residence for many centuries devoted to divine studies, religious retirement and the extensive exercise of charity and benevolence – a place where so many of your predecessors have led their lives in such sanctity as has thrown lustre on the pure religion they professed and adorned. I trust you will suppress them immediately, so that I may not have occasion to show any further marks of my displeasure or to interpose in a different manner.[13]

Thomas Tenison seems to have been particularly susceptible to female charms. He married the daughter of the master of his Cambridge college, but she died without issue. In 1712, when he was in his mid-seventies, he was evidently captivated by the 23-year-old Mary Pierrepont (better known as the adventurous Lady Mary Wortley Montagu) and wrote that he did 'still remember Her, and, perhaps . . . it wou'd be more for his repose cou'd he possibly forget her.'[14] Later that year she eloped with Edward Wortley and married him under special licence granted by Tenison. Tillotson, Wake, Potter, Hutton, Moore and Howley all had issue, but Tillotson's predeceased him, as did Howley's two sons. The most striking family dispute came when the younger John Potter, dean of Canterbury, was disinherited by his father after marrying a domestic servant. By way of contrast, Charles Manners Sutton (d. 1845), elder son of Archbishop Manners Sutton, achieved distinction as Speaker of the House of Commons and was ennobled as the first Viscount Canterbury. Archbishop Manners Sutton with his twelve children, ten of whom were daughters, was the primate as *paterfamilias*, far removed from the ideal of the medieval ascetic.

A large family required a substantial property and this Manners Sutton acquired with the purchase of the 1,200-acre Addington estate in Surrey in 1807. It became an exclave of the Canterbury diocese. Archbishop Cornwallis had severed the centuries-old connection with Croydon by selling the palace there in 1780. Since the Restoration, the primates had focused their building work on Lambeth Palace, with Juxon contributing the great hall and Tillotson, less ostentatiously but perhaps in keeping with the scientific spirit of the age, adding a greenhouse. Tenison bequeathed a palace much in need of repair, which Wake and Herring duly undertook. A minor revolution in the lives of the archbishops at Lambeth occurred in 1750 with the opening of Westminster Bridge. Under the Georgian archbishops, their wives and families, Lambeth became gradually more 'domesticated'. Archbishop Potter began the tradition of picture collecting, including the portraits of archbishops now hung in the Guard Room, and did his best to make gracious living possible in what had appeared a barrack-like or monastic pile. The hospitable Cornwallises provided a magnificent new drawing room and dining room, and the garden adjoining the Thames was much improved and landscaped.[15] At the end of the period came the most dramatic changes of all, when Archbishop Howley commissioned a report from Edward Blore, a Gothic revivalist architect, that paved the way for the demolition of much of the old palace in 1829 and its replacement by a great new west wing. Work was completed in 1833.

With the loss of Croydon, there was little or no option but for the late seventeenth- and eighteenth-century archbishops to be buried in Lambeth parish church. The acquisition of Addington brought with it the opportunity for archbishops and their families to have vaults beneath the medieval village church. Manners Sutton initiated this practice. His memorial in the north aisle of the church demonstrates in miniature the severity of Regency classicism; in neither the epitaph not the restrained decoration does it contain a hint of Christian sentiment. Archbishop Howley and his family are no less in evidence in the Addington church, but an initial hint at a possible return by the archbishops to their cathedral exists there in the empty canopied Gothic revival 'tomb', complete with recumbent effigy, erected to his memory.[16] Howley is also remembered at Canterbury Cathedral in the Howley-Harrison Library: Harrison was his domestic chaplain. Other archbishops of this period who contributed to the cathedral fabric included Juxon, who made a financial contribution towards the repair of gates to the precinct, and Tenison, who donated an elaborately carved wooden throne, the work of Grinling Gibbons.[17]

From the Reformation until the mid-nineteenth century, archbishops of Canterbury were not buried or, until Howley, even commemorated in their cathedral, from which they remained almost completely absent and in which they were installed by proxy. In the manner of his installation, Howley was very much the end of that tradition and, when he sent his proxy to Canterbury, he was taken to task by his former Winchester school fellow, the ever-quotable Sydney Smith: 'A proxy sent down in the Canterbury fly, to take the Creator to witness that the archbishop, detained in town by business or pleasure, will never violate that foundation of piety over which he presides – all this seems to me an act of the most extraordinary indolence ever recorded in history.'[18] When the archbishop visited Canterbury during the Reform Bill debate of 1832, he was mobbed and a dead cat thrown at his coach. So polite a reception had Manners Sutton received during his first visitation of his diocese that the congregation did not object when he preached on so 'popish' a subject as the history of confession: in common with many of his Anglican contemporaries, it should be pointed out, Manners Sutton considered the Church of England so inclusive and tolerant as to make Catholic Emancipation quite superfluous. In doing so he shared the predominant High Church teaching that the Church of England was a branch of the Catholic Church.[19] On 23 December 1752, Archbishop Herring had cause to write to

Dean Lynch of Canterbury concerning the relics of his predecessor Anselm, a letter that not only illustrates the physical and spiritual distance between the archbishop and his cathedral, but also the sheer contempt in which this seasoned anti-Jacobite held the Church of Rome:

I had a Request communicated to me to Day of a very singular Nature: and it comes from the Ambassador of a great Catholic Prince. Arch Bishop Anselm, it seems, lies buried in our Cathedral and the King of Sardinia has a great Desire to be possess'd of his Bones, or Dust and Coffin . . . You will believe I have no great Scruples on this Head, but if I had I would get rid of them all if the parting with the rotten Remains of a rebel to his King, a Slave to the Popedom & an Enemy to the married Clergy (all this Anselm was) would purchase Ease and Indulgence to one living Protestant . . . I should make no Conscience of palming on the Simpletons any other old Bishop with the Name of Anselm.[20]

The cathedral's Arundel Tower was seriously damaged in the 'great storm' of 1703, but was not rebuilt until the 1830s: it had not excited the nation's imagination. The rebuilding of St Paul's Cathedral, on the other hand, was a symbol of the reconstruction of the Church of England after the Civil War. Wren's architectural speculations allowed the clergy to think about what sort of church was suitable for the Restoration. The cathedral that was built (foundation stone laid 1675, structure completed 1710) represented a classical interpretation of a traditional cathedral form 'to reconcile, as near as possible, the Gothick to a better Manner of Architecture'.[21] Like St Paul's, the rebuilt Restoration Church combined elements of the new and the old. The renewed Church of England was celebrated in optimistic words by William Sancroft who, as dean of St Paul's, had made the initial contact with Wren:

If there be now in the world a Church to whom that eulogium, that she is a lily among thorns, is due and proper, it is this Church of which we are members, as it stands reformed now and established amongst us; the purest certainly upon earth, as being purified from those corruptions and abuses which the lapse of times, the malice of the devil and the wickedness of men had introduced insensibly into the doctrine and worship and government of it.[22]

They were sentiments that Archbishops Abbot and Laud would have recognised and applauded.

During the post-Restoration period the Royalist interpretation of the Civil War, pioneered by Peter Heylyn, Laud's biographer and chaplain, maintained that 'Presbyterianism' had caused the conflict. The return of the hereditary monarchy and the Anglican order of the Church bound the two institutions together. The clergy saw that they were servants of a personal monarchy and spokesmen for a national Church which was a bulwark against disorder. From 1660 many of the clergy became advocates of a high religious theory of kingship and used the opportunities provided by the celebrations of 30 January, the anniversary of Charles I's execution, and 19 May, that of Charles II's return, to preach the sanctity of monarchy and the sinfulness of rebellion. To the advocates of the revived Church, the Restoration was a confirmation of the Church of England's historic destiny: 'The Restoration was not only a divine attestation of the English Church, it was an attestation miraculous in such a degree that it dwarfed all the miracles of Rome, and stood on a level with the dry-shod passage of the Israelites through the Red Sea.'[23]

In 1664 the relationship between Church and State was refined when Archbishop Sheldon agreed to revive the ancient right of the clergy to be taxed separately from the laity; the result made convocation 'unnecessary to the Crown'. It did not meet again until 1689 and, when it was summoned, its Lower House expressed opposition to the measures of religious comprehension and toleration proposed by William of Orange, and it was prorogued again. In the century that followed, the non-functioning of convocation became a focus of discontent.[24] Its last eighteenth-century meeting was in 1717, but the suspension of regular sittings of convocation in that year was defended by Bishop Smalbroke, himself a High Churchman, as a necessary protection of 'the peace and Tranquility of the Publick' after the 'Heats and Animosities' of previous years.[25]

William Sancroft was a passionate monarchist and deeply influential at the court of Charles II, particularly after 1681 when parliaments ceased to be called. He gave solid support to the king's Catholic brother, James, duke of York, who he hoped might be won back to Anglicanism by a strong Church of England, and united with court politicians like the Hyde brothers, the earls of Clarendon and Rochester, to form a strong pro-James party against those who favoured the duke's exclusion from the line of succession. When Charles established the Ecclesiastical Commission for Ecclesiastical Promotions in 1681,

Sancroft used it to ensure that those promoted were solid Stuart royalists. Sancroft's national scheme for the reinvigoration of the Church included a desire to improve the status and educational quality of the clergy, who he regarded as the front-line warriors of Anglican dominance. His greatest care, though, was for the church courts, which were not just tribunals for recalcitrant clergy, but also exercised a comprehensive control over the religious duties and private lives of the laity. In 1682 he also made a metropolitan visitation. In short, it was so 'thorough' a programme as to be quite Laudian, though Sancroft went rather further than his predecessor when he suspended Thomas Wood, bishop of Lichfield and Coventry, for negligence: there were no half measures in Sancroft's Church.

Sancroft's theocratic inclinations were challenged by the king himself, who possibly imagined that a less rigid ecclesiastical framework would increase his personal patronage and power. Charles had been forced to climb down after his 1672 Declaration of Indulgence, but in the years that followed, Sancroft and his allies were sensitive to any call for 'toleration', which they saw as a threat to the hegemony of the national Church. Instead of 'toleration', Sancroft advocated 'comprehension', the relaxing of strictly Anglican principles to accommodate moderate Dissenters, but most certainly not Catholics. In 1685 the king's meaning was made perfectly clear when he died a Catholic: the archbishop visited him on his deathbed but, unlike previous primates, was not present for those crucial final moments.[26]

Despite his Catholic faith, the duke of York had promised to 'support and defend' the Church of England and he identified himself with Sancroft's episcopalian party. As king, James changed his mind. In 1687 his Declaration of Indulgence decreed that 'all and all manner of penal laws in matters ecclesiastical for not coming to Church or not receiving the sacrament, or for any other nonconformity . . . be immediately suspended.' The declaration, reissued in April 1688, was ordered to be read in London churches on 20 and 27 May and elsewhere on 3 and 10 June. Sancroft was in despair as he saw his whole system of church courts and discipline crumbling into ruin and his attempts to bring James back to the Protestant faith coming to nothing. In May, Sancroft and six other bishops petitioned the king against his declaration and called him back to the way of moderate authoritarianism. The six were Thomas Ken of Bath and Wells, a distinguished divine with considerable service as a royal chaplain, Jonathan Trelawney of Bristol, John Lake of Chichester, William Lloyd of St Asaph, Francis Turner of Ely, and Thomas

White of Peterborough. Their supporters included the future archbishops Tillotson and Tenison. In the same month the four vicars apostolic, missionary bishops appointed by Rome to serve the English Catholics, promulgated a triumphalist pastoral letter. In an episode of high drama, the 'Seven Bishops' were arrested, and taken to the Tower on 8 June. Just two days later, the queen gave birth to a son: a Catholic succession seemed inevitable. The bishops were put on trial for seditious libel on 29 June and acquitted the next day, prompting leading political figures to invite the Calvinist William of Orange, James's son-in-law, to come and defend English 'liberties'. The king's Catholicising policies had united the kingdom against him and his days as its monarch were numbered. The bishops' acquittal was a hollow triumph, for the flight of James to France and the invasion of William brought no comfort; indeed, it marked the end of the Sancroftian vision of alliance between Church and State, throne and altar.

On 28 January 1689 the English throne was declared vacant by the House of Commons, and a resolution of both Houses of the Convention Parliament in February offered the crown to William and Mary as joint monarchs. New oaths were to be sworn by all who held public office, including beneficed clergy. If Sancroft had presided over a Laudian Church, here was the measure that precipitated his own 'martyrdom'. Though no lover of James II's Catholic policies, Sancroft was not alone in regarding the Stuart king as the legitimate monarch, not least because he had performed the coronation himself. What God had ordained, parliament was powerless to change. When Sancroft heard his own chaplain, Henry Wharton, praying for William and Mary, he instructed him that 'he must thenceforth desist from offering prayers for the new king and queen, or else from performing the duties of his chapel, for as long as King James was alive no other persons could be sovereigns of the country'. The nonjurors, those clerics who refused to take the oaths of supremacy and allegiance to William and Mary, were deprived of their livings. They numbered more than four hundred. In addition to Sancroft, the deprived bishops were the former 'libellers' Ken, Lake, Turner and White, together with Robert Frampton of Gloucester, William Lloyd of Norwich and William Thomas of Worcester. Sancroft was suspended from office on 1 August 1689 and deprived on 1 February 1690, but remained defiant and refused to leave Lambeth. Another fourteen months passed before the government announced that John Tillotson was to be the new archbishop. Despite this, Sancroft remained defiant and it was late June before he bowed under the weight of the legal case made against him and finally vacated the palace where he had lived since 1678. For the last two years of his life he retreated once more to Fressingfield, his childhood home and his refuge during the interregnum. He mourned for the Stuart cause as Cranmer had for Henry VIII, by growing a long, white beard. His self-imposed exile had a pathetic quality about it and he was, indeed, the last archbishop of Canterbury to be deprived of office and die in any kind of exile.

The nonjurors were an important but increasingly eccentric group on the English Church scene. They claimed to be the true Church remnant in England and made genuine ecumenical efforts, particularly with regard to Orthodoxy, but they also lacked cohesion and provide a stark lesson in the dangers of schism. One commentator has described them as 'Utterly opposed to Rome, detesting the Lutheran and Reformed Churches, counting the English Dissenters as little better than heathen men and publicans, the Non-Jurors found it difficult to give practical expression to their zeal for the unity of all Christians.'[27] In 1692 Sancroft delegated his archiepiscopal powers to William Lloyd, the deprived bishop of Norwich, and in 1694 two bishops were secretly consecrated. One of them, George Hickes, consecrated three more bishops in his turn. A regular line of nonjuring bishops continued until 1779. The nonjurors' contribution to the study of history and liturgy was an important one, displaying as it did a 'fidelity to tradition – especially the tradition that the deprivation of bishops should not be carried out by the lay power'[28], and they remained an alternative model for the Established Church.

The Church of England could hardly be immune from the fierce party spirit which fractured the English ruling elite from the reign of William and Mary and became institutionalised in the eighteenth century. Groups and interests mingled in a plethora of patronage networks, Tory and Whig. The name Tory became current in the reign of Charles II for those who supported hereditary succession, the divine right of kings and loyalty to the Church of England. With the fall of James II many became Jacobites, supporters of the deposed king and his heirs, and between the risings of 1715 (on the death of Queen Anne) and 1745, the Tories were excluded from office under suspicion of being covert Jacobites. By the end of the eighteenth century, with Jacobitism crushed, the Tories were still associated with a high view of monarchy (even if it had to be Hanoverian monarchy), a resistance to parliamentary reform, and the removal of Catholic and Dissenting disabilities. Whigs were the defenders of parliament, Protestantism and ministerial responsibility under a constitutionally emasculated monarchy. They were the heirs of the 'Glorious Revolution' of 1688–9 and were the dominant political group for much of the eighteenth century.[29] They supported moderate parliamentary reform after the French Revolution and were the motor of the Reform Act of 1832.

In 1689 William of Orange approved the abolition of episcopacy in Scotland, and some saw the same fate awaiting the English bishops. The Church's day was saved by the earl of Nottingham, a moderate Tory, whose support for William came in exchange for concessions to the Church. 'I reckon,' Bishop Burnet noted, 'that I do not exceed the severe rules of history when I say that Nottingham's being in the ministry, together with the effects which it had, first preserved the Church and then the Crown.' Daniel Finch, second earl of Nottingham, went on to become largely responsible for the Toleration Act in 1689 and promoted a bill against occasional conformity in 1704. With the exception of John Tillotson, a close friend of Nottingham, many of the new bishops of 1689 and after were moderate Tories.

An initial indication of the political sympathies of the eighteenth-century primates can be gleaned from their university education, for Oxford tended to be more Tory and Cambridge, Tillotson's *alma mater*, more Whiggish. This rule certainly applied to Thomas Tenison, a Cambridge man who was not in favour with Queen Anne but fared rather better during the last months of his life, after the Hanoverian succession and Whig ascendancy. Archbishop Potter bucked the trend, for this distinguished Oxford scholar was a decided Whig. Manners Sutton restored the balance by being a Cambridge-educated Tory. At the end of the period, the Oxonian William Howley was a Tory of the more extreme sort.

In their churchmanship the primates were as variable as in their politics, ranging from latitudinarians to High Churchmen. Latitudinarians were broadly tolerant of religious Dissent, even to the extent of comprehending Unitarianism (or Socinianism; the Unitarian secession from the Church of England occurred in 1773). High Churchmen were Trinitarian, Arminian, apostolic and socially conservative and considered themselves theologically 'orthodox'.[30] The nonjurors did not retain the monopoly of High Churchmanship, and High Churchmen, within the Anglican tradition, saw a vital role for the Church's independent commission in matters spiritual. Again, the universities provided a useful rule of thumb for assessing the churchmanship of the various archbishops, for Cambridge was much more associated with latitudinarianism, which reached Lambeth in the person of the ecclesiastically supple John Tillotson, whose eucharistic theology had the distinction of being Zwinglian. Charles Leslie, an Irishman and a strong non-juring controversialist, characterised him thus:

> His politics are Leviathan, and his religion is Latitudinarian, which is none; that is nothing that is *positive*, but against every thing, that is *positive* in other religions; whereby to reduce all religions to an uncertainty, and determinable only by the civil power . . . He is own'd by the Atheistical wits of all *England* as their true Primate and Apostle . . . He leads them not only the length of Socinianism . . . but to call n question all revelation, to turn *Genesis* etc into a mere romance.[31]

As Cambridge men, Whigs and Low Churchmen, Archbishops Tillotson and Tenison shared an antipathy towards Roman Catholicism. The feeling was mutual, for James II dubbed Tenison a dull man. Dean Swift called him a solemn one – which he did not mean as a compliment – with a 'horror of anything like levity in the clergy, especially of whist'.[32] Tenison was not, however, lacking in vision and maintained a high pastoral profile. He became convinced that the Church could expect little from government assistance and should look towards voluntary action. He was much involved in the launching of the Society for the Propagation of the Gospel, the first meeting of which was held at Lambeth Palace on 27 June 1701. In 1712 a committee of the society drew up a scheme for colonial bishops which came to nothing, despite the fillip of a £1,000 legacy from Tenison. The Society for Promoting Christian Knowledge (SPCK) was established in 1699 and developed rapidly, embracing both High and Low Churchmen in its endeavour to propagate the Anglican way. The SPCK was the most visible aspect of a broad movement. Religious tracts of an 'improving' character were published and distributed, and 'societies for the reformation of manners' were founded with the same social objectives as Sancroft's church courts. Tenison's prosaic personality concealed a sincere devotion to Christianity.

Tenison's time at Lambeth entirely enveloped the reign of Queen Anne (1702–14), who had a great interest in religious matters and pursued a consistently High Church agenda. In 1704 she created 'Queen Anne's Bounty', which surrendered the claims of the throne to first fruits (annates) and tenths paid by bishops since Henry VIII's break with Rome.[33] The money went to endow poor clergy and, incidentally, financed the rebuilding of the

Arundel Tower at Canterbury over a century later. Queen Anne also showed favour towards Henry Sacheverell, the High Church polemicist, who was impeached for high treason and tried in Westminster Hall following his spirited attack on 'occasional conformity'.

It is as a champion of Anglican rights and institutions that William Wake is best remembered. His was not an easy primacy, beginning as it did with the 'Bangorian Controversy' of 1717. The one thing with which this episode was unconnected was the diocese of Bangor, for its bishop, the latitudinarian Benjamin Hoadly, never visited the place during his five years as diocesan. On 31 March 1717, Hoadly, a royal chaplain, preached before George I on the text 'My kingdom is not of this world', from which he argued that there was no scriptural authority for any visible Church whatsoever. It was a red rag to the High Church bull. In May the convocation of Canterbury sought to condemn Hoadly's sermon, but the king countered by proroguing it in order to defend his chaplain. It did not meet again until 1852.

In 1718, Wake sought to defend the Established Church by opposing a Bill for modification of the Corporation and Test Acts against Dissenters,[34] but it would be a mistake to label him as blindly conservative. Sykes argues that he pursued a middle way throughout: 'Compelled to essay the difficult task of navigating the barque of the Church amidst so many and conflicting cross-currents, Wake strove to repress heresy without stifling freedom of opinion and to discourage schism without denying tolerance to Dissenters,' The most creative and visionary aspect of his activities is revealed in his correspondence with other European Protestant churches and through his abiding contact with France. With the French divines he argued forcefully and with compelling evidence for the validity of Matthew Parker's consecration, recognition of which he saw as a step towards some kind of union between Anglicans and Gallicans. He always maintained a distinction between fundamental and non-essential doctrine and was the most fervent of pre-twentieth-century primatial ecumenists:

For whilst some of his predecessors like Laud had maintained a vigorous controversial exchange with Roman Catholic polemicists and others like Sancroft had shown great friendship to members of the foreign Reformed churches; and while a distinguished Irish primate, Bramhall, had laid the foundation of the defence of Anglican Orders, Wake was unique in combining all these aspects.[35]

Such activities required nerve in England when anti-Catholicism was endemic, hatred of the French above all other foreigners axiomatic, and the Jacobite rebellion of 1715 still a recent threat to Hanoverian complaisance.

Archbishop Potter was a Whig in politics but a High Churchman with a strong sense of episcopal authority. This he articulated in *A Discourse of Church-Government* (1707):

> As our Lord was sent by God the Father to establish a Church in the World, so the *Apostles* were authoriz'd by our *Lord* to enlarge and govern the Church after his Ascension, and that they deriv'd the same Authority to their Successors the Bishops, which was the thing at first propounded to be shewn.[36]

Theologically, Potter had much in common with the nonjurors but was willing to compromise on the ruling dynasty to protect the place of the Church.[37] It is with Potter that the history of the archbishops overlaps that of Methodism, for John Wesley was ordained both deacon and priest by Potter, in 1725 and 1728 respectively. Wesley's early preaching tours coincided with Potter's time as archbishop and they remained on friendly terms. In his younger days Thomas Herring was hardly less active than Wesley, undertaking a visitation of his diocese when bishop of Bangor and apparently confirming 'above thirty thousand people' as archbishop of York. Herring's Canterbury successor, the short-lived Matthew Hutton, was another Cambridge latitudinarian.

By the time of Thomas Secker's primacy Methodism, which promised a religious revival through a new enthusiasm, was making a major impact throughout the country. Secker was certainly concerned to win back the initiative by learning from the Methodist strategy, arguing that 'the only way is for the clergy to imitate and emulate what is good in them, avoiding what is bad.'[38] He received mixed reactions to his preaching. His disciple and biographer, Beilby Porteous, later bishop of London, saw his sermons as useful and scriptural. High Church critics found them lacking in doctrine; Bishop Hurd of Worcester could still detect a Dissenting influence. Horace Walpole regarded Secker's sermons as moral essays wanting in Gospel truths but nevertheless retaining a tone of fanaticism, however much Secker himself reeled from 'enthusiasm'. As befitted his Dissenting origins, he requested burial without a monument or epitaph: his wishes were respected and he was laid to rest in the covered passage leading from the private door of Lambeth Palace to the neighbouring parish church.

The lacklustre John Moore was archbishop at the time of the French Revolution, which not even the Anglo-French war could prevent from making an ideological impact in Britain. It was in the 1790s, therefore, that deism and atheism first established a popular following, often in alliance with democratic politics. 'In these years,' Hugh McLeod reminds us, 'we see the first signs of nineteenth-century England's characteristic religious pattern: the division between a conservative state church, a liberal Protestant Dissent and a radical secularism.'[39] From 1805 it fell to Manners Sutton to steady the Church and embody 'orthodoxy' in times of continuing change across the Channel. He was a High Churchman of the old school, and ensured that men of like minds were appointed to both the Canterbury chapter and the episcopal bench. So effective was his exercise of ecclesiastical patronage that there was talk of a 'Canterbury party' within the Church.[40] Among the lower but nevertheless High clergy, Manners Sutton cultivated a group known as the Hackney Phalanx, from which emerged in 1811 the National Society for the Education of the Poor in the Principles of the Established Church. Their foundations were the National Schools, which provided elementary education and remained in being throughout the nineteenth century, even after 1870 when the State established Board Schools. The archbishop himself chaired the first meeting of the National Society. Low Churchmen, including the Clapham Sect (another acknowledgement of London's urban or suburban sprawl) were not lacking in parallel initiatives and championed the burgeoning Sunday School movement. Manners Sutton was also actively interested in the management of the Canterbury estates, a concern he was able to project on a nationwide scale through his support for the Church Building Society, founded in 1818 for the repair of church fabric.

Archbishop Howley was another High Churchman, a thoroughly conservative figure in both religion and politics. Instinctively hostile to change, he opposed both Catholic emancipation and the Reform Bill in its early parliamentary stages. As we have seen, Howley was no rhetorician or confident public speaker. When successive Whig policies for reform of both Church and State passed into law, he was not the man to speak out against them. The young Oxford professor of poetry, John Keble was as articulate as Howley was bumbling and delivered his famous sermon on National Apostasy in the university church on 14 July 1833. Keble expressed the archbishop's sentiments and Howley was initially much in sympathy with the Oxford Movement. His enthusiasm for it waned when some of the Oxford men grew uncomfortably Romish. It is easy to forget that Howley was still archbishop when Newman argued in Tract 90 (1841) that the Thirty-nine Articles were quite compatible with the Tridentine decrees, and also when the future cardinal made his submission to the Holy See in 1845.

The historian may be tempted to parody the archbishops of Canterbury from the accession of William and Mary to the age of Victoria, as bewigged obscurantist gentlemen with great lawn sleeves living in cosseted isolation from the world of dynamic change that was the eighteenth century. 'The Georgian bench has been pilloried as a byword of sloth, inefficiency and neglect.'[41] This is to do the institution and its leaders an injustice. The Church, so damaged by the Civil War, was above all else steeling itself for survival. Eighteenth-century archbishops were defending their beliefs and position against a subversive world and were successful in fighting off the challenges of deism and Dissent. Seen from a churchman's perspective, the Church and its leaders provided a continuity which justified the State itself. As J.C.D. Clark has suggested, England was a 'confessional state' in which Anglicanism was a vital force and major player until the undermining of its political position and the effective end of the *ancien régime*, culminating in the emancipation of Protestant Dissenters in 1828, Catholic emancipation in 1829 and the Reform Act in 1832. Indeed, Clark suggests that, under the first two Georges, a powerful alliance was sustained between the Whig political establishment and the bishops, a combination so formidable that the numbers of Dissenters and Roman Catholics declined and, to all intents and purposes, Anglicanism and English society were coterminous.[42]

The archbishops of the long eighteenth century presided over a Church which had difficulties in coming to terms with the realities of industrialisation and the growth of Britain's population, especially in the towns, but it was a period of gradually expanding empire which brought opportunities to develop a broadening vision of a wider Anglican Church. Party politics and the impact of too much port and patronage did not stifle the beginnings of an international Anglicanism, which was eventually to bear fruit in the Anglican Communion. Restoration Anglicanism gave way to something much more hybrid and accommodating but, by this very fact, it was well suited for export overseas, though not to continental Europe. In spite of the fact that a Huguenot émigré was employed as librarian at Lambeth Palace for three decades in the eighteenth century, Anglicans were becoming increasingly insular in relation to international Protestantism. Perhaps the most notable Anglican traveller of the age, Frederick Augustus Hervey, the earl-bishop of Derry, was drawn not to the Protestant regions but to the Catholic world and died at Albano, near Rome, in 1803. Nevertheless, 'there was still a Protestant world in the eighteenth century to which the Church of England belonged, to which it was acknowledged to belong and to which it regarded itself as belonging.'[43] England turned to a Dutch Calvinist monarch and then a German Lutheran to keep out the Catholic Stuarts. English theology found its way into Dutch, German and other translations.

The Church of England in the eighteenth and early nineteenth centuries, experienced an overseas expansion hand-in-hand with the growth of the British Empire. In the sixteenth and seventeenth centuries Anglican chaplains had accompanied colonists and traders. As early as 1638 Laud had drawn up proposals for a bishop for the New England colonies and in the 1660s a bishop was nominated for Virginia, but nothing came of that. Archbishop Sancroft and his close associates were concerned to supervise the overseas congregations, but it was not until the American Revolution that much development could be made.[44] An Act of Parliament in 1786 cleared the way for the consecration of bishops overseas and the first self-governing independent church was that of the United States of America. In the colonies, too, bishoprics were established for Canada in 1787, India in 1814, the West Indies in 1824, Australia in 1836, New Zealand in 1841 and many thereafter. By Howley's death in 1848, the archbishop of Canterbury was the nominal head of an international communion.

1848–2005:
GAIN AND LOSS

Although an English or British legislative framework can aid understanding of the careers of the archbishops from Juxon to Howley, it cannot suffice when we turn to the more recent primates, the fourteen who have held office from John Bird Sumner to Rowan Williams. This time it is more useful to introduce them in the context of the worldwide Anglican Communion, a term which can itself be dated to 1851, at the beginning of the period under review. In that year the bishop of Vermont, writing to Archbishop Sumner, suggested the possibility of an international council of Anglican bishops, but this was not realised. The last two years of Sumner's archiepiscopate were clouded by a British theological dispute which had wider ramifications throughout the Anglican world: the publication of *Essays and Reviews* (1860), by seven authors who included the influential Oxford men Mark Pattison and Benjamin Jowett, as well as the future archbishop Frederick Temple, then headmaster of Rugby. Temple's essay on education was less contentious than others in the volume but his career was temporarily blighted by the liberalism of fellow authors' views, which caused serious disquiet among the more conservative clergy and led to Sumner's condemnation of the book. To the furore caused by *Essays and Reviews* was soon added the practices and published works of John William Colenso, the first bishop of Natal, which expressed rejection of a number of fundamental and long-held Christian doctrines. Matters reached a height during the six short years of Charles Thomas Longley's archiepiscopate (1862–8), when Colenso was deprived of office and excommunicated by the archbishop of Cape Town. He denied the authority by which this was done and successfully appealed to the Judicial Committee of the Privy Council. The Colenso saga, which rumbled on for decades, highlighted the need to define the source of authority within the fast-expanding Anglican Communion. What was the position of the archbishop of Canterbury in the various Anglican provinces? Was he or should he become an Anglican 'pope'?

Archbishop Longley's response to the rising tide of uncertainty was to summon the bishops of the Communion to Lambeth in 1867: this was the first Lambeth Conference. Seventy-six bishops attended and an *Address to the Faithful* was issued. Nothing can disguise the fact that this conference and its more immediate successors met in an imperial context: all the bishops were white and many of them, like Colenso, had been sent from the mother country to the colonies.

In 1868 Longley was succeeded at Canterbury by Archibald Campbell Tait. After initial reluctance, he called the second Lambeth Conference in 1878. This established the position of the archbishop of Canterbury as first among equals in the Anglican Communion. About a hundred bishops attended, one of them reflecting that 'the harmony and unanimity of the Conference were largely due to [Tait's] uniform affability and good temper and his masterly leadership'.[1] A central issue in 1878 was the rise of ritualism in the Church of England and, by extension, in the Anglican Communion. This was a by-product of the Oxford Movement – also known as Tractarianism from the *Tracts for the Times* (1833–41) – and a visible means of distinguishing Anglo-Catholics from other Anglicans. In 1883 Canterbury acquired its first 'ritualist' archbishop in the person of Edward White Benson, who had been an eager reader of the *Tracts* when they first appeared. Whereas Tait had preferred to think of the Church of England as a British phenomenon without a wider world mission, Benson was more catholic in his vision, and was particularly pleased by the establishment of an Anglican Church in Korea: over a century later the Church of Korea has a reputation for being the Church of the poor, while South Korea's professional class tends to be Roman Catholic. The Lambeth Conference of 1888 was therefore more congenial to Benson than that of 1878 had been to Tait. 145 bishops attended: Benson rejoiced in such a demonstration of episcopal collegiality. They issued the Lambeth Quadrilateral, four articles defining the central tenets of Anglicanism: the Old and New Testaments as the revealed Word of God; the Nicene Creed as its central statement of faith; ministry of the baptismal and eucharistic Sacraments; the historic episcopate effectively providing unity in the diversity of the Communion. The last conference of the nineteenth century met in 1897 under the presidency of Archbishop Frederick Temple. Temple was already aged seventy-five at the time of his translation from London to Canterbury the previous year, making him an archbishop in something of a hurry. The 1897 Lambeth Conference was much concerned with his personal interests, including temperance and the sanctity of marriage, but there was emphasis, too, on the importance of mission and the formalisation of the decennial conference: a Lambeth Consultative Body was established to facilitate this. It functioned until 1968.

In 1908, with the British Empire at its height, Dean Armitage Robinson of Westminster explained:

> The ideal function of the Anglican Communion is to express and guide the spiritual aspirations and activities of the Anglo-Saxon race. It has a duty besides to those other races whom Providence has in various degrees of closeness linked with that race; but towards some of them its ultimate responsibility may prove to be that of offering a type of Apostolic faith and order which they may hereafter appropriate and develop in independence.[2]

That year witnessed not only the fifth Lambeth Conference but also the Pan-Anglican Congress, which brought together 7,000 clerical and lay Anglicans from throughout the Communion. The suitably confident and competent archbishop who welcomed the delegates to both events was Randall Thomas Davidson. His confidence was surely enhanced by the fact that he had attended all the previous conferences except the first, and also by his personal experience of travel in North America (in 1904). Davidson's record became all the more remarkable when he presided over the next conference, postponed until 1920 on account of the First World War. The horrors of war provided the context for the *Appeal to all Christian People* issued by this assembly. As the strength of the octogenarian primate finally waned, he determined to resign the burdens of office, the first archbishop of Canterbury to do so. Essentially, this was designed to allow his expected successor, Cosmo Gordon Lang, to get his feet under the archiepiscopal table in time to prepare for the conference of 1930. Davidson need not have worried, for Lang took to the role so easily that the seventh Lambeth Conference was rather dominated by his thoroughly prelatical character, which made some visitors feel somewhat second-rate. After a period of ill health, exacerbated by direct hits on Lambeth Palace during the Blitz, Lang retired in 1942: his successor, William Temple, lived only until October 1944, so did not preside over a

Lambeth Conference, though he did chair the committee that debated church unity at the 1930 meeting. Lang outlived Temple by fourteen months.

In the wake of the Second World War, the British Empire evolved into the Commonwealth and air travel revolutionised contacts between the archbishop of Canterbury and the wider Anglican Communion. Archbishop Geoffrey Fisher and his wife were widely travelled:

> Apart from visits to the United States and Canada several times, they went to Australia and New Zealand in 1950, thus becoming the first Archbishop of Canterbury to visit the Antipodes, to West Africa in 1951, to Central Africa in 1955, to India, Japan and Korea in 1959, to Nigeria for Independence Day in 1960 and to East Africa in the same year.[3]

This was more or less the Commonwealth at prayer. Fisher's two Lambeth Conferences, in 1948 and 1958, witnessed a return to form. They were much concerned with challenges to family life, peace issues and the pressing need for church unity.

Since Fisher's time, a pattern has emerged of primates presiding over a single Lambeth Conference and serving as archbishop for more or less ten years before retiring. The more open nature of Archbishop Michael Ramsey's conference in 1968 matched that of the Second Vatican Council (1962–5), which had included Anglican observers and consultants, and made provision for the press. The previous conferences had been held at Lambeth Palace, with brief forays to Canterbury, but this one met at Church House, Westminster. It decided that a conference of bishops every ten years was insufficient to meet the needs of the Communion and therefore established the Anglican Consultative Council, a body of clergy and laity which has since met in every second or third year in different locations around the globe, initially in Kenya in 1971. Since 1978, the Lambeth Conferences have been held at the University of Kent at Canterbury and have witnessed growing rifts between the constituent Churches, reflecting the divisions – economic and otherwise – between the cultures in which they minister. Archbishop Donald Coggan came to Canterbury with experience of the Anglican world beyond England, for he had been a lecturer at Wycliffe College, Toronto, between 1937 and 1944. At his Lambeth Conference, in 1978, the principal bone of contention was the ordination of women, accepted by some provinces but not by others. Another initiative designed to paper over the cracks was the inauguration of regular meetings between the primates of the thirty-six self-governing provinces of the Communion. These began in Ely in 1979 and have not usually generated much media interest. This changed in 2003 with the emergency meeting called at Lambeth by Archbishop Rowan Williams, in response to the election of the openly homosexual Gene Robinson as bishop of New Hampshire. Even by the time of the 1988 Lambeth Conference, Archbishop Robert Runcie was able to identify the prevailing issue in the Anglican Communion as the choice between 'unity and gradual fragmentation'. Deepened by the nature and furious pace of global communications, the post-imperial fissures were all the more apparent when Archbishop George Carey met with his fellow bishops at the thirteenth Lambeth Conference in 1998. Latter-day parallels can easily be found for Bishop Colenso and his critics. For well over a century the Anglican Communion evolved to meet changing circumstances: are circumstances now changing too rapidly for it to be able to keep pace? In 2005 the Anglican Communion claims 70 million members, spread throughout more than 160 countries. Unlike the Petrine primacy, its source of authority is not set in stone and remains a matter for debate both in the Church of England and in the wider Anglican Communion.

Although Archbishop Lang 'once spoke of himself as the one through whom God chiefly speaks to the English people, evidently thinking of himself as another Vicar of Christ',[4] it not known whether the other archbishops from Sumner to Williams have entertained such notions. Otherwise, the most 'papal' elements of the archbishops' recent history are the dynastic threads, which are vaguely reminiscent of the Renaissance papacy. Davidson's career was very firmly moulded by his father-in-law, Archbishop Tait, and the two Temples were father and son. Sumner and Fisher also came from clerical dynasties. John Bird Sumner was the eldest son of an old Etonian vicar of Kenilworth; a younger brother, Charles Richard Sumner, was bishop of Winchester and it was Charles's daughter-in-law, Mary, who founded the Mothers' Union in 1876. Geoffrey Fisher came from a long line of parsons and was born at Higham-on-the-Hill, Leicestershire, where his father was the rector. Of the other primates, remarkably few came from solidly Anglican backgrounds. Longley, the son of a Rochester lawyer, possibly came closest to representing such solidity. Tait, the first Scot to be archbishop of Canterbury, was born in Edinburgh, the son of Presbyterian parents, and was not confirmed as an Anglican until he went to Oxford. The Davidsons were also Scottish Presbyterians and included a number of ministers. Randall

Davidson's father was a school friend of A.C. Tait and the two families remained on close terms. Lang, the third Scottish archbishop of Canterbury, was born in the manse at Fyvie in Aberdeenshire, the son and grandson of Presbyterian ministers. His distinctive name derived from that of his godfather, the local laird, William Cosmo Gordon. On his father's side, Robert Runcie was also of Scottish Presbyterian ancestry – and Irish on his mother's – but was born in Liverpool and confirmed as an Anglican in his teens. Continuing our tour of the Celtic fringe, much has been made of Rowan Williams as the first Welsh archbishop of Canterbury. He was born in Swansea in 1950 and his parents belonged to the Presbyterian Church of Wales in his childhood, but he soon developed an allegiance to the Anglo-Catholic tradition that distinguished the Anglican Church in Wales from its predominantly nonconformist surroundings. Even among the English-born primates, some had fervently nonconformist forebears. Ramsey's father, a Cambridge don, was a Congregationalist, though his mother was Anglican; Coggan's father was a successful London businessman and dedicated conservative evangelical. Carey's evangelicalism was not inherited, for his background was not in any sense 'churchy' and, as a young man, he acquired the enthusiasm of a neophyte. At no point in his career was this enthusiasm more apparent than during his seven years (1975–82) as incumbent of St Nicholas, Durham, where he drastically reordered the church interior to suit a non-traditional style of worship.

If George Carey's father, a hospital porter from Bow in London's East End, can be taken to represent one end of the social spectrum, the Temples belonged to the opposite pole, with most of the other archbishops representing variations on the theme of 'middle class'. In 1821 Frederick Temple was born on the Ionian island of Santa Maura (now Leucas), which was occupied by Britain from 1815 to 1864 and where Temple's father, Octavius Temple, was the official 'resident'. Octavius took up farming in Devon in 1825, but this work did not prosper and he returned overseas as lieutenant-governor of Sierra Leone, where he died young. Frederick was one of fifteen children, eight of whom survived infancy. He did not marry until he was fifty-five and was bishop of Exeter when his second son, William, was born in 1881. Frederick's wife, Beatrice Blanche Lascelles, was twenty-three years her husband's junior and a granddaughter of the second earl of Harewood on her father's side and of the sixth earl of Carlisle on her mother's. The marriage in 1922 of the Princess Royal and the sixth earl of Harewood had brought the Lascelles family into the royal line of succession by the time William Temple became archbishop in 1942, but he could already claim kinship through his mother with the Cavendishes, Howards, Lytteltons, Leveson-Gowers, Spencers, Churchills and Herveys who had for generations combined to form Britain's social-political elite. On the occasion of the 1901 census, Frederick, Beatrice and the nineteen-year-old William Temple had relatives staying with them at the Archbishop's Palace in Canterbury, among them Lucy Cavendish, the noted campaigner for women's education and widow of Lord Frederick Cavendish, who had been murdered in Phoenix Park, Dublin, in 1882.[5]

Archbishop Benson's family had enjoyed prominent social standing and even the company of royalty, but was in 'reduced circumstances' by the time he was born in Birmingham in 1829. Benson lost both parents during his formative years: his father while he was a pupil at King Edward VI's Grammar School, Birmingham, and his mother during his undergraduate years at Trinity College, Cambridge. Benson was a 'born priest' and always more comfortable in an ecclesiastical milieu. This was little wonder: his school friends Brooke Foss Westcott and Joseph Barber Lightfoot both became bishops of Durham, and were deeply influential in the development of the Victorian Church. Whereas most of the eighteenth-century primates had been the products of grammar schools, the nineteenth century was the great age of the English public schools and this is amply reflected in the academic records of the archbishops: Sumner at Eton (albeit before 1801), Longley at Westminster, Davidson at Harrow, William Temple at Rugby, and Fisher at Marlborough (founded in 1843 for 'sons chiefly of clergymen of the Church of England'). In the twentieth century Ramsey was a pupil at Repton during Fisher's time as headmaster there, Coggan went to Merchant Taylor's in London (Archbishop Juxon's school) and Runcie to its Liverpool namesake, a grammar school. Williams attended his local grammar school in Swansea and Carey a secondary modern in Hackney, which he left at the age of fifteen. Some years later Carey's education was resumed at the London College of Divinity and King's College, London, making him the first archbishop of Canterbury, since Roger Walden at the end of the fourteenth century, not to be a graduate of one or other of the two ancient universities. Carey was no less a man of his time in being called up for National Service. Runcie, his immediate predecessor, was the only archbishop to have served in the regular army, which he did during the Second World War; thereafter he went up to Brasenose College, Oxford, and took a first in Greats in 1948.

The other Oxford men in this group were Longley (Christ Church), Tait (Balliol; previously at Glasgow University), Frederick Temple (Balliol), Davidson (Trinity), Lang (Balliol; also previously at Glasgow), William Temple (Balliol), and Fisher (Exeter). Firsts were the norm, a triple first in Fisher's case, his academic and sporting prowess undiminished by the heavy pipe-smoking he adopted during his Oxford years. Of the Balliol men, only Lang was a member of the college during the mastership of Benjamin Jowett, who upbraided him for his involvement with Samuel Barnett's Toynbee Hall: 'Mr Lang, you are making a great mistake. You forget that your business here is not to reform the East End of London, but to get a First Class in the School of Literae Humaniores'.[6] Davidson was the least distinguished of the Oxonians, managing only a third in law and modern history. Lang and William Temple were both presidents of the Oxford Union. Tait and both the Temples gained college fellowships, but Lang effectively upstaged them all by becoming a fellow of All Souls. In Chichele's venerable institution he fulfilled the slightly less venerable office of Lord Mallard, a master of revels whose duty is to sing on specified occasions the song of the Mallard:

> The Griffin, Bustard, Turkey and Capon
> Let other hungry mortals gape on,
> And on their bones with stomach full hard,
> But let All Souls men have their Mallard . . .

Lang served as Lord Mallard from 1898 until 1928, which gave him the distinction of presiding at the Mallard Feast, held at All Souls at the beginning of each century since early modern times. Thus it was that, in January 1901, four fellows carried the Lord Mallard in a chair throughout the college and even over the roofs, as he brandished a dead mallard on a long pole, all the while singing the Mallard Song.[7] Even before this episode, Oxford had made such an impression on Lang that he decided to become an Anglican, was confirmed by Bishop King of Lincoln, rejected a legal career on the eve of being called to the Bar and determined upon ordination. To that end he studied at Cuddesdon, the theological college near Oxford, thereby becoming the first future archbishop of Canterbury to train for the priesthood at such an establishment. A single term at Wells Theological College was sufficient preparation for Fisher's career as a prelate.

The Cambridge men were Sumner (King's), Benson (Trinity), Ramsey (Magdalene, where the master, A.C. Benson, son of the archbishop, found him 'a distressing object'), Coggan (St John's) and Williams (Christ's). In contrast to their Oxford counterparts, they proved to be peculiarly interested in theology, while collectively embodying the full Anglican ecclesiological spectrum. Sumner fell under the influence of Charles Simeon, a fellow of King's, and became a convinced evangelical. The genially eccentric Ramsey was president of the Union, and followed his first in theology with a year at Cuddesdon, prior to ordination. Williams appears to have inherited the mantle of the late nineteenth- and early twentieth-century Christian Socialists, devoting his Cambridge years to a combination of academic work, social concerns and political activism. He took a double first in the theological tripos, before moving to Oxford to undertake doctoral research on the Russian Orthodox theologian Vladimir Lossky (d. 1958).

If any one figure in modern English ecclesiastical history can assist our appreciation of Williams's career and ecclesiology it is arguably Charles Gore, the High Church theologian who sought 'to put the Catholic faith into its right relation to modern intellectual and moral problems'. This was the purpose behind his edited volume of essays *Lux mundi* (1889), which caused such a stir among Tractarians of the older school. At that point Gore (another Balliol man) was principal of Pusey House, Oxford, but went on to an episcopal career, beginning as bishop of Worcester in 1902. Newman had already recognised that the spiritual needs of industrial cities like Birmingham were not being met in the nineteenth century, and Gore followed that lead by carving out the new Anglican diocese of Birmingham, becoming its first bishop in 1905. From 1911 he was bishop of Oxford. By way of parallel, Rowan Williams acquired a formidable academic reputation, first in Cambridge and then, from 1986, as Lady Margaret professor of divinity at Oxford. In 1991 came his election as bishop of Monmouth and the opportunity for ministry among the post-industrial communities of south-east Wales. Nor do the parallels end there, for Gore is also remembered as the founder of the Community of the Resurrection, the most notable survival of nineteenth-century Anglicanism's 'call of the cloister'. In 1898 the community moved from Radley to Mirfield in Yorkshire, since when they have been known as the Mirfield Fathers. Upon completion of his D.Phil. in 1975, Rowan Williams became a lecturer at Mirfield's College of the Resurrection: a clear reflection of his interest in the monasticism of both the western and eastern traditions.

Most of the archbishops of the last century and a half have sought to fulfil their ministry through the published word, even if the output of some was limited to a few sermons. In 1872 Tait assessed *The Present Position of the Church of England*, in 1884 Frederick Temple addressed *The Relation between Religion and Science*, and in 1905 Lang glimpsed *The Opportunity of the Church of England* as disbelief spread through society and the modern age presented a host of new challenges to the aspirant priest. Benson's work on St Cyprian was published posthumously, but only three of the archbishops stand out as significant thinkers and writers: William Temple, Michael Ramsey and Rowan Williams. Temple was trained as a philosopher and, at the same time, was instinctively drawn to work of a social nature, which he was able to express through his teaching for the Workers' Educational Association and membership of the Labour Party. Both of these influenced his writings, which included *Church and Nation* (1915), *Mens creatrix* (1917), *Christus veritas* (1924), *Christian Faith and Life* (1931), *Nature, Man and God* (1934), and culminated in the best-selling *Christianity and Social Order* (1942), in which he articulated a vision of postwar society; it partly inspired the creation of the Welfare State. As earlier Christian Socialists had done, he looked for a synthesis which would allow Christianity to make its case in an unfriendly world. Temple's work can be understood in relation to that of his lifelong friend R.H. Tawney, his near contemporary at Rugby and Balliol, who regretted that Christianity, especially among the urban poor, was 'gradually and reluctantly drifting out of the lives of no inconsiderable part of society'. For his sheer industry and sense of moral purpose, Maurice Cowling has compared Temple to the great Whig historian Macaulay, except that 'where Macaulay had been a book in breeches, Temple was a book in gaiters'.[9] Temple's output combined scholarly publications with popular journalism and he was the first archbishop to recognise the pastoral potential of broadcasting.[10]

Michael Ramsey was no means loath to address social questions, but his literary strength lay in academic theology. Of his first book, *The Gospel and the Catholic Church* (1936), Adrian Hastings comments:

It brought together Scripture, liturgy and tradition, in a rich synthesis which made sense of a key 'Catholic' idea of the church, vastly richer than was customary in Protestant or Anglican circles, yet without the authoritarian legalism which so damaged most Roman Catholic accounts of the Catholic Church at that time was with a sense of scriptural rootedness which made this sort of high church vision attractive for many who had thought of themselves as Protestants.[11]

His later works, including *The Glory of God and the Transfiguration of Christ* (1949), are written in a richly nuanced style but belong to a fundamentally Anglican tradition.

Though politically astute, Ramsey created an impression of holiness and was given to long silences, which could be awkward and embarrassing in social situations. This was not a problem shared by those archbishops who had been schoolmasters, as most of his predecessors since Sumner had been, honing their preaching skills in school chapels. Sumner taught at Eton, but it was with Longley at Harrow that the line of headmaster-archbishops began. Archbishop Tait maintained that the headmaster's calling was a 'proper profession for a clergyman',[12] though his own reputation as a headmaster possibly suffers from the fact that he had to succeed the great Dr Thomas Arnold at Rugby in 1842. Before the decade was out, Tait's health had suffered so much that he was forced to resign and take the less arduous position of dean of Carlisle. There was, though, no relief from his woes, for it was at Carlisle that five of his young daughters died of scarlet fever. Shortly after Tait's departure, Rugby managed to break E.W. Benson in a similar fashion, though he was only a junior master. Thereafter Benson made his mark as the first headmaster of Wellington College. By 1857 Frederick Temple had been the last principal of Kneller Hall, a teacher training college near Twickenham, and a government inspector of similar institutions, before he too accepted the Rugby challenge and proved himself equal to it. As Rugby united three of the nineteenth-century archbishops, so Repton united three of those in the twentieth century. William Temple had been headmaster there for four years when he was succeeded in 1914 by the 27-year-old Geoffrey Fisher. Fisher's eighteen-year rule at Repton has been the subject of controversy. Some boys were certainly traumatised by the severity of his punishments for sometimes unlikely offences, but others could take the pace and have spoken out in his defence. Soon after Ramsey's appointment to Canterbury in 1961, Prime Minster Harold Macmillan found himself in conversation with the new primate and commented 'Fisher seems to disapprove of you.' Ramsey replied: 'Yes, he was my headmaster and headmasters often know the worst.'[13] Bernard Palmer, historian of the headmaster-archbishops, suggests that only Frederick Temple was indisputably a great headmaster, though Benson and Fisher were 'very near to greatness . . . William Temple was a great man but emphatically *not* a great headmaster, while Longley and Tait were middle-of-the-road heads who kept their shows on the road without breaking any box office records.'[14] Fisher was the last of that particular line, after which the archbishops emerged from a different type of educational milieu: Ramsey served on the staff of Lincoln Theological College (founded by Benson as chancellor of Lincoln Cathedral in 1874); Coggan, Runcie and Carey were all principals of such foundations.[15]

Schoolmastering provided the future primates with more opportunities to enjoy female company than could life in Oxford and Cambridge, even after the foundation of the women's colleges. Marriage and Oxbridge fellowships were still incompatible in the nineteenth century: Sumner had to resign his fellowship at King's when he married in 1803, but carried on teaching at Eton. Benson and Fisher married the daughters of their fellow masters. Among the modern archbishops, only Lang did not marry. Hints had been dropped about his sexuality – for example, with regard to his loneliness following the death of one of his chaplains in the First World War – but it was left to the outspoken A.L. Rowse, in his acidic memoirs of *Friends and Contemporaries* (1989), to leave his readers in no doubt of Lang's homosexual nature. Most of the archbishops had children. So interconnected were the Taits and the Davidsons that Randall Davidson not only married Archbishop Tait's second daughter, Edith, but served as his father-in-law's chaplain and secretary. Thus Davidson was eminently well placed to co-author a life of Tait in 1891. Neither this nor the Temple dynasty have generated half as much biographical interest as the Benson family, whose collective genius tipped over the edge into insanity in the case of the archbishop's daughter Margaret. There were six children altogether, of whom three died relatively young: 'At least four possessed talents bordering on genius; also most remarkable energy in intellectual activity, coupled with a tendency to lapse into acute mental depression and sometimes morbid introspection.'[16] Arthur Christopher, Edward Frederick and Robert Hugh were all prolific writers, A.C. Benson producing a reverential two-volume life of his father in 1899 and another encomium, *The Trefoil*, in 1923. R.H. Benson personified the exotic intensity of late nineteenth-century Anglo-Catholicism: he tried Mirfield, but it was not exotic enough and he was received into the Roman Catholic Church in 1903.

He befriended F.W. Rolfe and they collaborated on a life of St Thomas of Canterbury, but the friendship degenerated in a stream of invective from the notoriously difficult Rolfe. None of the Benson children married, and the archbishop's widow, Mary Sidgwick, created no less interest for biographers and by becoming the inseparable companion of Lucy Tait, another of A.C. Tait's daughters.

When Gladstone proposed Benson for Canterbury in 1883, Queen Victoria objected that he was too young at the age of fifty-three. Yet his credentials were eminently sound, for he had not only been the first headmaster of Wellington, but also the first bishop of Truro (from 1877). Not since St Germans was suppressed in the eleventh century had Cornwall had its own see. Courtesy of the architect J.L. Pearson, Benson acquired at Truro the first Anglican cathedral to be built in England since St Paul's and the first in the Gothic style since before the Reformation. Relatively few of the modern archbishops matched Benson by making their names in the predominantly rural dioceses of southern England. Davidson, for example, was successively dean of Windsor, bishop of Rochester and of Winchester, but there was a sense in which those appointments were merely a way of filling in time before his inevitable promotion to Canterbury. Reputations tended to be made in the industrial north, after which prelates had either proved themselves tough enough for London or in need of the relative ease of Canterbury. When Sumner was bishop of Chester between 1828 and 1848 the diocese still included much of newly industrialised Lancashire. Churches were built in new urban areas and Christian education was promoted through the foundation of the teacher training college in Chester in 1841. Like Benson, Longley was a pioneer, being appointed as the first bishop of Ripon in 1836; William Temple was the fifth bishop of Manchester and Donald Coggan the third bishop of Bradford. Temple's sympathy with Manchester's large working class population tended to make him unpopular with their middle class employers, but his work in the city is recalled in the dedication of the William Temple Memorial Church, built in the new suburb of Wythenshawe in 1964–5. Longley, William Temple, Ramsey and Coggan were all translated from northern dioceses to York, and from York to Canterbury. This sense of York as the new London, the natural stepping-stone to Canterbury, is enhanced when Lang's nineteen years there are also taken into consideration. Unlike the other northern primates, he built on his Toynbee Hall experience by ministering in urban areas in the south of England, as well as in Leeds. A photograph of him as vicar of Portsea, which had a population of some 40,000 in the 1890s, shows the putative bishop with an impressively large staff of eleven curates (and two dogs). From 1901 to 1908 he was suffragan bishop of Stepney and devoted much time and energy to fund-raising for the East London Church Fund. By 1900 work in slum parishes was one of the archetypal expressions of 'ritualist' Anglo-Catholicism, one of the leading exponents of which was Father Robert Dolling, who would have been a neighbour of Lang had he not resigned from St Agatha's, Landport, in 1896, the year that Lang arrived at Portsea. The following year, elaborate copes and stoles were much in evidence on the steps of St Paul's for the celebration of Queen Victoria's diamond jubilee: half a century earlier the Establishment would not have countenanced such a display, considering it the thin end of a popish wedge.

In 1848, Lord John Russell chose Sumner for Canterbury because of his 'fervent Protestantism', the very foundations of which, Sumner argued, were being undermined by the Tractarians. Sumner used every opportunity, parliamentary and otherwise, in his endeavours to stamp out ritualism. It was no coincidence, therefore, that the bishop with whom he most famously crossed swords was the High Churchman, Henry Phillpotts of Exeter, who was not only impressed by the Tractarians but supported the creation of Anglican religious communities. In 1847 Phillpotts had cause to doubt the orthodoxy of the Reverend G.C. Gorham, who had been presented to a living in his diocese, and refused to institute him. The matter was referred to the Judicial Committee of the Privy Council, which decided in Gorham's favour. Phillpotts announced that he would 'repudiate communion' with anyone who intervened and instituted Gorham; Sumner accepted the challenge and did precisely that. It was a case that convulsed the Church of England. After Sumner, Archbishop Longley was another decided anti-ritualist, as he demonstrated during his time as bishop of Ripon, when he suppressed 'Roman Catholic teaching and practices' at St Saviour's, Leeds, the slum parish founded by E.B. Pusey. Come 1862, Longley was Palmerston's choice for Canterbury, a safe pair of hands whose moderate High Churchmanship meant that he was committed to the alliance of Church and State.

At Longley's death in 1868, Bishop Samuel Wilberforce of Oxford might well have been translated to Canterbury had Gladstone been in office. Disraeli did not share his rival's intense interest in ecclesiastical matters and it was Victoria, a particularly interventionist supreme governor, who insisted on

Tait's move from London to the primacy. The prime minister had reservations but concurred with her wishes. What attracted the queen was Tait's Scottishness, his air of bereavement after the loss of so many children, and a shared favourite hymn, 'Lead kindly light'. He acted as a kind of personal chaplain to the royal family, baptising royal children and conducting royal confirmations, marriages and funerals. He was also entirely devoted to the cause of national unity and the role of the Church of England as a force for patriotic national cohesion. As his epitaph at Canterbury expressed it: 'He had one aim: to make the Church of England more and more the church of the people'.[17] The *Church Times* put it more caustically in 1877: 'What music is to a man with no ear, that religion is to Archbishop Tait.' Thus he came into the later nineteenth-century category of Broad Churchmen, whose theological liberalism distinguished them from convinced evangelicals and Rome-leaning Tractarians alike. In parliament he supported what he regarded as 'inclusive' legislation, such as the 1880 Burial Act, which allowed nonconformists to be buried in parish churchyards. What he refused to tolerate was ritualism, which he regarded as a threat to national unity and to the Established Church because it tended to lead its adherents to Rome. When the Papal States fell to the forces of Vittorio Emanuele in 1870 and Victoria offered sympathy to Pius IX as a fellow sovereign, it coincided with a collapse in Tait's health so severe that he was compelled to consecrate his former pupil, Edward Parry, as bishop of Dover in order that pastoral work might continue. The bishop of Dover continues to undertake much of the pastoral work of the Canterbury diocese. Tait was repeatedly overwhelmed by anxiety: in 1870–1 he retreated to San Remo to recover; in 1882 medical advice prompted him to return to the Riviera. Like the European travels of Queen Victoria and those of so many other notable Britons of Tait's era, these expeditions need not be interpreted as ventures into 'enemy territory', for the Mediterranean region was amply supplied with Anglican chaplaincies, organised into the diocese of Gibraltar from 1842.

With Tait's example before him, Archbishop Benson ought to have collapsed under the weight of the socio-political forces ranged against him. The Education Act of 1870, for example, effectively removed the education of the young from the hands of the Church, whose National Schools were steadily phased out. Benson felt beleaguered as the Church of England seemed to be losing its traditional control over the hearts and minds of the people. This loss was already apparent in the results of the 1851 religious census; had that exercise been repeated there seems little doubt that the findings would have proved increasingly uncomfortable for the Church of England. The need to re-engage the laity lay behind Benson's creation of a consultative House of Laymen in 1886, as did the growing realisation that parliament was no longer an adequate forum for debate on ecclesiastical matters. He even contemplated a 'college of cardinals' to provide him with support among the clergy. Benson was too English and too much of a High Churchman to achieve a rapport with the queen, but he had the consolation of a genuine friendship with W.E. Gladstone, who was no less imbued with the spirit of Tractarianism. Low Churchmen could no longer be sure of support in high places. In 1888, a particularly high-profile accusation of ritualism was brought by the convinced Protestants of the Church Association against Bishop King of Lincoln, whose celebration of the Eucharist was all too evidently Catholic in nature. Benson made his 'Lincoln Judgement' on 21 November 1890, finding in favour of almost all King's practices. William Stubbs, the historian who was bishop of Oxford from 1889, muttered that Benson's court was nothing more than the archbishop sitting in his library, but Dean Church regarded it 'as the most courageous thing to have come out of Lambeth for the last two hundred years'. Westcott thought in even larger terms and declared that it 'vindicated beyond reversal one master principle of his faith, the historic continuity of our Church. The Reformation was shown to be not its beginning but a critical stage in its growth.'

Like Becket, Benson expired on consecrated ground. A plaque in the choir stalls at Hawarden parish church, marks the spot where he collapsed with heart failure during Holy Communion on 11 October 1896, while staying at Gladstone's country home near Chester. Lord Salisbury, the prime minister, chose the bishop of London, Frederick Temple, as his successor. If Benson had been too young, Temple was arguably too old and Victoria considered him 'eminently unsuited to the post'.[18] Her favourite was the courtly Randall Davidson, but he had to wait another seven years for the top job. Temple was certainly past the prime that had caused him to be described as 'granite on fire' and did not relish his parliamentary responsibilities. As for the controversy over ritualism which had so exercised some of his predecessors, it proceeded in more measured tones when, in 1899 and 1900, the archbishops of Canterbury and York together issued the Lambeth Opinions on the liturgical use of incense, the carrying of lights in processions, and reservation of the Sacrament. Each of these practices was declared to be not legitimate

Anglican practice, the only crumb of comfort for the ritualists being the admission that incense might be used to sweeten the air in churches.

Randall Davidson's time finally came in 1903, courtesy of Arthur Balfour, the first of seven prime ministers (four Conservative, two Liberal and one Labour) with whom he dealt in the course of his quarter century at Lambeth. In such a changing political climate, it helped that Davidson was a master of diplomacy and a formidable parliamentarian. His diplomacy was to the fore in 1926 when he argued for reconciliation during the General Strike: this was quite an achievement for a prelate who had never soiled his hands in the East End settlements and was a natural courtier, 'an unrivalled ecclesiastical authority on royal ritual'. Davidson provided gravitas at the coronation of George V, in contrast to Howley's misfortune with the ring in 1838 and Frederick Temple placing the crown back to front on Edward VII's head in 1902. In short, Davidson would have made a consummate nineteenth-century archbishop, but his skills were tested in the more challenging circumstances of the early twentieth. The Church's powers and prerogatives were attacked by both Liberal and Conservative governments and never more so than in 1911, when the newly introduced Parliament Act forced Welsh Disestablishment over the heads of the House of Lords. The independent Church in Wales became a reality in 1919; in 1920 Canterbury lost its primatial status in the principality as Wales gained its first archbishop. Rowan Williams was the eleventh holder of that office, which is held in rotation by the Welsh diocesan bishops. Davidson kept his nerve under assault and effectively turned the Welsh model to the Church of England's advantage. 1919 saw the passing of an Enabling Act to recognise the powers of the Church Assembly, a body that had evolved out of Benson's House of Laymen, to take over many aspects of the running of the Church. This was a limited triumph for Davidson, for there remained the possibility of a parliamentary veto on the Assembly's actions. Still in the sphere of Church-State relations, his archiepiscopate witnessed the repeal of the 1874 Public Worship Regulation Act, the centrepiece of Tait's anti-ritualist campaign. A line could still not be drawn under ecclesiological factionalism, the High and Low Churchmen of the previous century having become Anglo-Catholics and evangelicals. The Prayer Book revision of 1927 was Davidson's nemesis. The revised Prayer Book was supported by the Church Assembly and by all but four of the forty-three English diocesan bishops. It reflected sound scholarship but it also reflected a predominantly Anglo-Catholic view of the liturgy: this time, in contrast to the Lambeth Opinion of 1900, reservation of the Sacrament was permitted. Amid widespread cries of 'No popery!' parliament vetoed the Prayer Book, rendering it 'unofficial': the Church was still at the mercy of the State. When Davidson became the first archbishop to resign (and accept a life peerage) in November 1928, it was not because of this defeat, but on account of his advanced years.

On the wider stage, the world in which Davidson had cut his Establishment teeth – particularly as dean of Windsor – was that of Victoria, the grandmother of Europe. When the nations of Europe descended into war in 1914, his innately patriotic nature longed for British and imperial victories, but his principal concerns were pastoral. Davidson refused to condone hatred of the German people, condemned the use of gas against the enemy, and visited the troops and their chaplains. One of the chaplains, writing about the archbishop's visit to the Western Front in May 1916, commented: 'I saw him in a motor in his archiepiscopal robes with a tin helmet on his head. That I think must surely be one of the sights of the war.'[19]

Few archbishops of Canterbury have made a greater visual impact than Cosmo Gordon Lang, either in his handsome youth or distinguished maturity. Stanley Baldwin's appointment of Lang to Canterbury in 1928 was effectively engineered by Davidson, who had enjoyed an excellent working relationship with his counterpart in the northern province. In spite of Baldwin's acute sense of Englishness, he much appreciated this second successive Scottish primate. In Baldwin's eyes Lang was evidently an honorary Englishman, perhaps even an honorary Worcestershire man. For his part, Lang appreciated all that went with belonging to the Establishment, including being chairman of the British Museum trustees, and acted the part to perfection. In politics he considered himself a liberal Conservative, though he retained important friendships with Churchmen well to the left of him, including Henry Scott Holland, one of the *Lux mundi* authors. As a young man, he fancied himself as a Conservative prime minister, with three country seats, an aristocratic wife and eight equally imaginary children.[20] Lang was a skilled speaker, an accomplished debater and an effective parliamentarian, even when dealing with tough issues like the Tithe Measure of 1936, which cost the Church of England dearly. His clarity of purpose is well illustrated by a speech to the Lords in 1933: 'To govern India has been the greatest achievement this country has ever attempted . . . It will be an even higher achievement, an even nobler task, to assist India to govern itself.'[21] In 1936 came the real crisis of Lang's archiepiscopate, when he supported Baldwin and the pro-abdication 'respectable tendency' that unseated Edward VIII. His BBC broadcast on Sunday 13 December rebuked the king for preferring 'a craving for private happiness' over duty to his country; he had 'disappointed hopes so high and abandoned a trust so great' in 'a manner inconsistent with the Christian principles of marriage'. To Baldwin, Lang's was 'the voice of Christian England'; to the wider public – whether or not they had a facility for puns – the archbishop had attacked a much loved figure:

> My Lord Archbishop, what a scold you are!
> And when your man is down, how bold you are!
> Of Christian charity how scant you are!
> And, auld Lang swine, how full of cant you are![22]

However much Lang's admirers revel in the splendid anecdotes related by his biographer J.G. Lockhart, it is the popular criticism of him during the abdication crisis that tends to be perpetuated in political histories of the period. Fortunately for Lang, his natural showmanship was given full rein in the *Crown Imperial* coronation of 1937. This event was broadcast on the wireless, and its popularity caused Lang to 'wonder whether any event in history has been so realised throughout the whole world'.[23] He regarded it as confirmation that improved ceremonial could engender 'a deeper religious sense'. This was the culture of the slum parishes writ large. Lang reached the age of seventy-five in 1939; the Second World War tested him to the limit. While Archbishop William Temple of York retained a pacifist agenda, Lang was prepared to pray for Allied victory, but nevertheless recognised his duty to uphold spiritual values during the conflict. He was one of the signatories of the 'Ten points of a Christian order' laid out in a letter to *The Times* on 21 December 1940 and took an interest in the Sword of the Spirit movement which prayed for an end to totalitarianism and a just lasting peace. By November 1941, when he went to All Souls and sang the Mallard Song, his mind was made up: he resigned in January 1942.

Winston Churchill's appreciation of the deeply patriotic Cardinal Arthur Hinsley of Westminster served to underline the reservations he felt in appointing to Canterbury a dedicated campaigner for peace at the height of the war. Any idea of appeasement was repugnant to the prime minister. To Clement Attlee, Churchill expressed that reluctance by describing Temple as the 'only half-a-crown in a sixpenny bazaar.'[24] From the Left, Bernard Shaw was gleeful: 'an Archbishop of Temple's enlightenment was a realized impossibility'. Lang also favoured the succession of the prophetic Temple, whose vision of postwar reconstruction was set out in *Christianity and Social Order* (1942). Once at Canterbury, Temple expressed that vision in two campaigns: 'The Church looks forward' (1942) and 'Religion and life' (1944). He went 'further than any other Anglican archbishop had ever done in saying that peace according to the will of God, not a national military victory, must be the chief aim.'[25] Temple was probably the most actively political of all the modern archbishops of Canterbury, and never more so than in his contribution to the 1944 Education Act, which expressed a détente in the Church/State struggle that had dominated educational debate for over half a century. William Temple was the archbishop of the 1945–51 Labour government in every sense but one: he did not live to see it. His place as one of the greatest twentieth-century archbishops is nevertheless assured, even if only for 'the richness of his attempt to give Christianity a pivotal function in modern thought'.[26]

After Temple's death on 26 October 1944, the succession soon became a choice between the bishops of London and Chichester, Geoffrey Fisher and G.K.A. Bell. Bell was distrusted by some on account of his outspoken advocacy of Church/State reform – a natural enough cry from Davidson's former chaplain and biographer – and effectively disqualified himself by his vociferous denunciations of Allied bombing raids. Even Temple had regarded Fisher as his natural successor, musing, with unconscious reference to Fisher's Repton reputation, 'I must give up in time to let Geoffrey have a whack.' If Owen Chadwick's law of elective constitutions may be applied not to modern papal elections but to the selection of archbishops of Canterbury in the same period, Fisher emerged as the victor because he was the physical, political and cultural antithesis of Temple. He was certainly no prophet, more primate as head prefect, which was the role he had performed during his own school days at Marlborough. Fisher was a pragmatic man and what he lacked in imagination he made up for in the energy that he poured into travel, administration and other responsibilities. He also represented the Masonic element in the Church of England and was no friend to the political Left, as his turbulent relationship with Hewlett Johnson, the famous 'red dean' of Canterbury, only served to accentuate. Then again, Johnson was no moderate, but rather the most prominent supporter of Communism in the Anglican

Church: 'if Temple was the epitome of theological seriousness and socialist moderation, Johnson was the embodiment of radical rebellion.'[27] Johnson could match Lang in prelatical appearance, but his prominence was no less a consequence of his longevity: only Dean Lynch in the eighteenth century held the office for longer than Johnson's thirty-two years. The dean was decorated by Stalin for his work in promoting the cause of Communist Russia and was in constant conflict with Fisher; their correspondence was at times as incendiary as the bombs that fell on Canterbury during the Second World War. While Johnson promoted another country, Fisher was a fervent British nationalist: 'The greatest creation of our nation,' he said in 1951, 'has been a way of life, a tradition of how men and women and children may live together in the freedom of mutual respect and trust, free to be themselves, free to be generous to others – with a grand sense of proportion and patience and a grand power of laughing at ourselves.'[28] The archbishop himself was affable and approachable, providing the conversation did not turn to religion. The last prime minister with whom he had to deal while in office was Harold Macmillan, a keen Anglican, yet Macmillan did not find Fisher easy: 'I try to talk to him about religion, but he seems quite uninterested and reverts all the time to politics.'[29] In spite of giving the impression of being the leader of 'the Tory Party at prayer', Fisher's taste for national affairs frequently placed him in opposition to Labour and Conservative administrations alike, especially with regard to colonial or post-colonial matters. This included a robust critique of the Suez affair in 1956, in which Eden's government 'had not only lost a very good opportunity of doing the right thing but . . . had done the wrong thing'.[30] On the domestic front he was conscious of changing social trends and duly pronounced on a range of moral issues. In 1956, for example, he spoke out against gambling in general and made a pointed attack on the introduction of Premium Bonds as 'a second-rate expedient which may attract savings, but which adds nothing to the spiritual capital of the nation and which insinuates on a large scale this undignified and unedifying adulteration of public duty by motives of private gain.'[31]

Churchill was not the only one to cast himself as something of a father-figure to the young Elizabeth II when she succeeded to the throne in 1952; Fisher, the father of six sons but no daughters, was another contender. In 1947 he had presided at her wedding to Philip Mountbatten, but her coronation in 1953 was Fisher's finest hour. Building on the success of George VI's coronation in 1937, tradition continued to be invented.[32]

A scholarly commission supervised the reintroduction of much arcane ceremonial to create a triumph of realised antiquarianism: Lang would have revelled in it. At the same time, the use of television cameras inside Westminster Abbey made the coronation the greatest leap of the Church and the monarchy into the modern world. The well-known film footage conveys the resonance of Fisher's voice, while the prematurely venerable Michael Ramsey, standing on the monarch's right in his capacity as bishop of Durham, makes a particularly striking impact on the viewer. From that day onwards the archbishop of Canterbury was no longer an exclusively Establishment figure, confined to the world of public schools, Oxbridge, the House of Lords and the clubs of St James's; he had become known to the wider public. It took some decades for familiarity to reach the level of popular satire in the television programme *Spitting Image*, in which the puppets of Archbishops Runcie and Carey illustrated how much the mystique of office had evaporated. Fisher himself came in for popular criticism in 1955, for his alleged part in the ending of the romance between Princess Margaret, third in line to the throne, and the divorcé Peter Townsend. Those who saw Fisher as instrumental in persuading the princess to put her public duty before her private emotions called for his resignation. It was like a re-run of the abdication crisis.

In reality, Fisher's resignation had to wait until 1961. He was less than pleased by Macmillan's choice of Ramsey as his successor, but informed opinion felt that the prime minister had done well in providing a High Churchman (Ramsey) to one archbishopric and a Low Churchman (Coggan) to the other. Macmillan's long years of reading Trollope had clearly paid off.[33] His relations with Fisher had certainly not been smooth, partly accounting for the appointment of a contrasting character to Canterbury. For so profound a thinker and so eminent a theologian, Ramsey was remarkably jolly. A comic photograph publication, *The Canterbury Pewside Book* (s.d.), was dedicated to him as 'the genial Friar Tuck of a man . . . whose unfailing good humour and generosity of spirit is an example to Christians and non-Christians alike'.[34] A Canadian newspaper considered him the stage model of an archbishop: 'Vigorous, silver haired with a high forehead, great shaggy eyebrows, a majestic mien, looking older than his years, but always smiling and ever ready to break into bellowing laughter.'[35] He attracted anecdotes as Lang had done, but there was no hint of pomposity about Archbishop Ramsey. In 1961, at the time of his appointment, he was required in the usual fashion to identify himself at St Paul's Cathedral as the real Michael Ramsey and heard himself described as 'Arthur Michael Ramsey, freeborn and no bastard', at which he could be heard to comment 'How do *they* know?'[36] For all his refreshing humanity, Ramsey was no political lightweight nor did he shirk his responsibilities with regard to defining Christian morality in a time of accelerating social change. Already Fisher's assault on Premium Bonds seemed almost a luxury issue, as Ramsey addressed fundamental questions about life, death and basic human rights. On the question of capital punishment, he was a committed abolitionist and consistently voted against hanging; in 1965 he was almost persuaded to pilot an anti-hanging bill through parliament. Racism and race relations formed one of the strongest threads running through his public interventions. The apartheid regime in South Africa was a constant concern to him, as were Ian Smith's Rhodesia and the various immigration bills introduced into the British parliament, of which he was a leading opponent. At Harold Wilson's invitation he accepted the chairmanship of the National Committee for Commonwealth Immigrants, but remained aloof from party politics and was not afraid to speak out against government policy when his duty and his conscience required. Such an example was the Divorce Reform Bill of 1968/9, which did not concur with a church report, *Putting Asunder*, submitted to parliament by the archbishop in 1966. At the same time, he supported liberalisation of the law on homosexuality, took a 'pastoral' approach to abortion and was measured in his assessment of what constituted pornography. Ramsey's high profile in parliament coincided with significant loosening of the ties between the State and the Church of England. In 1970 the Church Assembly ceased to exist and the powers of the convocations of York and Canterbury were limited in order to make way for synodical government, by which diocesan synods of bishop, clergy and laity send their representatives to the general synods held two or three times a year.

Donald Coggan's translation from York to Canterbury in 1974 was so widely expected that it met with little reaction. Anglican evangelicals hoped for much, but were disappointed. The new archbishop's approach to life and politics was straightforward and excited no particular interest. His one serious attempt to break into public life, *Call to the Nation* (1975), made little impact. There were not even any royal weddings to raise Coggan's profile with the general public. This was the calm before the storm.

Between 1983 and 1996 four biographies of the mild, urbane, pig-keeping Archbishop Runcie were published.[37] None attracted as much controversy as

Humphrey Carpenter's in 1996, revealing as it did the retired archbishop's indiscreet thoughts on a variety of subjects and individuals. Runcie was an unlikely hero, but he mattered to biographers because of the socio-political role urged upon and assumed by the Churches in Margaret Thatcher's Britain; he mattered also because the Church of England experienced such serious fragmentation over the ordination of women that a complete fracture was seriously contemplated. Runcie was generally a shrewd operator, but at least twice he courted public relations disaster, first with the diplomatic activities of his 'envoy' Terry Waite, leading to Waite's kidnapping in Beirut, and second when the attack on him in the anonymous preface of the 1987 edition of *Crockford's Clerical Directory* resulted in the suicide of its author, G.V. Bennett, a distinguished historian of the Church of England. Far less controversially, Runcie was the first archbishop to be appointed under the latest procedure, according to which a commission presented the prime minister with just two names from which to choose. As Adrian Hastings somewhat impishly points out, that made his appointment the first since the Reformation 'to conform to clause 1 of Magna Carta', on the freedom of church elections.[38] Just sixteen months later he acquired a highly public profile as he presided and preached at the 'fairy tale' wedding of Prince Charles and Lady Diana Spencer. A year after that spectacle he was again centre stage in St Paul's for the service of remembrance after the Falklands conflict. Under the gaze of the 'Iron Lady', he did not flinch from his pastoral responsibility and spoke with the authority that came from being a decorated ex-serviceman: 'War is a sign of human failure and everything we say and do in this service must be in that context.'[39] The politicising of the Church of England to meet the challenges of Thatcherism did not really emerge until the publication of its report on *Faith in the City* (1985), which provided a vision for the future of the troubled inner cities and led to the creation of the Church Urban Fund, with the archbishop as its patron. Runcie found himself cast as an unofficial leader of the opposition, championing the victims of a society which was alleged not to exist. Meanwhile, in 1987, the archbishop made ecclesiastical history by sanctioning the first ordinations of women to the diaconate in the Church of England. It was suggested that he became the subject of a whispering campaign engineered by opponents of women's ordination.[40] Whatever the truth of that, he was much appreciated in certain Establishment circles.

As long as the Church of England remains 'established', the archbishop of Canterbury has a unique opportunity to provide a Christian presence in the corridors of power and a Christian perspective on the issues of the day. George Carey expressed a primate's angle on this: 'Accused as I sometimes am of meddling in politics or affairs that do not concern me, I have to reply that a Christianity which is not concerned about the whole of life is not a Christianity I want or the modern world deserves.'[41] At his enthronement in February 2003 Rowan Williams presented another variation on the theme: 'Jesus' followers grieve or protest about war, debt, poverty and prejudice because of the fear we feel when insult and violence blot out the divine image in human relations.'[42]

In 2002, Archbishop Williams was appointed in the most extraordinary glare of publicity and the right-wing press was not slow to accuse him of being too closely associated with the Labour Party to be a truly impartial moral voice. The irony of this lay in the emphasis which was also placed on him as the first archbishop to be appointed from outside the Church of England, a prophetic outsider of the sort that does not usually emerge from appointment-by-committee. Even as Williams was enthroned, the Labour Party and the Labour government were divided over the Anglo-American invasion of Iraq. Williams spoke out against this military action, and there was much debate over what constitutes a 'just' war. Against this bloody backdrop, Williams had to strive hard to interest the media and thereby the general public in other moral issues, either through the conventional means of speeches in the House of Lords or through televised 'conversations' on subjects including medical ethics and the 'loss' of childhood. Carey was the first archbishop to have a website and Williams's speeches on a variety of national and international issues have been made available to the public through that medium. Any archbishop of Canterbury would be challenged by the task of communicating the Christian message to an increasingly secular society characterised by pervasive consumerism: even the name Whitgift now refers to a shopping centre in Croydon.

An instinct for survival in such hostile surroundings is among the less idealistic explanations for the rise in ecumenical initiatives in Britain over the last century. Whatever their origins, a survey of the archbishops' role in relations between the Church of England and other Christian denominations can provide a useful guide to the relatively short history of ecumenism in Britain. In the nineteenth century ecumenical initiatives tended to be aimed at the Protestant Churches, much as they had been in the eighteenth. International movements like the evangelical revivals crossed denominational barriers and the Bible Societies brought together many different local churches. With regard to the Roman Catholic Church, the nineteenth century witnessed more inter-denominational rivalry and suspicion than co-operation and mutual respect. John Bird Sumner, the first evangelical archbishop, was faced with an emancipated Catholic community and a growing Catholic constituency, especially of immigrants in the industrial cities. The Oxford Movement, which to some extent inherited the evangelicals' search for holiness, presented the Church of England as a *via media* between Roman errors and Protestant excesses. The restoration of the Catholic hierarchy in 1850, and the emergence of the bombastic Cardinal Wiseman as its leader, promoted fears of a Roman resurgence and an attack on Establishment principles. Archbishop Tait, the model of archbishop as national unifier, was not prepared to join the new Protestant Alliance against the reformed hierarchy in 1850 on the grounds that, 'Popery in this country is better met by every Protestant clergyman and layman zealously doing his duty in the position God has assigned him, than by the agitation which seems implied in the formation of a Society for the defence of Protestantism.'[43] It was clear that Wiseman saw himself as the fulfilment of Gregory the Great's plan for a London metropolitan see and therefore as the true successor to St Augustine. No archbishop of Canterbury could have easy dealings with a man like that. The young Wiseman had befriended the Tractarians and saw them as part of an English Catholic revival; throughout the century there were prophetic figures who looked forward to a great united Church. With the growth of ultramontanism and the prominence of Cardinal Manning – the former archdeacon of Chichester who rejected Anglicanism and embraced a highly papalist Catholicism – any possibility of accommodation between Rome and Canterbury grew even dimmer. As Rome came under attack from the unifying Italian states, the papacy responded to the forces of nationalism and secularism with increasingly triumphalist interpretations of papal authority, culminating in Pius IX's declaration of papal infallibility in 1870. Again, this only served to alienate Anglicans.

Although Archbishop Benson was of a ritualist inclination, that did not mean he was personally favourable towards the Catholicism later adopted by his own son. As long as Newman and Manning lived, Benson also had to deal with national figures who in some senses outclassed him. Newman died in 1890, Manning in 1892. Benson's own end came at a particularly acute crisis in relations between Rome and Canterbury. Ironically, it was not the ultra-papalist Pius, but the much more outward-looking Leo XIII who brought matters to a head with his bull of 13 September 1896, *Apostolicae curae*. This condemned Anglican Orders as 'null and void', not because the apostolic succession might have been lost with Matthew Parker's consecration in 1559, but because the wording of the Edwardian Ordinal did not make it explicit that priests so ordained would have the power to offer the sacrifice of the Mass.[44] Benson's death at Hawarden occurred less than a month later. Responding to *Apostolicae curae* was therefore one of the first tasks that faced Archbishop Frederick Temple. On 29 March 1897 he and Archbishop William Maclagan of York issued their *responsio*, a measured defence of the sufficiency of the Ordinal, firmly inimical to the Roman position and, it has been said, written in better Latin than that of Rome: a reflection of the quality of teaching at King Edward VI's, Rugby and Wellington.

It was during the archiepiscopate of Randall Davidson that the first signs of a thaw between Rome and Canterbury became apparent. In 1920 the sixth Lambeth Conference called on all Christian people to unite, basing this summons on the historic episcopate. This chimed with the long-held opinions of Lord Halifax, the future viceroy of India, who initiated a series of Anglican/Catholic 'conversations' at Malines in Belgium in 1922. These informal meetings were chaired by Cardinal Désiré Joseph Mercier; contributors included Charles Gore and the historian Pierre Batiffol. Much agreement was reached on issues such as the papal primacy and the real presence of Christ in Eucharist, but Archbishop Davidson was all too aware of the furore caused by the Prayer Book revision and urged caution in his correspondence with Mercier:

> It is I think possible that our Roman Catholic friends, unfamiliar perhaps with the strength of opinion on these subjects which is prevalent in large sections of the English Church and people, may suppose us to be ready for a more accommodating acceptance of Roman Catholic contentions and claims than I for one, can regard as being either possible or in accordance with our deliberate belief as to what is true.[45]

Meanwhile, less inhibited ecumenical initiatives continued among the Protestant Churches. The 1924 COPEC conference (Conference on Christian Politics, Economics and Citizenship) duly led to the Life and Work movement, formed in 1937, and in turn to the World Council of Churches, established in

1948 with Archbishop Fisher as its first chairman.[46] In 1925 Anglican Orders were formally recognised by the Old Catholic Church of the Netherlands, which sent a delegation to Lang's Lambeth Conference in 1930. Lang was a committed ecumenist. Mention has already been made of the inter-denominational wartime Sword of the Spirit movement, supported by all the principal church leaders in Britain. Behind the scenes, relations between Lang and Cardinal Hinsley were facilitated by the scholarly Catholic bishop David Mathew, an Oxford historian, friend of Lang, and Hinsley's right-hand man. So far had personal relations between the English archbishops improved since the days of Sumner and Wiseman that Lang even proposed Hinsley for membership of the Athenaeum, by tradition the archbishop of Canterbury's London club. After Lang's resignation, the rigours of war continued to offer William Temple opportunities to further Anglican/Catholic relations.

Archbishop Fisher's initial contribution to ecumenism came with his suggestion, in 1946, that unity might be possible between the Church of England and the Free Churches (as the nonconformists had become) providing that the non-Anglicans could overcome their opposition to episcopacy. It was no small stumbling block. Methodism was thought to present the most promising prospect, for it had emerged directly out of the Church of England in the eighteenth century; decades of Anglican–Methodist dialogue followed but the proposed covenant was rejected by the General Synod in 1972.[47]

Peace in 1945 did not bring ecumenical dividends in the wider Rome-Canterbury relationship: on one side there was the resolute papal monarch Pius XII; on the other, Britain's global significance was on the wane, so why should its national Church loom large in Rome's view of the world? The breakthrough, when it finally came, featured one of twentieth-century Canterbury's less likely ecumenists: the Freemason Geoffrey Fisher. The opportunities presented by air travel meant that he was familiar with much of the Anglican world, so it seemed appropriate that he should complete his period in office with an historic pilgrimage to Jerusalem, Istanbul (formerly Constantinople, the heart of Orthodox Christianity) and Rome. His meeting with Pope John XXIII on 2 December 1960 lasted an hour or so: it was low key, there were no official photographs, but the ice had been broken and it effectively ended centuries of alienation. An Anglican spokesman offered a measured account of the encounter: 'It was never intended that this should be a consideration of particular problems or issues and the meeting retained throughout, the character of a visit of courtesy. It was marked by a happy spirit of cordiality and sympathy, such as befitted a notable event in the history of Church relations.' Fisher himself was more effusive in recollection: 'It was the final achievement of my archiepiscopate, without any doubt, and it arose in the simplest of ways, as a simple matter of a simple visit to a simple Pope.'[48] So inclusive was the vision of John XXIII that provision was bound to be made for Anglicans in the Second Vatican Council. Not only were there official Anglican observers at the council, but its decree on ecumenism (1964) contains the statement: 'Among those in which some Catholic traditions and institutions continue to exist, the Anglican Communion occupies a special place.' Two years later Michael Ramsey donned a Canterbury cap and paid his visit to Pope Paul VI. This time there were photographs to witness to the joy of the occasion, which the archbishop regarded as one of the highlights of his life. He was particularly impressed by the ring with which the pope presented him: 'As we walked down St Paul's-without-the-Walls, he took off his ring, he took off his ring and he put it on my finger, just like a wedding, very nice and we got in to our big black cars, and we drove off in opposite directions.'[49] In the wake of that encounter the Anglican Roman Catholic International Commission (ARCIC) was established in 1969, with ARCIC II following in 1982.

Visits to Rome have become regular features of the archiepiscopal itinerary, but their symbolic significance still generates more interest than most of the primate's extensive international travels. In September 1989, for example, there was much for the historically sensitive observer to appreciate in Robert Runcie's five-day visit to Pope John Paul II, whether in their attendance at vespers in the church of S. Gregorio Magno, the place from which Gregory the Great originally sent Augustine to England, or even in the small anti-papal protest by the Ulster Unionist leader Ian Paisley as Runcie attended the papal Mass outside St Peter's basilica. By the time Rowan Williams performed the hugely symbolic act of kissing the pope's ring in October 2003, ARCIC had identified the exercise of authority in the Church as a 'gift' and the gesture seemed less an act of submission (as his fundamentalist critics might see it) than a mark of respect for a great church leader.

Rowan Williams is equally well known for his interest in Orthodox Christianity. In this he is the inheritor of a long Anglican tradition stretching back to the seventeenth century. In more recent times, Davidson, Lang and William Temple had all encouraged Anglican relations with the Orthodox

Churches before Fisher's symbolic visit to Istanbul. In the ecumenically optimistic climate of the 1960s Michael Ramsey raised interest to new levels by inviting a number of senior Orthodox figures to Britain and in 1973 an Anglican-Orthodox Theological Commission was established. What remains unique, though, is the visit of John Paul II to England in May 1982, which included a time of silent prayer with Archbishop Runcie at the site of Becket's martyrdom.

If it was extraordinary for a Polish pope to visit Canterbury, it should be remembered that, just a century and a half earlier, it was remarkable for the archbishop himself to put in an appearance there. That state of affairs changed when it became possible to travel by train from London to Canterbury (via Ashford) in 1846. On 28 April 1848 a new era opened in the relationship between the archbishop and his cathedral when John Bird Sumner was enthroned there, with only as much ceremonial as an anti-ritualist could tolerate. There was, as yet, no question of the archbishops returning to live at Canterbury on a permanent basis or of them being buried there. Their parliamentary responsibilities required their presence at Lambeth, while Addington remained more of a family home and the resting place of Archbishops Sumner, Longley and Tait. Sumner's memorial in the village church is in the Gothick style; Longley's illustrates in miniature the renaissance of the Italian Renaissance in nineteenth-century Britain. The memorial window to Archbishop Tait suggests something about his perceived place in history, flanked as he is by Augustine preaching to the pagans of Kent, and Langton signing Magna Carta. When Benson arrived at Canterbury in 1883, he came with firm ideas of how a cathedral should operate and had published a book on the subject in 1878.[50] Benson also took a medieval bishop's interest in the city, and received a medieval bishop's tomb courtesy of the leading architect T.G. Jackson, whose canopied design is clearly inspired by the tomb of Archbishop Pecham. Benson's friends were left to commemorate him at Addington with the most spectacular of the archiepiscopal memorials there: the highly decorated chancel attributed to Heywood Sumner. Small statues depict Archbishops Cranmer, Theodore, Benson and Laud, the last inaccurately clad in full priestly vestments. It was left to Frederick Temple to realise Benson's vision. In 1897 Addington was sold for £70,000 and the primate ceased to be a 'country gentleman'.[51] Ironically enough, Archbishop Benson's son, Monsignor Robert Hugh Benson, bequeathed his own home, Hare Street House in Hertfordshire, to the archbishops of Westminster as a kind of Catholic Addington. For the moment, that left Temple with only his residence at Lambeth, where he made his mark by reducing the grounds to create the public space of Archbishop's Park. Meanwhile, W.D. Caroë, architect to the Church Commissioners, was engaged to design a new residence for him in Canterbury. This he did on the site of the Old Palace, where the new palace was completed by 1901. The archbishop's private chapel there was dedicated to his predecessor St Anselm and consecrated that same year.

Throughout the twentieth century the archbishops were regularly invited by the dean and chapter to preside in their own cathedral at the great festivals of the Church. As the example of Fisher and Dean Johnson illustrates, this did not mean that relations between the archbishop and the dean and chapter were always cordial. By way of contrast, Cosmo Gordon Lang was among those primates who enjoyed a more positive relationship with his Canterbury colleagues. Lang was utterly enchanted by his cathedral: 'Surely the view of the choir and apse at Canterbury is one of the most beautiful pictures in stone in England, perhaps in the world.'[52] His enthronement on 4 December 1928 was an occasion of great magnificence, masterminded by Dean Bell, Randall Davidson's sometime secretary. Vaughan Williams composed a Te Deum for the event and even the Southern Railway Company played its part with the provision of a special train to transport the guests from London.[53] In 1941 it was to Canterbury that Lang retreated when the bombing in London became too intense. In the aftermath of war, Archbishop Fisher and his wife lived through the ten-year programme of repairs to the devastated palace at Lambeth and, in the process, endeavoured to create a more modest and homely living environment in what had been a somewhat barrack-like building. The reception rooms for official functions remain, and the Library has a new reading room named after Archbishop Runcie, but the archbishop's personal accommodation is now located in a small self-contained apartment.

For seven of the twentieth-century archbishops Lambeth was not their last home: Davidson, Lang, Fisher, Ramsey, Runcie, Coggan and Carey all accepted life peerages and retired. Indeed, between Coggan's retirement in 1974 and Ramsey's death in 1988 there were two ex-archbishops of Canterbury still alive. Lang remained active during the three years of his retirement, which he was able to spend at Kew, courtesy of the generosity of his friend J. Pierpont Morgan. There was a dramatic dimension even to his death, which occurred after he collapsed in the street when hurrying to catch a train at Kew station. Posthumous appreciation of him has even included a cameo role in a Susan Howatch novel.[54] Only Archbishop Fisher retained pastoral duties in his retirement, settling with his wife in the picturesque Dorset village of Trent and serving the village church. The Ramseys initially retired to Durham, before moving to Bishopthorpe and, finally, to Oxford; the Coggans took up residence just outside the walls of Winchester's cathedral close. It had been with great reluctance that Runcie made the move from St Albans to Lambeth in 1980, so it came as no surprise when he retired to his former cathedral city, though he continued to be in demand for social and cultural events. In 2004 Carey made headlines as never before when he went beyond Archbishop Secker's example by not only compiling memoirs, but publishing them as well. Carey's observations on the marriage of the prince and princess of Wales were devoured by the media with much greater ardour than were the earlier chapters of the book, which chronicle the unlikely early life of a future archbishop. Reticence and episcopal distance were sacrificed to 'transparency'.

Though it is not altogether certain that Fisher was, as he maintained, the ninety-ninth archbishop of Canterbury, the long history of the Canterbury primates nevertheless reflects continuity and evolution in Christian witness within and beyond England's southern province. It also allows us to appreciate in microcosm the chronicle of relations between Church and State, the mitre and the crown. Of many of the earlier archbishops we know little or nothing beyond what their hagiographers chose to convey. There followed the age of the princes, whose exalted status may still be glimpsed in the decayed magnificence of their tombs. The letters, diaries and interviews of recent archbishops present a considerably more human picture: when he confided in his journal for 1888 that he felt 'full of fears, self-misgivings, anxieties, perplexities', Archbishop Benson may well have articulated the feelings of many holders of the office.[55] Their individual ministries can reveal much about England's social, political and ecclesiastical history, but their collective achievement over the span of more than fourteen centuries is a remarkable story of survival, adaptation and careful cultivation of the seed sown by Gregory the Great and Augustine of Canterbury.

ENGLISH AND WELSH DIOCESES HELD BY PRELATES WHO BECAME OR WHO HAD BEEN ARCHBISHOPS OF CANTERBURY

Archbishops-elect are not included in this table.

Diocese *with date of foundation*	**Bishop**
Bangor *late 6C*	Henry Deane 1494–1500
	Thomas Herring 1737–43
	Matthew Hutton 1743–7
	John Moore 1775–83
Bath and Wells: see Wells	
Bradford *1920*	Donald Coggan 1955–61
Bristol *1542*	Thomas Secker 1735–7
Chester *1541*	John Bird Sumner 1828–48
	Geoffrey Fisher 1932–9
Chichester *1075*	John Kemp 1421
Durham *995*	Charles Thomas Longley 1856–60
	Michael Ramsey 1952–6
Elmham *c. 672*	Stigand 1043–7

Ely *1108*

Simon Langham 1362–6
Thomas Arundel 1374–88
Thomas Bourchier 1436–7 and
1443–54
John Morton 1478–86

Exeter *1050*

Frederick Temple 1869–85

Hereford *676*

Cuthbert 736–40
Willliam Courtenay 1369–75

Lichfield and Coventry *c.* 669

George Abbot 1609–10
Frederick Cornwallis 1750–68

Lincoln *1072*

Thomas Tenison 1692–5
William Wake 1705–16

London *604*

Mellitus 604–19
Dunstan 959–60
Robert of Jumièges 1044–51
Simon Sudbury 1361–75
William Courtenay 1375–81
Roger Walden 1405–06
John Kemp 1421–5
Willliam Warham 1502–3
Edmund Grindal 1559–70
Richard Bancroft 1597–1604
George Abbot 1610–11
William Laud 1628–33
William Juxon 1633–60
Gilbert Sheldon 1660–3
William Howley 1813–28
Archibald Campbell Tait 1856–68
Frederick Temple 1885–96
Geoffrey Fisher 1939–45

Manchester *1847*

William Temple 1921–9

Monmouth *1921*   Rowan Williams 1992–2002
                           (Archbishop of Wales 2000–2)

Norwich *1094/96*   Charles Manners Sutton 1792–1805

Oxford *1542*   John Potter 1715–37
                           Thomas Secker 1737–58

Ramsbury *c. 909*   Oda *c.* 925–41
                           Sigeric *c.* 985–90
                           Ælfric *c.* 990–5

Ripon *1836*   Charles Thomas Longley 1836–56

Rochester *604*   Justus 604–24
                           Ralph d'Escures 1108–14
                           William Whittlesey 1361–4
                           John Kemp 1419–21
                           Randall Thomas Davidson 1891–5

Salisbury *1078*   Hubert Walter 1189–93
                           Henry Deane 1500–1

Selsey *c.* 681   Æthelgar 980–8

St Albans *1877*   Robert Runcie 1970–80

St Davids *6C*   Henry Chichele 1408–14
                           William Laud 1621–6

Truro *1877*   Edward White Benson 1877–83

Wells *c. 909*   Athelm *c.* 909–23x25
                           Wulfhelm 923x25–6
Bath and Wells   Byrhthelm 956–9
united 1245   Lyfing 998x99–1013
                           John Stafford 1424–43

William Laud 1626–8
George Carey 1987–91

Winchester *660*   Ælfheah (Alphege) 984–1006
                             Stigand 1047–52
                             John Stratford 1323–33
                             Randall Thomas Davidson 1895–1903

Worcester c. *680*   Dunstan 957–9
                             Baldwin 1180–4
                             Walter Reynolds 1308–13
                             William Whittlesey 1364–8
                             Thomas Bourchier 1435–6
                             John Whitgift 1577–83

York *625*   Thomas Arundel 1388–96
                             John Kemp 1425–52
                             Edmund Grindal 1570–6
                             Thomas Herring 1743–7
                             Matthew Hutton 1747–57
                             Charles Thomas Longley 1860–2
                             Cosmo Gordon Lang 1908–28
                             William Temple 1929–42
                             Michael Ramsey 1956–61
                             Donald Coggan 1961–74

Uniquely among the archbishops of Canterbury, Boniface of Savoy had been a bishop outside the provinces of Canterbury and York, at Belley, 1234–41.

TOMBS AND MEMORIALS

With the exception of John Offord (d. 1349), archbishops-elect are not included in this table.

Archbishop	Date of death	Place of burial/tomb/memorial
Augustine	26 Feb. 604	St Peter and St Paul, Canterbury (which or 609 was rededicated in 978 as St Augustine's Abbey)
Laurence	2 Feb. 619	St Peter and St Paul (St Augustine), Canterbury
Mellitus	24 Apr. 624	St Peter and St Paul (St Augustine), Canterbury
Justus	10 Nov. 627 or 631	St Peter and St Paul (St Augustine), Canterbury: porch
Honorius	30 Sept. 653	St Peter and St Paul (St Augustine), Canterbury: west porch
Deusdedit	14 July 664	St Peter and St Paul (St Augustine), Canterbury
Theodore	19 Sept. 690	St Peter and St Paul (St Augustine), Canterbury
Berhtwald	13 Jan. 731	St Peter and St Paul (St Augustine), Canterbury
Tatwine	30 July 734	St Peter and St Paul (St Augustine), Canterbury
Nothhelm	17 Oct. 739	St Peter and St Paul (St Augustine), Canterbury
Cuthbert	26 Oct. 760	Canterbury Cathedral (Christ Church)
Bregowine	764	Canterbury Cathedral (Christ Church)
Jænberht	12 Aug. 792	St Peter and St Paul (St Augustine), Canterbury
Æthelheard	12 May 805	Canterbury Cathedral (Christ Church): chapel of St John the Baptist

Wulfred	24 Mar. 832	Canterbury Cathedral (Christ Church)
Feologild	30 Aug. 832	(Possibly) Canterbury Cathedral (Christ Church)
Ceolnoth	4 Feb. 870	Canterbury Cathedral (Christ Church)
Æthelred	30 June 888	Canterbury Cathedral (Christ Church): crypt
Plegmund	2 Aug. 923	Canterbury Cathedral (Christ Church)
Athelm	8 Jan. 926	(Possibly) Canterbury Cathedral (Christ Church)
Wulfhelm	12 Sept. 941	Canterbury Cathedral (Christ Church)
Oda	2 June 958	Canterbury Cathedral (Christ Church): shrine in corona, south side
Byrhthelm	dep. 959 d. 15 May 973	(Possibly) Canterbury Cathedral (Christ Church)
Dunstan	19 May 988	Canterbury Cathedral (Christ Church): shrine to south of high altar
Æthelgar	12/13 Feb. 990	(Possibly) Canterbury Cathedral (Christ Church)
Sigeric	28 Oct. 994	Canterbury Cathedral (Christ Church): crypt
Ælfric	16 Nov. 1005	Abingdon Translated to Canterbury Cathedral (Christ Church) in early eleventh century
Ælfheah (Alphege)	19 Apr. 1012	London, St Paul's Cathedral Translated to Canterbury Cathedral (Christ Church) 1023; shrine to north of high altar, corresponding to that St Dunstan's shrine on south side
Lyfing	12 June 1020	Canterbury Cathedral (Christ Church)
Æthelnoth	28/29 Oct. or 1 Nov. 1038	Canterbury Cathedral (Christ Church)
Eadsige	29 Oct. 1050	Canterbury Cathedral (Christ Church): crypt
Robert of Jumièges	depr. Sept. 1052 d. c. 1052/3	Jumièges (Normandy), abbey church: near high altar

Stigand	depr. 11 Apr. 1070 d. 21/22 Feb. 1072	Old Minster, Winchester probably translated to Winchester Cathedral *c.* 1093–4 and later located in mortuary chest on top of presbytery screen wall; location of bones uncertain, but possibly distributed among the Winchester mortuary chests
Lanfranc	28 May 1089	Canterbury Cathedral (Christ Church): north-east transept, where translated 1180
Anselm	21 Apr. 1109	Canterbury Cathedral (Christ Church): St Anselm's Chapel, where no memorial survives
Ralph d'Escures	20 Oct. 1122	Canterbury Cathedral (Christ Church)
William of Corbeil	21 Nov. 1136	Canterbury Cathedral (Christ Church)
Theobald	18 Apr. 1161	Canterbury Cathedral (Christ Church): Trinity Chapel translated to (former) Lady Chapel, eastern bay of north nave aisle, 1180
Thomas Becket	29 Dec. 1184	Canterbury Cathedral (Christ Church): originally buried in crypt translated to Trinity Chapel 7 July 1220; shrine dismantled 1538; location of bones uncertain
Richard (of Dover)	16 Feb. 1184	Canterbury Cathedral (Christ Church): near tomb of Archbishop Theobald
Baldwin	19/20 Nov. 1190	Acre
Hubert Walter	13 July 1205	Canterbury Cathedral (Christ Church): Purbeck marble tomb chest in south ambulatory
Stephen Langton	9 July 1228	Canterbury Cathedral (Christ Church): St Michael's Chapel; tomb curiously placed beneath altar, half in and half out of building
Richard le Grant (Wethershed)	3 Aug. 1231	Convent of Friars Minor, S. Gemini (between Narni and Todi, Umbria)

Edmund Rich of Abingdon	16 Nov. 1240	Pontigny (Champagne): apse of abbey church
Boniface of Savoy	18 July 1270	Hautecombe (Savoie): abbey church; tomb and fifteenth-century effigy destroyed during French Revolution, but rebuilt 1839, based on an engraving of the original
Robert Kilwardby	res. 5 June 1378 d. 10 Sept. 1279	Dominican church of S. Maria in Gradi, Viterbo
John Pecham	8 Dec. 1292	Canterbury Cathedral (Christ Church): north-west transept; wooden effigy beneath wall-mounted Decorated ogee canopy
Robert Winchelsey	11 May 1313	Canterbury Cathedral (Christ Church): south-east transept; tomb destroyed 1540s because of cult associated with it
Walter Reynolds	16 Nov. 1327	Canterbury Cathedral (Christ Church): south choir aisle; Purbeck marble effigy
Simon Mepham	12 Oct. 1333	Canterbury Cathedral (Christ Church): in form of screen across entrance to chapel of St Peter and St Paul (now St Anselm's Chapel); Purbeck marble tomb-chest but no effigy
John Stratford	23 Aug. 1348	Canterbury Cathedral (Christ Church): between presbytery and south choir aisle; alabaster effigy beneath vaulted canopy
John Offord	20 May 1349	Canterbury Cathedral (Christ Church): north-west transept
Thomas Bradwardine	26 Aug. 1349	Canterbury Cathedral (Christ Church): chapel of St Peter and St Paul (now St Anselm's Chapel)
Simon Islip	26 Apr. 1366	Canterbury Cathedral (Christ Church): nave; removed 1787
Simon Langham	res. 28 Nov. 1368 d. 22 July 1376	Carthusian church near Avignon; translated to St Benedict's Chapel,

		Westminster Abbey, 1379; tomb by Henry Yevele and Stephen Lote; alabaster effigy
William Whittlesey	5/6 June 1374	Canterbury Cathedral (Christ Church): nave; removed 1787
Simon Sudbury	14 June 1381	Canterbury Cathedral (Christ Church): between presbytery and south choir aisle, near tomb of Archbishop Stratford; Purbeck marble tomb-chest with vaulted stone canopy but no effigy; Sudbury's severed head preserved at St Gregory's church, Sudbury, Suffolk
William Courtenay	31 July 1396	Canterbury Cathedral (Christ Church): Trinity Chapel, to south of St Thomas's shrine and next to tomb of the Black Prince; alabaster tomb-chest and effigy
Thomas Arundel	19 Feb. 1414	Canterbury Cathedral (Christ Church): east end of north aisle; destroyed 1540
Roger Walden	depr. 19 Oct. 1399 d. Jan. 1406	London, St Paul's Cathedral: All Saints' Chapel; destroyed 1666
Henry Chichele	12 Apr. 1443	Canterbury Cathedral (Christ Church): between presbytery and north choir aisle; effigy on tomb-chest with cadaver below; mutilated during Commonwealth; repaired 1663–4; heavily restored 1897–99
John Stafford	25 May 1452	Canterbury Cathedral (Christ Church): north-west transept; marble slab, no effigy
John Kemp	22 Mar. 1454	Canterbury Cathedral (Christ Church): between presbytery and south choir aisle, corresponding to Archbishop Chichele's tomb on north side; remarkably tall canopy, but no effigy
Thomas Bourchier	30 Mar. 1486	Canterbury Cathedral (Christ Church): between presbytery and north choir

aisle, close to shrine of St Alphege and corresponding to Archbishop Sudbury's tomb on south side; vaulted canopy, elaborate carving, but no effigy

John Morton · 15 Sept. 1500 · Canterbury Cathedral (Christ Church): Our Lady Undercroft Chapel; effigy; decoration includes Tudor roses, Beaufort portcullises and cardinal's hats; damage to tomb resulted in loss of Morton's bones and odyssey of his skull, which is now at Stonyhurst College, Lancashire

Henry Deane · 15 Feb. 1503 · Canterbury Cathedral (Christ Church): north-west transept 'under a flat stone of marble', which has not survived

William Warham · 22 Aug. 1523 · Canterbury Cathedral (Christ Church): north-west transept, next to Archbishop Pecham's tomb; effigy beneath large vaulted canopy

Thomas Cranmer · depr. 13 Nov. 1553 · Martyrs' Memorial, St Giles, Oxford, designed by G. G. Scott and erected
d. 21 Mar. 1556 · 1841–3, remembers H. Latimer and N. Ridley, as well as Cranmer; memorial in chapel of Jesus College, Cambridge, bears single word 'CRANMER'.

Reginald Pole · 17 Nov. 1558 · Canterbury Cathedral: corona, north side; restored at expense of Cardinal H. Vaughan, 1897–1900

Matthew Parker · 17 May 1575 · Lambeth Palace chapel

Edmund Grindal · 6 July 1583 · St John the Baptist, Croydon: tomb destroyed in fire of 1867; charred inscription remains on south wall of chancel

John Whitgift · 29 Feb. 1604 · St John the Baptist, Croydon: St Nicholas Chapel; tomb with polychrome effigy in English Renaissance style; includes Whitgift's bearings of

		archbishop of Canterbury, bishop of Worcester, dean of Lincoln, as well as those of his Cambridge colleges, Peterhouse, Pembroke Hall and Trinity.
Richard Bancroft	2 Nov. 1610	St Mary's, Lambeth
George Abbot	4 Aug. 1633	Holy Trinity, Guildford: Lady Chapel; monument with effigy erected by his brother Sir Maurice Abbot
William Laud	10 Jan. 1645	All Hallows, Barking; translated to chapel of St John's College, Oxford, 24 July 1663, where there is a memorial on south wall of sanctuary
William Juxon	4 June 1663	St John's College, Oxford: buried in chapel, but no memorial
Gilbert Sheldon	9 Nov. 1677	St John the Baptist, Croydon: south aisle; improbably mitred effigy by J. Latham
William Sancroft	depr. 1 Feb. 1690 d. 24 Nov. 1693	St Peter and St Paul, Fressingfield (Suffolk): tomb chest in churchyard
John Tillotson	22 Nov. 1694	St Lawrence Jewry, London: wall monument; also a statue (1796) by J. Wilton in St Peter's, Sowerby
Thomas Tenison	14 Dec. 1715	St Mary, Lambeth: chancel
William Wake	24 Jan. 1737	St John the Baptist, Croydon: tomb destroyed in fire of 1867; memorial plaque dated 1988
John Potter	10 Oct. 1747	St John the Baptist, Croydon: chancel; tomb destroyed in fire of 1867
Thomas Herring	13 Mar. 1757	St John the Baptist, Croydon: tomb destroyed in fire of 1867; memorial plaque in St Nicholas Chapel
Matthew Hutton	19 Mar. 1758	St Mary, Lambeth: buried in chancel vault
Thomas Secker	3 Aug. 1768	St Mary, Lambeth: buried in covered passage leading to Lambeth Palace
Frederick Cornwallis	19 Mar. 1783	St Mary, Lambeth: buried in chancel vault

John Moore	18 Jan. 1805	St Mary, Lambeth
Charles Manners Sutton	21 July 1828	St Mary the Blessed Virgin, Addington: buried in family vault beneath vestry; memorial in church
William Howley	11 Feb. 1848	St Mary the Blessed Virgin, Addington: buried in church; tomb-like memorial north of altar; also memorial in form of tomb-chest with effigy by R. Westmacott the Younger in Canterbury Cathedral, between presbytery and north choir aisle, between tombs of Archbishops Chichele and Bourchier
John Bird Sumner	6 Sept. 1862	St Mary the Blessed Virgin, Addington: buried in churchyard; memorial in church
Charles Thomas Longley	28 Oct. 1868	Addington, St Mary the Blessed Virgin: buried in churchyard; memorial in church
Archibald Campbell Tait	1 Dec. 1882	St Mary the Blessed Virgin, Addington: buried in churchyard; memorial window in church; also memorial in form of tomb-chest with effigy by J.E. Boehm in Canterbury Cathedral, north-east transept, near burial place of Archbishop Lanfranc.
Edward White Benson	11 Oct. 1896	Canterbury Cathedral: buried in crypt; memorial in western bay of north aisle of nave in form of tomb-chest by T.G. Jackson, modelled on Archbishop Pecham's tomb, with effigy by T. Brock; chancel of St Mary the Blessed Virgin, Addington decorated as memorial.
Frederick Temple	22 Dec. 1902	Canterbury Cathedral: buried in cloister garth; memorial in corona in form of tomb-chest with kneeling figure by W.D. Caroë

Randall Thomas Davidson	res. 12 Nov. 1928 d. 25 May 1930	Canterbury Cathedral: buried in cloister garth; tomb-chest with effigy by C. Thomas in Trinity Chapel
Cosmo Gordon Lang	res. 31 Mar. 1942 d. 5 Dec. 1945	Canterbury Cathedral: ashes buried in St Stephen's Chapel
William Temple	26 Oct. 1944	Canterbury Cathedral: ashes buried cloister garth; chapel of St John the Evangelist refurnished 1951 by S. Dykes-Bower as memorial
Geoffrey Fisher	res. 31 May 1961 d. 15 Sept. 1972	Trent (Dorset), St Andrew: vault in churchyard memorial chapel in south transept; memorial in St Gregory's chapel, Canterbury Cathedral
Michael Ramsey	res. 15 Nov. 1974 d. 23 Apr. 1988	Canterbury Cathedral: ashes buried cloister garth; memorial in cloister
Donald Coggan	res. 25 Jan. 1980 d. 18 May 2000	Canterbury Cathedral: ashes buried in cloister garth; memorial in cloister
Robert Runcie	res. 31 Jan. 1991 d. 11 July 2000	St Albans Cathedral: buried in north churchyard

Notes

Introduction

1. So called from the fact that the court sat in the church of St Mary-le-Bow (S. Maria de Arcubus), the archbishop's exempt deanery in the City of London.

2. See J. Sayers (ed.), *Medieval Records of the Archbishops of Canterbury*, London, 1962; I.J. Churchill, *Canterbury Administration: the Administrative Machinery of the Archbishops of Canterbury Illustrated from Original Records*, 2 vols, London, 1933; F. Makower, *The Constitutional History and Constitution of the Church of England*, London, 1895.

3. The model was a Roman imperial one and metropolitan rights were defined by the Council of Nicaea in 325. The title of archbishop, after being originally applied to patriarchs, became in the western Church synonymous with metropolitans.

4. See B. Palmer, *High and Mitred: Prime Ministers as Bishop-makers 1837–1977*, London, 1992.

5. See J.W. Lamb, *The Archbishopric of Canterbury: from its Foundation to the Norman Conquest*, London, 1971.

6. M. Fuller, *The Throne of Canterbury; or the Archbishop's Jurisdiction*, London, 1891, p. 312. See S. Platten, *Augustine's Legacy: Authority and Leadership in the Anglican Communion*, London, 1997, for a considered contemporary view of Anglican authority.

7. *The Times* (T2), 9 January 2004, p. 1.

8. Debrett's *Peerage*, 1894, p. xxv.

9. G. Garimberti, *La prima parte delle vite, overo fatti memorabili d'alcuni papi, et di tutti cardinali passati*, Venice, 1567; A Chacón (d. 1599), corrected by A. Oldoino, *Vitae et res gestae pontificium romanorum et S.R.E. cardinalium*, Rome, 1677.

10. In 1949 Archbishop Geoffrey Fisher was keen to discover his own number in the line of archbishops and concluded that he was ninety-nine. The Church of England's official figure has remained faithful to that conclusion.

Chapter 1

1. Dates after the names of popes refer to the span of their pontificates, not their lives.
2. Bede, *Ecclesiastical History II*, 1.
3. R. Fletcher, *The Conversion of Europe*, London, 1997, p. 116.
4. C.M. Cusack, *The Rise of Christianity in Northern Europe*, 300–1000, London, 1999, p. 99.
5. N. Brooks, 'The Anglo-Saxon Cathedral Community, 597–1070', in P. Collinson, N. Ramsay and M. Sparks, eds, *A History of Canterbury Cathedral*, Oxford, 1995, p. 36.
6. R.A. Markus, *Gregory the Great and his World*, Cambridge, 1997, p. 180.
7. N. Brooks, *The Early History of the Church of Canterbury*, London, 1984, pp. 67–71. Reculver's Romanesque twin towers remain as landmarks, but its great seventh-century church, with its bands of Roman tiles, stood intact as late as 1809. Fragments of Reculver's church are preserved in the crypt of Canterbury Cathedral. They include two monolithic columns, 20 feet high and Byzantine in inspiration. The Anglo-Saxon monks were part of a European culture comprising the then undivided Church of East and West.
8. D.H. Farmer, *The Oxford Dictionary of Saints*, 2nd edn, Oxford, 1987, p. 437. Lyminge was a double house of monks and nun endowed by Æthelberga in 633. The present parish church preserves traces of the original buildings.
9. N. Brooks, 'Anglo-Saxon Cathedral', p. 11.
10. N. Brooks, *Early History*, p. 125.
11. For Sigeric's journey (including a map) and his visit to Rome, see F. Barlow, *The English Church 1000–1066*, London, 1963, pp. 12–13 (map) and pp. 292–3.
12. N. Brooks, *Early History*, p. 304.
13. F. Barlow, *English Church*, p. 55.
14. F.R.H. Du Boulay, *The Lordship of Canterbury: an Essay on Medieval Society*, London, 1966, p. 51.

15. Prevailing notions of Stigand's patriotism are even reflected in the third chapter of *Alice in Wonderland*. See J. Crook, 'The Mortuary Chests and the Bones of Archbishop Stigand', *Winchester Cathedral Record* 73 (2004), pp. 21–31.

16. M. Lapidge, ed., *Archbishop Theodore: Commemorative Studies on his Life and Influence*, Cambridge, 1995, p. 29.

17. D.H. Farmer, *Saints*, p. 359.

18. N. Brooks, 'Anglo-Saxon Cathedral', p. 37.

19. H. Mayr-Harting, 'The West: the Age of Conversion (700–1050)', in J. McManners, ed., *The Oxford Illustrated History of Christianity*, Oxford, 1990, p. 94.

20. D.H. Farmer, *Benedict's Disciples*, 2nd edn, Leominster, 1995, p. 43.

21. The oldest extant manuscript of the Rule of St Benedict, now in the Bodleian Library (MS Hatton 48), dates from the eighth century. Its production has sometimes been located to Kent, and therefore Canterbury, by the general aspect of the script; it is closer to the Kentish uncial than to the Wearmouth-Jarrow versions. Its long association with Worcester and lack of clear evidence makes its localisation at Canterbury problematic: R. Gameson, 'The Earliest Books of Christian Kent', in R. Gameson, ed., *St Augustine and the Conversion of England*, Stroud, 1999, p. 360.

22. See D. Parsons, ed., *Tenth-Century Studies*, London, 1975, and for Ethelwold, B. Yorke, ed., *Bishop Aethelwold: his Career and Influence*, Woodbridge, 1988.

23. D.J. Dales, 'The spirit of the *Regularis Concordia* and the hand of St Dunstan', in N. Ramsay, M. Sparks and T. Tatton-Brown, *St Dunstan: His Life, Times and Cult*, Woodbridge, 1992, p. 54.

24. N.P. Brooks, 'The Career of St Dunstan', in Ramsay, Sparks and Tatton-Brown, *Dunstan*, p. 23. For Dunstan's visual impact see N. Ramsay and M. Sparks, *The Image of St Dunstan*, Canterbury, 1988.

25. See I. Wood, *The Missionary Life: Saints and the Evangelisation of Europe 400–1050*, Harlow, 2001.

Chapter 2

1.   Dates after the names of kings refer to the span of their reigns, not their lives.

2.   See C.R. Cheney, *Hubert Walter*, London, 1967.

3.   Barlow, *English Church 1066–1154*, p. 256.

4.   Apart from Paris, Salerno (founded 1173) was the sole rival to Oxford, while Cambridge (founded 1209) was only predated by Bologna (1200) and Palencia (1208).

5.   See J.I. Catto, ed., *The History of the University of Oxford, I: The Early Oxford Schools*, Oxford, 1984, for the teaching career and posthumous impact of Edmund in Oxford.

6.   R.W. Southern has written several seminal studies on Anselm, culminating in *Saint Anselm: a Portrait in a Landscape*, Cambridge, 1991. *Anselm's Prayers and Meditations* have been edited by B. Ward, Harmondsworth, 1973, and an accessible guide to his thought has been written by G.R. Evans, *Anselm*, London, 1989. D.E. Luscombe and G.R. Evans (eds), *Anselm, Aosta, Bec and Canterbury*, Sheffield, 1996, has much of interest including a lecture by R.W. Southern, pp. 17–35.

7.   L.E. Wilshire, 'Boniface of Savoy, Carthusian and archbishop of Canterbury 1207–1270', *Analecta Cartusiana* 31 (1977), p. 22.

8.   See M. Walsh, *Warriors of the Lord: the Military Orders of Christendom*, Alresford, 2003.

9.   For Bec see M. Morgan, *The English Lands of the Abbey of Bec*, Oxford, 1946.

10. M. Gibson, *Lanfranc of Bec*, Oxford, 1978 contextualises the archbishop in the world of contemporary learning, and H.E.J. Cowdrey, *Lanfranc*, Oxford, 2003, concentrates on his work as archbishop and metropolitan.

11. *The Monastic Constitutions of Lanfranc*, ed. and trans D. Knowles, rev. edn, C.N.L. Brooke, Oxford, 2002.

12. M. Gibson, 'Normans and Angevins, 1070–1220', in Collinson, Ramsey and Sparks, *Canterbury Cathedral*, p 47.

13. See R.W. Southern, ed., *The Life of St Anselm by Eadmer*, Oxford, 1962.

14. Gibson, 'Normans and Angevins', in Collinson, Ramsey and Sparks, *Canterbury Cathedral*, p. 55.

15. *Ibid.*, p. 61.

16. See J.C. Robertson and J.B. Sheppard, *Materials for the History of Thomas Becket*, 7 vols, Rolls Series, London, 1875–85. D.C. Douglas and G.W. Greenaway, *English Historical Documents*, vol. 2, 1042–1189, London, 1953, provides translations of many of the accounts of Becket's death,

pp. 702–76. There is now also *The Correspondence of Thomas Becket, Archbishop of Canterbury 1162–1170*, ed. and trans. A.J. Duggan, 2 vols, Oxford, 2000.

17. Knowles's celebrated lecture on Becket, 'Archbishop Thomas Becket', is in *The Historian and Character*, Cambridge, 1963.

18. T. Tatton-Brown, *Lambeth Palace*, London, 2000, pp. 19–20.

19. C. Knightly, ed., *A Mirror of Medieval Wales: Gerald of Wales and his Journey of 1188*, Cardiff, 1988.

20. It was not until 1942 that another son of a bishop, William Temple, was selected for the archbishopric, though the high medieval period also offers the possibility that Baldwin of Forde was the son of an archdeacon of Totnes.

21. Quoted by E. Carpenter, *Cantuar*, p. 67.

22. J. Butler, *The Quest for Becket's Bones*, New Haven and London, 1995, pp. 25–6.

23. E. Jones, *The English Nation; the Great Myth*, Stroud, 1998, p. 127.

24. B. Rackham, *The Stained Glass Windows of Canterbury Cathedral*, Canterbury, 1957, pp. 49–51.

25. *The Life of St Edmund by Matthew Paris*, trans., ed. and with bibliography by C.H. Lawrence, Stroud, 1996, and Farmer, *Oxford Dictionary of Saints*, pp. 132–3.

26. See A. J. Duggan, 'Totius christianitas caput: the popes and the princes', in B. Bolton and A.J. Duggan (eds), *Adrian IV, the English Pope (1154–1159): Studies and Texts*, Aldershot, 2003, pp. 138–55 for the most recent summary.

27. See D.A. Bellenger and S. Fletcher, *Princes of the Church*, Stroud, 2000, pp. 3–5; J. Sayers, *Papal Judges Delegate in the Province of Canterbury 1198–1254*, Oxford, 1971.

28. Bellenger and Fletcher, *Princes*, pp. 5–6. See also B. Bolton and A.J. Duggan (eds), *Adrian IV*.

29. Six other archbishops were recipients of red hats: Robert Kilwardby (1278), Simon Langham (1368), John Kemp (1439), Thomas Bourchier (1467), John Morton (1493) and Reginald Pole (1536). In 1378 Archbishop William Courtenay refused to accept the honour.

30. C. Duggan, 'From the Conquest to the death of John', in C.H. Lawrence, ed., *The English Church and the Papacy in the Middle Ages*, new edn, Stroud, 1999, p. 115.

31.   F. Barlow, *The English Church 1066–1154*, London, 1979, p. 60.
32.   Barlow, *English Church*, p. 86. See also M. Brett, *The English Church Under Henry I*, Oxford, 1975.
33.   *English Historical Documents 2*, p. 705.
34.   See D. Knowles, *The Epsicopal Colleagues of Thomas Becket*, Cambridge, 1951.
35.   *English Historical Documents 2*, p. 758.
36.   Cheney, *Hubert Walter*, pp. 185–6.
37.   M.T. Clanchy, *From Memory to Written Record: England 1066–1307*, 2nd edn, Oxford, 1993, p. 73.
38.   C.R. Cheney, *From Becket to Langton*, Manchester, 1956, p. 177.

Chapter 3

1.   Kilwardby and the other archbishops who doubled up as cardinals are featured in Bellenger and Fletcher, *Princes of the Church*, chapters 1–2.
2.   Among the thirty variant spellings of his name, J.L. Peckham lists Patcham, Peccanus, Pecciano, Pectzan and Piccianor: *Archbishop Peckham as a Religious Educator*, Scottdale, Pennsylvania, 1934, p. 141. For a full biography of Pecham, see D.L. Douie, *Archbishop Pecham*, Oxford, 1952.
3.   J.H. Denton, *Robert Winchelsey and the Crown 1294–1313*, Cambridge, 1980, p. 5.
4.   St Augustine's was a running sore: half a century later Archbishops Sudbury and Courtenay experienced similar jurisdictional problems when they attempted to conduct visitations.
5.   On Stratford see N. M. Fryde, 'John Stratford, Bishop of Winchester, and the Crown, 1323–30', *Bulletin of the Institute of Historical Research* 44 (1971), pp. 153–61; R.M. Haines, *Archbishop John Stratford*, Pontifical Institute of Medieval Studies, Studies and texts 76, Toronto, 1986.
6.   W.L. Warren, 'A reappraisal of Simon Sudbury, bishop of London (1361–75) and archbishop of Canterbury (1375–81)', *Journal of Ecclesiastical History* 10 (1959), pp. 139–52.
7.   This was the treaty that transferred Calais to the diocese of Canterbury.
8.   F.R.H. Du Boulay, 'The fifteenth century', in C.H. Lawrence (ed.), *The English Church and the Papacy in the Middle Ages*, new edn, Stroud, 1999, p. 198.

9. A detailed account of his pre-Canterbury career is provided by M. Aston, *Thomas Arundel: a Study of Church Life in the Reign of Richard II*, Oxford, 1967.

10. Mowbray died in Venice in 1399.

11. See R.L. Storey, 'Episcopal king-makers in the fifteenth century', in B. Dobson (ed.), *The Church, Politics and Patronage in the Fifteenth Century*, Gloucester and New York, 1984, pp. 82–98.

12. A recent account of the Lancastrian usurpation is provided by N. Saul, *Richard II*, New Haven and London, 1997.

13. See M. Harvey, *England, Rome and the Papacy, 1417–1464: the Study of a Relationship*, Manchester and New York, 1993.

14. G.L. Harriss, *Cardinal Beaufort: a Study of Lancastrian Ascendancy and Decline*, Oxford, 1988, p. 272.

15. C. Allmand, *Henry V*, new edn, New Haven and London, 1997, p. 269.

16. The future primate Thomas Bradwardine accompanied Edward III in the invasion of Normandy which led to the Crécy campaign in 1346.

17. 25 October was also the feast of the translation of the relics of the eighth-century bishop of York, John of Beverley, one of those native saints who attracted great devotion in fifteenth-century England.

18. Archbishops Richard Scrope, Thomas Rotherham and Thomas Wolsey appear for York in the same series.

19. Arundel's other sister, Alice, married Thomas Holland, 2nd earl of Kent, which made her a sister-in-law to Richard II.

20. It has been calculated that Oxford produced 70% (98) of the bishops appointed between 1399 and 1499, and Cambridge 21% (29): H. Jewell, 'English bishops as educational benefactors in the later fifteenth century', in B. Dobson (ed.), *The Church, Politics and Patronage in the Fifteenth Century*, Gloucester and New York, 1984, p. 147.

21. A.B. Emden, *A Biographical Register of the University of Oxford to A.D. 1500*, vol. II, Oxford, 1958, pp. 1006, 1261; vol. III, Oxford, 1959, p. 1796. Emden is the most convenient source of biographical information about all the archbishops featured in this chapter who had any connection with Oxford.

22. On which see G. Leff, *Bradwardine and the Pelagians*, Cambridge, 1957.

23. See P. Partner, *The Pope's Men: the Papal Civil Service in the Renaissance*, Oxford, 1990.

24. B. Dobson, 'The monks of Canterbury in the later middle ages, 1220–1540', in P. Collinson, N. Ramsay and M. Sparks (eds), *A History of Canterbury Cathedral*, Oxford, 1995, p. 79.

25. J. Dahmus, *William Courtenay Archbishop of Canterbury 1381–1396*, University Park and London, 1966, pp. 107–60.

26. Douie, *Archbishop Pecham*, pp. 95–142.

27. Warren, 'A reappraisal of Simon Sudbury', p. 151.

28. Quoted by Dahmus, *William Courtenay*, p, 37.

29. T. Jones, R. Yeager, T. Dolan, A. Fletcher, J. Dor, *Who Murdered Chaucer? A Medieval Mystery*, London, 2003.

30. Aston, *Thomas Arundel*, p. 1.

31. Quoted by E.F. Jacob, *Henry Chichele*, London, 1967, p. 79.

32. *The Book of Margery Kempe*, trans. B. A. Windeatt, Harmondsworth, 1985, p. 72

33. Tatton-Brown, *Lambeth Palace*, pp 48–49.

34. Even in Lambeth, the archbishop did not always stay in his own palace. Thomas Bradwardine died in the neighbouring palace of the bishop of Rochester, five weeks and four days after his consecration, but without being enthroned.

35. Dobson, 'The monks of Canterbury', p. 110.

36. Dunstan was also a popular native saint in the early fifteenth century: Allmand, *Henry V*, p. 416

37. Dobson, 'The monks of Canterbury', p. 81.

Chapter 4

1. More, *Utopia*, ed. G.M. Logan, R.M. Adams and C.H. Miller, Cambridge, 1995, p.55.

2. *Ibid.*

3. F. Heal, *Of Prelates and Princes: a Study of the Economic and Social Position of the Tudor Episcopate*, Cambridge, 1980, pp. 330–3.

4. From the first year of Edward IV's reign, Deane was prior of the Gloucester Llanthony, daughter house of the original Llanthony in Monmouthshire. The mother house was the weaker of the two and, in 1481, Prior Deane obtained royal consent to unite the two foundations.

5. Attitudes towards Becket were a key feature of Pole's visitation articles in the 1550s.

6. At the same time the province of Canterbury acquired five new bishoprics with cathedrals in former monastic houses: Bristol, Gloucester, Oxford, Peterborough and Westminster. The last survived only from 1540 to 1550.

7. D. MacCulloch, *Thomas Cranmer; a Life*, New Haven and London, 1996; T.F. Mayer, *Reginald Pole: Prince and Prophet*, Cambridge, 2000.

8. Tatton-Brown, *Lambeth Palace*, p. 62; Mayer, *Reginald Pole*, pp. 320–30.

9. On Cranmer's library see D. G. Selwyn, *The Library of Thomas Cranmer*, The Oxford Bibliographical Society, 3rd series, I, Oxford, 1996.

10. *Matthew Parker's Legacy* (exhibition catalogue), Cambridge, 1975, p. 6.

11. *The Remains of Edmund Grindal*, DD, ed. W. Nicholson, Cambridge, 1843.

12. Collinson, P., *Archbishop Grindal 1519–1583: the Struggle for a Reformed Church*, London, 1979, p. 280.

13. Bancroft's last will and testament is printed in S.B. Babbage, *Puritanism and Richard Bancroft*, London, 1962, pp. 386–89. For details of his library see M.R. James, 'The history of Lambeth Palace Library', *Transactions of the Cambridge Bibliographical Society 3* (1959), pp. 1–31, and A. Cox-Johnson, 'Lambeth Palace Library, 1610–44', *Transactions of the Cambridge Bibliographical Society 2* (1955), pp. 105–26.

14. The school at Farnworth had been founded in 1507 by Bishop William Smith of Lincoln, who flourished through the patronage of Lady Margaret Beaufort. That Bancroft went on to Christ's College, Cambridge, is explained by the residual impact of the Smith-Beaufort connection.

15. Clarendon, *The History of the Rebellion and Civil Wars in England*, ed. W.D. Macray, Oxford, 1888, I, p. 118.

16. H.R. Trevor-Roper, *Archbishop Laud*, London, 2nd edn, 1962, p. 117.

17. P. Collinson, *The Religion of Protestants: the Church in English Society, 1559–1625*, Oxford, 1982, p. 90.

18. Quoted by Trevor-Roper, *Archbishop Laud*, p. 56.

19. One such is C. Carlton, *Archbishop William Laud*, London and New York, 1987. In his biography of Pole, Thomas Mayer has made an argument for the cardinal's homosexuality, but critics have drawn attention to the lack of supporting evidence.

20. Quoted by C. Hill, *The Economic Problems of the Church from Archbishop Whitgift to the Long Parliament*, Oxford, 1956, p. 28.

21. MacCulloch, *Thomas Cranmer*, p. 585.

22. Peter Gwyn suggests that the younger William Warham was the archbishop's son, rather than his nephew, but this is possibly coloured by what is known of Thomas Wolsey as a family man: P. Gwyn, *The King's Cardinal: the Rise and Fall of Thomas Wolsey*, London, 1990, p. 302.

23. At Salisbury and Canterbury Deane was assisted by John Bell, bishop of Mayo.

24. Gwyn, *The King's Cardinal*, p. 52.

25. *Ibid.*, p. 32.

26. *Ibid.*, p. 278.

27. MacCulloch, *Thomas Cranmer*, p. 31.

28. Mayer, *Reginald Pole*, pp. 47–8.

29. Apart from John Fisher of Rochester, Warham and his fellow bishops seem to have had little problem with Henry's request for an annulment and with the implications of the same.

30. At some point the second Mrs Cranmer travelled to England and bore her husband three children. She probably lived at the manor of Ford near Canterbury. The Act of Six Articles (1539) enforced clerical celibacy, but Mrs Cranmer remained a shadowy presence even after its repeal in 1547.

31. G. Redworth, *In Defence of the Church Catholic: the Life of Stephen Gardiner*, Oxford, 1990, p. 51.

32. MacCulloch, *Thomas Cranmer*, pp. 637–8.

33. See D. Fenlon, *Heresy and Obedience in Tridentine Italy: Cardinal Pole and the Counter Reformation*, Cambridge, 1972.

34. MacCulloch, *Thomas Cranmer*, pp. 354–5, 379–83.

35. Detailed coverage of Pole's years in England, first as legate and then as archbishop, is provided by Mayer, *Reginald Pole*, pp. 203–355.

36. *Correspondence of Matthew Parker, DD, Archbishop of Canterbury*, ed. J. Bruce and T.T. Perowne, Parker Society, Cambridge 1853, p. 57.

37. Quoted by G. Rupp, *Matthew Parker, a Man*, Cambridge, 1975, p 8.

38. Quoted by S.B. Babbage, *Puritanism and Richard Bancroft*, p. 5.

39. *Correspondence of Matthew Parker*, p. 478.

40. *Ibid.*, p. 70.

41. See P. Lake, *Moderate Puritanism and the Elizabethan Church*, Cambridge, 1982.

42. Brook, *Whitgift and the English Church*, p. 87.
43. R. Williams, *Anglican Identities*, London, 2004.
44. T. Fuller, *Worthies of England*, London, 1662.
45. Much of the former bishop's palace at Abergwili, now the Carmarthen-shire County Museum, post-dates a fire in 1903, but the chapel is still identified as that of Archbishop Laud.
46. P.A. Welsby, *George Abbot, the Unwanted Archbishop, 1562–1633*, London, 1962, p. 21.
47. *Ibid.*
48. See K. Fincham, *Prelate as Pastor: the Episcopate of James I*, Oxford, 1990.
49. W.B. Patterson, *King James I and VI and the Reunion of Christendom*, Cambridge, 1997, p. 219.
50. *Ibid.*, pp. 214–15.
51. Welsby, *George Abbot*, pp. 57–73.
52. *Ibid.*, pp. 77–8.
53. Archbishop Cranmer had been an enthusiastic hunter, perhaps making a point about rejection of the canon law of Rome through his choice of recreation.
54. Trevor-Roper, *Archbishop Laud*, pp. 110–11.
55. W. Laud, *Works*, ed. J. Bliss and W. Scott, Oxford 1847–60, VI, part 1, p. 133.
56. K. Sharpe, *The Personal Rule of Charles I*, New Haven and London, 1992, p. 286.
57. Quoted by Hill, *Economic Problems*, p 5.
58. Sharpe, *Personal Rule*, p. 288.
59. Quoted by Gwyn, *The King's Cardinal*, p. 35.
60. Quoted by Hill, *Economic Problems*, p. 27.
61. *Ibid.*, p. 41.
62. Sharpe, *Personal Rule*, pp. 333–45.
63. J. Milton, *Of Reformation in England and the Causes that Hitherto Have Hindered It*, 1651.

Chapter 5

1. Lady Holland, *Memoir*, vol. 1, London, 1855, p. 309.
2. The Ecclesiastical Commissioners remained in being until 1948, when

their responsibilities and those of the governors of Queen Anne's Bounty were assumed by the Church Commissioners.

3. A wealth of biographical details may be found in Secker's autobiography, compiled between 1766 and 1768, when the archbishop was well into his seventies: *The Autobiography of Thomas Secker, Archbishop of Canterbury*, ed. J. S. Macauley and R. W. Greaves, Lawrence, Kansas, 1988.

4. J.C.D. Clark, *English Society 1660–1832: Religion, Ideology and Politics During the Ancien Regime*, 2nd edn, Cambridge, 2000 pp. 100–2. See also N. Sykes, *Edmund Gibson*, Oxford, 1926.

5. A.E. McKilliam, *A Chronicle of the Archbishops of Canterbury*, London, 1913, p. 364.

6. *Ibid.*, p. 366.

7. N. Sykes, William Wake, *Archbishop of Canterbury, 1657–1737*, vol. I, Cambridge, 1957, p. 253.

8. *Ibid.*, pp. 242–3. An appendix (pp. 246–51) records the wide-ranging activity of his visitations.

9. J. Swift, *Intelligencer* 3, in *Works*, vol. 9, ed. W. Scott, Edinburgh, 1814, p. 298.

10. McKilliam, *Chronicle*, pp. 392–3.

11. O. Chadwick, *The Victorian Church*, vol. I, London, 1966, p. 12.

12. J. Gregory, 'Canterbury and the *ancien régime*: the dean and chapter, 1660–1828', in Collinson, Ramsay and Sparks (eds), *Canterbury Cathedral*, p. 216.

13. McKilliam, *Chronicle*, p. 387.

14. I. Grundy, *Lady Mary Wortley Montagu*, Oxford, 1999, p. 55.

15. Tatton-Brown, *Lambeth Palace*, p. 82.

16. K. Eustace, 'The post-Reformation Monuments', in Collinson, Ramsay and Sparks (eds), *Canterbury Cathedral*, pp. 538–9

17. Gregory, 'Canterbury and the *ancien régime*', pp. 213, 235.

18. Quoted by A.M.C. Stephenson, *The Victorian Archbishops of Canterbury*, Blewbury, 1991, p. 11.

19. Gregory, 'Canterbury and the *ancien régime*', p. 234.

20. J. Wickham Legg, *English Church life from the Reformation to the Tractarian Movement*, London, 1914, pp. 9–10.

21. W.R. Matthews and W.M. Atkins (eds), *A History of St Paul's Cathedral*, London, 1957, p. 337.

22. N. Sykes, *From Sheldon to Secker*, Cambridge, 1959, p. 223.

23.   B.H.G. Wormald, *Clarendon: Politics, History and Religion 1640–1660*, Cambridge, 1951, p. 239.

24.   See G. Rupp, *Religion in England 1688–1791*, Oxford, 1986, pp. 56–64, and G. Bennett, *The Tory Crisis in Church and State, 1688–1730*, Oxford, 1975.

25.   R. Sharp, 'New perspectives on the High Church tradition: historical background 1730–1780', in G. Rowell, ed., *Tradition Renewed*, London, 1986, p. 8.

26.   G. D'Oyly, *The Life of William Sancroft*, 2nd edn, London, 1860, p. 123.

27.   G.E. Rupp, *Religion in England*, p. 19.

28.   J. Gregory, *Restoration, Reformation and Reform, 1660–1828: Archbishops of Canterbury and their Diocese*, Oxford, 2000, p. 93.

29.   See J.C.D. Clark, *The Dynamics of Change*, Cambridge, 1982.

30.   *Ibid.*, p. xii.

31.   From T. Birch, *The Life of Dr John Tillotson*, London, 1752, pp. 323–4, quoted by P. Searby, *A History of the University of Cambridge* III: 1750–1870, Cambridge, 1997, p. 277.

32.   McKilliam, *Chronicle*, p. 368. Much good material is provided by A.W. Rowden, *The Primates of the Four Georges*, London, 1916.

33.   See G.F.A. Best, *Temporal Pillars: Queen Anne's Bounty, the Ecclesiastical Commission and the Church of England*, Cambridge, 1964.

34.   N. Sykes, *William Wake*, vol. 2, pp. 257–71.

35.   *Ibid.*, p. 267.

36.   J. Potter, *A Discourse of Church-Government*, London, 1707, p. 11.

37.   Clark, *English Society*, pp. 111–12.

38.   N. Sykes, *From Sheldon to Secker*, p. 222.

39.   H.M. McLeod, *Religion and the People of Western Europe 1789–1989*, 2nd edn, Oxford, 1997, p. 16.

40.   P.B. Nockles, *The Oxford Movement in Context: Anglican High Churchmanship 1760–1857*, Cambridge, 1994, p. 271.

41.   N. Sykes, *Church and State in England in the XVIIIth Century*, Cambridge, 1934, p. 144.

42.   J.C.D. Clark, *English Society*, p. 26. 'The bulk of the people submit,' wrote Bishop Samuel Horsley in 1790, 'with much complacency, to the religion of the state; and, where no undue arts are employed to perplex their understandings, do not usually trouble themselves or their neighbours with theological niceties.'

43. W.R. Ward, 'The eighteenth-century Church: a European view', in J Walsh, C. Haydon and S. Taylor (eds), *The Church of England c. 1689–c. 1833: from Toleration to Tractarianism*, Cambridge, 1993, p. 285

44. See W. Jacob, 'The development of the Anglican Communion', in S. Platten (ed.), *Anglicanism and the Western Christian Tradition: Continuity, Change and the Search for Communion*, Norwich, 2003, pp. 192–206.

Chapter 6

1. A.M.G. Stephenson, *Anglicanism and the Lambeth Conferences*, London, 1978, p. 72.

2. *Ibid.*, p. 2.

3. W. Purcell, *Fisher of Lambeth*, London, 1969, p. 218. In contrast, Lang disliked travel. As archbishop he made just one train journey and only then with reluctance: see T. Beeson, *The Bishops*, London, 2002, p. 23.

4. A.L. Rowse, *Friends and Contemporaries*, London, 1989.

5. In addition to the Temples and their guests, twelve servants were listed in the census for the Archbishop's Palace in Canterbury. The same source records that Randall and Edith Davidson were then residing at the Castle, Farnham, together with a chaplain and eighteen servants. Meanwhile, the thirty-seven-year-old Cosmo Gordon Lang headed an entirely clerical household at the vicarage in Fratton Road, Portsmouth, where his half dozen resident curates included Cyril Garbett, who went on to succeed him as archbishop of York and was tipped for Canterbury in 1942 but passed over as too elderly. Geoffrey Fisher appears in the 1901 census as a thirteen-year-old boarder at Marlborough College.

6. J.G. Lockhart, *Cosmo Gordon Lang*, London, 1949, p. 40.

7. *Ibid.*, pp. 57–8; p. 462 for the text of the Mallard Song.

8. M. Cowling, *Religion and Public Doctrine in Modern England III*, Cambridge, 2001, p. 281.

9. *Ibid.*, pp. 271–2.

10. For a detailed study of broadcasting, see K.M. Wolfe, *The Churches and the British Broadcasting Corporation*, London, 1984, especially pp. 60–5 for the work of F. A. Iremonger, Temple's biographer, and pp. 543–6 for a transcript of a 1942 talk between Ronald Selby Wright and Temple,

'The padre asks the archbishop'. For the political implications of William Temple's broadcasting, see A. Briggs, *The History of Broadcasting in the United Kingdom*, vol 3: *The War of Words*, London, 1970, pp. 621–2. Temple's enthronement ceremony was broadcast in 1942.

11. A. Hastings in Carpenter, *Cantuar*, 3rd edn, p. 526.

12. B. Palmer, *A Class of their Own*, Lewes, 1997, p. 2.

13. B. Palmer, *High and Mitred*, London, 1992, p. 261.

14. Palmer, *A Class of their Own*, p. 189.

15. The London College of Divinity, Cuddesdon and Trinity College, Bristol, respectively. The pre-Canterbury careers of the primates from Longley to Carey are neatly tabulated by Adrian Hastings in *Robert Runcie*, London, 1991, p. 29.

16. D. Newsome, *Godliness and Good Learning*, London, 1961, p. 195.

17. D.L. Edwards, *Leaders of the Church of England, 1828–1944*, London, 1971, p. 123.

18. Palmer, *High and Mitred*, p. 125.

19. A. Wilkinson, *The Church of England and the First World War*, London, 1978, p. 151.

20. Lockhart, *Cosmo Gordon Lang*, pp. 460–1.

21. *Ibid.*, p. 382.

22. *Ibid.*, p. 406, n. 1.

23. *Ibid.*, p. 421.

24. Palmer, *High and Mitred*, p. 221.

25. Edwards, *Leaders*, p. 327.

26. Cowling, *Religion and Public Doctrine*, III, p. 291.

27. C. Bryant, *Possible Dreams: a Personal History of the British Christian Socialists*, London, 1996, p. 212.

28. Purcell, *Fisher of Lambeth*, p. 211.

29. Palmer, *High and Mitred*, p. 253.

30. Carpenter, *Cantuar*, p. 508.

31. Purcell, *Fisher of Lambeth*, p. 216.

32. See D. Cannadine, 'The context, performance and meaning of ritual: the British monarchy and the "invention of tradition", *c.* 1820–1977', in E. Hobsbawm and T. Ranger, *The Invention of Tradition*, Cambridge, 1983.

33. Palmer, *High and Mitred*, p. 253.

34. Quoted by O. Chadwick, *Michael Ramsey: a Life*, Oxford, 1990, p. 353.

35. *Ibid.*, p. 210.

36. *Ibid.*, p. 157.

37. M. Duggan, *Runcie: the Making of an Archbishop*, London, 1983; M. De-la-Noy, *Michael Ramsey*, London, 1990; J. Mantle, *Archbishop: a Portrait of Robert Runcie*, London, 1991; H. Carpenter, *Robert Runcie: the Reluctant Archbishop*, London, 1996.

38. Hastings in Carpenter, *Cantuar*, 3rd edn, p. 538.

39. H. Carpenter, *Robert Runcie*, p. 256. Runcie was awarded the Military Cross in 1945.

40. *Ibid.*, pp. 284–5.

41. G. Carey, *Sharing a Vision*, London, 1993, p. 73.

42. R. Shortt, *Rowan Williams: an Introduction*, London, 2003, p. 125.

43. R. Davidson and W. Benham, *Life of Archibald Campbell Tait*, London, 1891, vol I, p. 184.

44. See R.W. Franklin (ed.), *Anglican Orders*, London, 1966.

45. B. and M. Pawley, *Rome and Canterbury Through Four Centuries*, London, 1974, p. 289.

46. Ramsey was a later chairman, but Coggan declined the invitation when his turn came, contributing to his lower international profile.

47. See J.M. Turner, *Conflict and Reconciliation: Studies in Methodism and Ecumenism in England 1740–1982*, London, 1985.

48. Purcell, *Fisher of Lambeth*, p. 288.

49. M. De-la-Noy, *Michael Ramsey*, p. 152.

50. E.W. Benson, *The Cathedral: its Necessary Place in the Life and Work of the Church*, London, 1978.

51. In recent times the house has been home to the Royal School of Church Music, but is currently advertised as a venue for weddings.

52. Lockhart, *Cosmo Gordon Lang*, p. 318.

53. K. Robbins, 'The Twentieth Century, 1898–1994', in P. Collinson, N. Ramsay and M. Sparks (eds), *A History of Canterbury Cathedral*, Oxford, 1995, p. 315.

54. S. Howatch, *Glittering Images*, London, 1987.

55. Quoted by D. Edwards, *Leaders*, p. 199.

Bibliography

General

N. Aston and M. Cragoe (eds), *Anticlericalism in Britain c. 1500–1914*, Stroud, 2000

D.A. Bellenger and S. Fletcher, *Princes of the Church: a History of the English Cardinals*, Stroud, 2000

I. Bradley, *God Save the Queen: the Spiritual Dimension of Monarchy*, London, 2002

The Canons of the Church of England, London, 1969

E. Carpenter, with additional material by Adrian Hastings, *Cantuar: the Archbishops in their Office*, 3rd edn, London, 1997

The Church of England Year Book

P. Collinson, N. Ramsay and M. Sparks (eds), *A History of Canterbury Cathedral*, Oxford, 1995

Crockford's Clerical Directory

G.J. Cuming, *A History of Anglican Liturgy*, London, 1969

E. Duffy, *Saints and Sinners: a History of the Popes*, London, 1997

W.F. Hook, *Lives of the Archbishops of Canterbury*, 12 vols, London, 1860–76

E. Jones, *The English Nation: the Great Myth*, Stroud, 1998

Oxford Dictionary of National Biography, Oxford, 2004

B. and M. Pawley, *Rome and Canterbury Through Four Centuries: a Study of the Relations between the Church of Rome and the Anglican Churches, 1530–1973*, London, 1974

T. Tatton-Brown, *Lambeth Palace: a History of the Archbishops of Canterbury and their Houses*, London, 2000

1   597–1070: Conversion and Consolidation

F. Barlow, *The English Church 1000–1066*, London, 1963

Bede, *Ecclesiastical History of the English People*, ed. B. Colgrave and R.A.B. Mynors, Oxford, 1969

N. Brooks, *The Early History of the Church of Canterbury*, London, 1984

——, 'The career of St Dunstan', in N. Ramsay, M. Sparks and T. Tatton-Brown, *St Dunstan: His Life, Times and Cult*, Woodbridge, 1992, pp. 1–23

——, 'The Anglo-Saxon cathedral community, 597–1070', in P. Collinson, N. Ramsay and M. Sparks (eds), *A History of Canterbury Cathedral*, Oxford, 1995, pp. 1–37

J. Crook, 'The mortuary chests and the bones of Archbishop Stigand', *Winchester Cathedral Record* 73 (2004), pp. 21–31.

C.M. Cusack, *The Rise of Christianity in Northern Europe, 300–1000*, London, 1999

D.J. Dales, 'The spirit of the *Regularis concordia* and the hand of St Dunstan', in N. Ramsay, M. Sparks and T. Tatton-Brown, *St Dunstan: His Life, Times and Cult*, Woodbridge, 1992, pp. 45–56

F.R.H. Du Boulay, *The Lordship of Canterbury: an Essay on Medieval Society*, London, 1966

D.H. Farmer, *The Oxford Dictionary of the Saints*, 2nd edn, Oxford, 1987

——, *Benedict's Disciples*, 2nd edn, Leominster, 1995

R. Fletcher, *The Conversion of Europe*, London, 1997

R. Gameson (ed.), *St Augustine and the Conversion of England*, Stroud, 1999

R. Gem (ed.), *English Heritage Book of St Augustine's Abbey*, Canterbury, London, 1997

J.W. Lamb, *The Archbishopric of Canterbury: from its Foundation to the Norman Conquest*, London, 1971

M. Lapidge (ed.), *Archbishop Theodore: Commemorative Studies on his Life and Influence*, Cambridge, 1995

R.A. Markus, *Gregory the Great and His World*, Cambridge, 1997

H. Mayr-Harting, 'The West: the age of conversion (700–1050)', in J. McManners, (ed.), *The Oxford Illustrated History of Christianity*, Oxford, 1990

V. Ortenberg, *The English Church and the Continent in the Tenth and Eleventh Centuries: Cultural, Spiritual and Artistic Exchanges*, Oxford, 1992

D. Parsons (ed.), *Tenth-Century Studies*, London, 1975

N. Ramsay and M. Sparks, *The Image of St Dunstan*, Canterbury, 1988

B. Yorke (ed.), *Bishop Aethelwold: his Career and Influence*, Woodbridge, 1988

I. Wood, *The Missionary Life: Saints and the Evangelisation of Europe 400–1050*, Harlow, 2001

2   1070–1270: Ecclesia anglicana reformata

Anselm, *Prayers and Meditations*, ed. B. Ward, Harmondsworth, 1973

F. Barlow, *The English Church 1066–1154*, London, 1979

——, *Thomas Becket*, London, 1986

The Correspondence of Thomas Becket, Archbishop of Canterbury 1162–1170, ed. and trans. A. J. Duggan, 2 vols, Oxford, 2000

B. Bolton, '101 uses for a dead archbishop' in H. Chadwick (ed.), *Not Angels, but Anglicans: a History of Christianity in the British Isles*, London, 2000, pp. 66–75

B. Bolton and A.J. Duggan (eds.), *Adrian IV, the English Pope (1154–1159): Studies and Texts*, Aldershot, 2003

M. Brett, *The English Church Under Henry I*, Oxford, 1975.

J. Butler, *The Quest for Becket's Bones*, New Haven and London, 1995

J.I. Catto (ed.), *The History of the University of Oxford, I: The Early Oxford Schools*, Oxford, 1984

C.R. Cheney, *From Becket to Langton*, Manchester, 1956

——, *Hubert Walter*, London, 1967

M.T. Clanchy, *From Memory to Written Record: England 1066–1307*, 2nd edn, Oxford, 1979

H.E.J. Cowderey, *Lanfranc*, Oxford, 2003

D.C. Douglas and G.W. Greenaway, *English Historical Documents*, vol. 2: 1042–1189, London, 1953

A.J. Duggan, '*Totius Christianitas caput*: the popes and the princes', in B. Bolton and A.J. Duggan (eds), *Adrian IV, the English Pope (1154–1159): Studies and Texts*, Aldershot, 2003, pp. 138–55

——, *Thomas Becket*, London, 2004

C. Duggan, 'From the Conquest to the death of John', in C.H. Lawrence, ed., *The English Church and the Papacy in the Middle Ages*, new edn, Stroud, 1999, pp.

G.R. Evans, *Anselm*, London, 1989

R. Foreville, *Thomas Becket: Actes du Colloque International de Sédières*, Paris, 1975

M. Gibson, *Lanfranc of Bec*, Oxford, 1978

——, 'Normans and Angevins, 1070–1220', in P. Collinson, N. Ramsay and M. Sparks (eds), *A History of Canterbury Cathedral*, Oxford, 1995, pp. 38–68

Lanfranc, *The Monastic Constitutions of Lanfranc*, ed. and trans D. Knowles, rev. edn, C.N.L. Brooke, Oxford, 2002

D.E. Luscombe and G. R. Evans (eds), *Anselm, Aosta, Bec and Canterbury*, Sheffield, 1996

C. Knightly (ed.), *A Mirror of Medieval Wales: Gerald of Wales and his Journey of 1188*, Cardiff, 1988

D. Knowles, *The Episcopal Colleagues of Thomas Becket*, Cambridge, 1951

——, 'Archbishop Thomas Becket', in *The Historian and Character*, Cambridge, 1963

——, *Thomas Becket*, London, 1970

C.H. Lawrence, *St Edmund of Abingdon: a Study in Hagiography and History*, Oxford, 1960

M. Morgan, *The English Lands of the Abbey of Bec*, Oxford, 1946

The Life of St Edmund by Matthew Paris, trans., ed. and with bibliography by C.H. Lawrence, Stroud, 1996

B. Rackham, *The Stained Glass Windows of Canterbury Cathedral*, Canterbury, 1957

J.C. Robertson and J. B. Sheppard, *Materials for the History of Thomas Becket*, 7 vols, Rolls Series, London, 1875–85.

A. Saltman, *Theobald Archbishop of Canterbury*, London, 1956

J. Sayers, *Papal Judges Delegate in the Province of Canterbury 1198–1254*, Oxford, 1971

R.W. Southern, ed., *The Life of St Anselm by Eadmer*, Oxford, 1962

——, *Saint Anselm: a Portrait in a Landscape*, Cambridge, 1991

M. Walsh, *Warriors of the Lord: the Military Orders of Christendom*, Alresford, 2003

L. E. Wilshire, 'Boniface of Savoy, Carthusian archbishop of Canterbury 1207–70', *Analecta Cartusiana* 31 (1977), pp. 1–90

3   1270–1486: From Mendicants to Princes

C. Allmand, *Henry V*, new edn, New Haven and London, 1997

M. Aston, *Thomas Arundel: a Study of Church Life in the Reign of Richard II*, Oxford, 1967

J.I. Catto (ed.), *The History of the University of Oxford, I: The Early Oxford Schools*, Oxford, 1984

J.I. Catto and R. Evans (eds), *The History of the University of Oxford, II: Late Medieval Oxford*, Oxford, 1992

J. Dahmus, *William Courtenay Archbishop of Canterbury 1381–1396*, University Park and London, 1966

R.G. Davies, 'Thomas Arundel as archbishop of Canterbury, 1396–1414', *Journal of Ecclesiastical History* 14 (1973), pp. 9–21

J.H. Denton, *Robert Winchelsey and the Crown 1294–1313*, Cambridge, 1980

B. Dobson (ed.), *The Church, Politics and Patronage in the Fifteenth Century*, Gloucester and New York, 1984

——, 'The monks of Canterbury in the later Middle Ages, 1220–1540', in P. Collinson, N. Ramsay and M. Sparks (eds), *A History of Canterbury Cathedral*, Oxford, 1995, pp. 69–153

D.L. Douie, *Archbishop Pecham*, Oxford, 1952

——, 'The fifteenth century' in C.H. Lawrence (ed.), *The English Church in the Middle Ages*, new edn, Stroud, 1999, pp. 195–242

A.B. Emden, *A Biographical Register of the University of Oxford to AD 1500*, 3 vols, Oxford, 1957–9

N.M. Fryde, 'John Stratford, Bishop of Winchester, and the Crown, 1323–30', *Bulletin of the Institute of Historical Research* 44 (1971), pp. 153–61

A. Goodman, *John of Gaunt: the Exercise of Princely Power in Fourteenth-Century Europe*, Harlow, 1992

G.L. Harriss, *Cardinal Beaufort: a Study of Lancastrian Ascendancy and Decline*, Oxford, 1988

R.M. Haines, *Archbishop John Stratford*, Pontifical Institute of Medieval Studies, Studies and texts 76, Toronto, 1986

——, *Ecclesia Anglicana: Studies in the English Church of the Later Middle Ages*, Toronto, 1989

G. Holmes, *The Good Parliament*, Oxford, 1975

E.F. Jacob, *Henry Chichele and the Ecclesiastical Politics of His Age*, London, 1952

——, *Archbishop Henry Chichele*, London, 1967

H. Jewell, 'English bishops as educational benefactors in the later fifteenth century', in B. Dobson (ed.), *The Church, Politics and Patronage in the Fifteenth Century*, Gloucester and New York, 1984, pp. 146–167

T. Jones, R. Yeager, T. Dolan, A. Fletcher, J. Dor, *Who Murdered Chaucer? A Medieval Mystery*, London, 2003

G. Leff, *Bradwardine and the Pelagians*, Cambridge, 1957

W.E. Lunt, *Financial Relations of the Papacy with England, 1327–1534*, 2 vols, Cambridge, Mass, 1962

M.H. Keen, *English Society in the Later Middle Ages 1350–1500*, Harmondsworth, 1990

The Book of Margery Kempe, trans. B. A. Windeatt, Harmondsworth, 1985

J.L. Kirby, *Henry IV of England*, London, 1970

D. Knowles, *The Religious Orders in England* ii: *The End of the Middle Ages*, Cambridge, 1955

W.M. Ormrod, *The Reign of Edward III: Crown and Political Society in England 1327–77*, New Haven and London, 1990

J.L. Peckham, *Archbishop Peckham as a Religious Educator*, Yale Studies in Religion 7, Scottdale, Pennsylvania, 1934

N. Saul, *Richard II*, New Haven and London, 1997

R.L. Storey, 'Episcopal king-makers in the fifteenth century', in B. Dobson (ed.), *The Church, Politics and Patronage in the Fifteenth Century*, Gloucester and New York, 1984, pp. 82–98

W.L. Warren, 'A reappraisal of Simon Sudbury, bishop of London (1361–75) and archbishop of Canterbury (1375–81)', *Journal of Ecclesiastical History* 10 (1959), pp. 139–152

C. Wilson, 'The medieval monuments', in P. Collinson, N. Ramsay and M. Sparks, (eds), *A History of Canterbury Cathedral*, Oxford, 1995, pp. 451–510

B.P. Wolffe, *Henry VI*, London, 1981

J.R. Wright, *The Church and the English Crown, 1305–1334: a Study based on the Register of Archbishop Walter Reynolds*, Toronto, 1980

4   1486–1660: Canterbury between Rome and Geneva

P. Ayris and D. Selwyn (eds), *Thomas Cranmer, Churchman and Scholar*, Woodbridge, 1993

S.B. Babbage, *Puritanism and Richard Bancroft*, London, 1962

V.J.K. Brook, *A Life of Archbishop Parker*, Oxford, 1962

——, *Whitgift and the English Church*, London, 1957

P.N. Brooks, *Cranmer in Context*, Cambridge, 1989

C. Carlton, *Archbishop William Laud*, London and New York, 1987

P. Collinson, *Archbishop Grindal 1519–1583: the Struggle for a Reformed Church*, London, 1979

——, *The Religion of Protestants: the Church in English Society, 1559–1625*, Oxford, 1982

——, D. McKitterick and E. Leedham-Green, *Andrew Perne: Quatercentenary Studies*, Cambridge, 1991

——, 'The Protestant cathedral, 1541–1660', in P. Collinson, N. Ramsay and M. Sparks (eds), *A History of Canterbury Cathedral*, Oxford, 1995, pp. 154–203

A Cox-Johnson, 'Lambeth Palace Library, 1610–1644', *Transactions of the Cambridge Bibliographical Society* 2 (1955), pp. 105–26

C.S.L. Davies, 'Bishop John Morton, the Holy See and the accession of Henry VII, *English Historical Review* 102 (1987), pp. 2–30

J. Davies, *The Caroline Captivity of the Church*, Oxford, 1992

A.B. Emden, *A Biographical Register of the University of Oxford to AD 1500*, 3 vols, Oxford, 1957–59

D. Fenlon, *Heresy and Obedience in Tridentine Italy: Cardinal Pole and the Counter Reformation*, Cambridge, 1972

K. Fincham, *Prelate as Pastor: the Episcopate of James I*, Oxford, 1990

—— (ed.), *The Early Stuart Church, 1603–1642*, Basingstoke, 1993

T. Fuller, *Worthies of England*, London, 1662

The Remains of Edmund Grindal, DD, ed. W. Nicholson, Cambridge, 1843

P. Gwyn, *The King's Cardinal: the Rise and Fall of Thomas Wolsey*, London, 1990

F. Heal, *Of Prelates and Princes: a Study of the Economic and Social Position of the Tudor Episcopate*, Cambridge, 1980

——, 'The archbishops of Canterbury and the practice of hospitality', *Journal of Ecclesiastical History* 33 (1982), pp. 544–63

C.M. Hibbard, *Charles I and the Popish Plot*, Chapel Hill, North Carolina, 1983

C. Hill, *The Economic Problems of the Church from Archbishop Whitgift to the Long Parliament*, Oxford, 1956

S.M. Holland, 'George Abbot: the "wanted archbishop"', *Church History* 56 (1987), pp. 172–87

W.S Hudson, *The Cambridge Connection and the Elizabethan Settlement of 1559*, Durham, North Carolina, 1980

M.R. James, 'The history of Lambeth Palace Library', *Transactions of the Cambridge Bibliographical Society* 3 (1959), pp. 1–31

M.K. Jones and M.G. Underwood, *The King's Mother: Lady Margaret Beaufort, Countess of Richmond and Derby*, Cambridge, 1992

P. Lake, *Anglicans and Puritans? Presbyterianism and English Conformist Thought from Whitgift to Hooker*, Cambridge, 1988

——, *Moderate Puritanism and the Elizabethan Church*, Cambridge, 1982

W. Laud, *Works*, ed. J. Bliss and W. Scott, 7 vols, Oxford, 1847–60

D. Lindley, *The Trials of Frances Howard: Fact and Fiction at the Court of King James*, London and New York, 1993

D.M. Loades, *The Oxford Martyrs*, London, 1970

R. Lockyer, *Buckingham: the Life and Political Career of George Villiers, First Duke of Buckingham 1592–1628*, Harlow, 1981

D. MacCulloch, *Thomas Cranmer: a Life*, New Haven and London, 1996

——, *Reformation: Europe's House Divided 1490–1700*, London, 2003

J. McConica (ed.), *The History of the University of Oxford*, III: *The Collegiate University*, Oxford, 1986

A. McGrath, *In the Beginning: the Story of the King James Bible and How it Changed a Nation, a Language and a Culture*, London, 2001

Matthew Parker's Legacy, exhibition catalogue, Cambridge, 1975

T.F. Mayer, *Reginald Pole: Prince and Prophet*, Cambridge, 2000

J. Milton, *Of Reformation in England and the Causes that Hitherto have Hindered it 1651*

T. More, *Utopia*, ed. G.M. Logan, R.M. Adams and C.H. Miller, Cambridge, 1995

Correspondence of Matthew Parker, DD, Archbishop of Canterbury, ed. J. Bruce and T.T. Perowne, Cambridge, 1853

W.B. Patterson, *King James I and VI and the Reunion of Christendom*, Cambridge, 1997

G. Redworth, *In defence of the Church Catholic: the Life of Stephen Gardiner*, Oxford, 1990

J. Ridley, *Thomas Cranmer*, Oxford, 1966

G. Rupp, *Matthew Parker, a Man*, Cambridge, 1975

J.J. Scarisbrick, *Henry VIII*, London, 1968

D.G. Selwyn, *The Library of Thomas Cranmer*, The Oxford Bibliographical Society, 3rd series, I, Oxford, 1996

K. Sharpe, *The Personal Rule of Charles I*, New Haven and London, 1992

M. Stieg, *Laud's Laboratory: the Diocese of Bath and Wells in the Early Seventeenth Century*, East Brunswick, NJ, 1982

H. Trevor-Roper, *Archbishop Laud*, 2nd edn, London, 1962

——, 'Laudianism and Political Power', in *Catholics, Anglicans and Puritans: 17th century Essays*, Chicago and London, 1987

N. Tyacke, *Anti-Calvinism: the Rise of English Arminianism, c. 1590–1640*, Oxford, 1987

—— (ed), *The History of the University of Oxford*, III: *Seventeenth-century Oxford*, Oxford, 1997

P.A. Welsby, *George Abbot: the Unwanted Archbishop 1562–1633*, London, 1962

The Work of Archbishop John Williams, ed. B. Williams, Sutton Courtenay, 1980

R. Williams, *Anglican Identities*, London, 2004

5   1660–1848: Ecclesia Anglicana Instaurata

L. Adams (ed.), *William Wake's Gallican Correspondence and Related Documents, 1716–1731*, 2 vols, New York, 1988

G.W.O. Addleshaw and F. Etchells, *The Architectural Setting of Anglican Worship*, London, 1958

G. Bennett, *The Tory Crisis in Church and State, 1688–1730*, Oxford, 1975

G.F.A. Best, *Temporal Pillars: Queen Anne's Bounty, the Ecclesiastical Commissioners and the Church of England*, Cambridge, 1964

O. Chadwick, *The Victorian Church*, vol. 1, London, 1966

J.C.D. Clark, *The Dynamics of Change*, Cambridge, 1982

——, *English Society 1688–1832: Religion, Ideology and Politics During the Ancien Regime*, 2nd edn, Cambridge, 2000

E. Cruickshanks, *The Glorious Revolution*, London, 2000

G. D'Oyly, *The Life of William Sancroft*, 2nd edn, London, 1860

K. Eustace, 'The post-Reformation monuments', in P. Collinson, N. Ramsay and M. Sparks (eds), *A History of Canterbury Cathedral*, Oxford, 1995, pp. 511–52

G. Every, *The High Church Party 1688–1718*, London, 1956

J. Gregory, 'Canterbury and the *ancien régime*: the dean and chapter, 1660–1828', in P. Collinson, N. Ramsay and M. Sparks (eds), *A History of Canterbury Cathedral*, Oxford, 1995, pp. 204–255

——, *Restoration, Reformation and Reform, 1660–1828: Archbishops of Canterbury and their Diocese*, Oxford, 2000

I. Grundy, *Lady Mary Wortley Montagu*, Oxford, 1999

W. Jacob, 'The development of the Anglican Communion', in S. Platten (ed.), *Anglicanism and the Western Christian Tradition: Continuity, Change and the Search for Communion*, Norwich, 2003, pp. 192–206

D. Keene, A. Burns and A. Saint (eds), *St Paul's: the Cathedral Church of London 604–2004*, London, 2004

W.R. Matthews and W. M. Atkins (eds), *A History of St Paul's Cathedral*, London, 1957

A.E. McKilliam, *A Chronicle of the Archbishops of Canterbury*, London, 1913

H.M. McLeod, *Religion and the People of Western Europe 1789–1989*, 2nd edn, Oxford, 1997

P.B. Nockles, *The Oxford Movement in Context: Anglican High Churchmanship 1760–1857*, Cambridge, 1994

A.W. Rowden, *The Primates of the Four Georges*, London, 1916

G. Rupp, *Religion in England 1688–1791*, Oxford, 1986

P. Searby, *A History of the University of Cambridge*, III: 1750–1870, Cambridge, 1997

The Autobiography of Thomas Secker, Archbishop of Canterbury, ed. J. S. Macauley and R.W. Greaves, Lawrence, Kansas, 1988

R. Sharp, 'New perspectives on the High Church tradition: historical background 1730–1780', in G. Rowell (ed.), *Tradition Renewed*, London, 1986, pp. 4–23

R.A. Soloway, *Prelates and People: Ecclesiastical Social Thought in England 1783–1852*, London, 1969

W.M. Spellman, *The Latitudinarians and the Church of England, 1660–1700*, London, 1983

A.M.C. Stephenson, *The Victorian Archbishops of Canterbury*, Blewbury, 1991

V.D. Sutch, *Gilbert Sheldon: Architect of Anglican Survival, 1640–1675*, The Hague, 1973

N. Sykes, *Edmund Gibson*, Oxford, 1926.

——, *Church and State in England in the XVIIIth Century*, Cambridge, 1934

——, *William Wake, Archbishop of Canterbury, 1657–1737*, 2 vols, Cambridge, 1957

——, *From Sheldon to Secker*, Cambridge, 1959

W.R. Ward, 'The eighteenth-century Church: a European view', in J. Walsh, C. Haydon and S. Taylor (eds), *The Church of England c. 1689-c. 1833: from Toleration to Tractarianism*, Cambridge, 1993, pp. 285–98

J. Wickham Legg, *English Church Life from the Reformation to the Tractarian Movement*, London, 1914

B.H.G. Wormald, *Clarendon: Politics, History and Religion 1640–1660*, Cambridge, 1951

6   1848–2004: Gain and Loss

P. Barrett, *Barchester: English Cathedral Life in the Nineteenth Century*, London, 1993

S. Bates, *A Church at War: Anglicans and Homosexuality*, London, 2004

T. Beeson, *The Bishops*, London, 2002

G.K.A. Bell, *Randall Davidson, Archbishop of Canterbury*, 2 vols, Oxford, 1935

A. Briggs, *The History of Broadcasting in the United Kingdom*, vol 3: *The War of Words*, London, 1970

O.J. Brose, *Church and Parliament: the Reshaping of the Church of England 1828–1860*, Stanford, California, 1951

C. Bryant, *Possible Dreams: a Personal History of the British Christian Socialists*, London, 1996

G. Carey, *Sharing a Vision*, London, 1993

——, *Know the Truth: a Memoir*, London, 2004

E. Carpenter, *Archbishop Fisher: his Life and Times*, Norwich, 1991

H. Carpenter, *Robert Runcie: the Reluctant Archbishop*, London, 1996

O. Chadwick, *Michael Ramsey: a Life*, Oxford, 1990

M. Cowling, *Religion and Public Debate in Modern England*, 3 vols, Cambridge, 1980, 1985 and 2001

H. Davies, *Worship and Theology in England: the Ecumenical Century, 1900–1965*, Princeton, New Jersey, 1965

R. Davidson and W. Benham, *Life of Archibald Campbell Tait*, 2 vols, London, 1891

M. De-la-Noy, *Michael Ramsey*, London, 1990

M. Duggan, *Runcie: the Making of an Archbishop*, London, 1983

D. Edwards, *Leaders of the Church of England 1828–1944*, London, 1971

R.W. Franklin (ed.), *Anglican Orders*, London, 1966

A.S. Frere, (ed.), *Grand Lodge 1717–1967*, Oxford, 1967

A. Hastings, *A History of English Christianity, 1920–1985*, London, 1986

——, *Robert Runcie*, London, 1991

——, addition to E. Carpenter, *Cantuar*, 3rd edn, London, 1997, pp. 516–60

S. Howatch, *Glittering Images*, London, 1987

F.A. Iremonger, *William Temple*, Oxford, 1948

W.M. Jacob, *The Making of the Anglican Church Worldwide*, London, 1997

J. Kent, *William Temple: Church, State and Society in Britain, 1880–1950*, Cambridge, 1992

R. Lloyd, *The Church of England 1900–1965*, London, 1966

F. Longford, *The Bishops: a Study of Leaders in the Church Today*, London, 1986

J. Mantle, *Archbishop: a Portrait of Robert Runcie*, London, 1991

P.T. Marsh, *The Victorian Church in Decline: Archbishop Tait and the Church of England 1868–1882*, London, 1969

D. Newsome, *Godliness and Good Learning: Four Studies on a Victorian Ideal*, London, 1961

P.B. Nockles, 'Aspects of cathedral life, 1828–1898', in P. Collinson, N. Ramsay and M. Sparks (eds), *A History of Canterbury Cathedral*, Oxford, 1995, pp. 256–96

E. Norman, *Church and Society in England 1770–1970: a Historical Study*, Oxford, 1967

——, *The Victorian Christian Socialists*, Cambridge, 1987

——, *An Anglican Catechism*, London, 2001

——, *Anglican Difficulties: a New Syllabus of Errors*, London, 2004

D. O'Connor (ed.), *Three Centuries of Mission: the United Society for the Propagation of the Gospel 1701–2000*, London, 2000

W. Oddie, *The Crockford's File: Gareth Bennett and the Death of the Anglican Mind*, London, 1989

G. Palmer and N. Lloyd, *Father of the Bensons: the Life of Edward White Benson Sometime Archbishop of Canterbury*, Harpenden, 1998

B. Palmer, *High and Mitred: Prime Ministers as Bishop-makers 1837–1977*, London, 1992

——, *A Class of Their Own*, Lewes, 1997

M. Pawley, *Donald Coggan: Servant of Christ*, London, 1987

W. Purcell, *Fisher of Lambeth: a Portrait from Life*, London, 1969.

K. Robbins, 'The twentieth century, 1898–1994', in P. Collinson, N. Ramsay and M. Sparks (eds), *A History of Canterbury Cathedral*, Oxford, 1995, pp. 297–340

A.L. Rowse, *Friends and Contemporaries*, London, 1989

G. Rowell (ed.), *Tradition Renewed: the Oxford Movement Conference Papers*, London, 1986

E.G. Sandford (ed.), *Memoirs of Archbishop Temple by Seven Friends*, 2 vols, London, 1906

N. Scotland, *The Life and Work of John Bird Sumner, Evangelical Archbishop*, Leominster, 1995

R. Shortt, *Rowan Williams: an Introduction*, London, 2003

M. Sparks, 'The post-Reformation monuments', in P. Collinson, N. Ramsay and M. Sparks (eds), *A History of Canterbury Cathedral*, Oxford, 1995, pp. 511–52

A.M.G. Stephenson, *Anglicanism and the Lambeth Conferences*, London, 1978

—— *The Victorian Archbishops of Canterbury*, Blewbury, 1991

K.A. Thompson, *Bureaucracy and Church Reform*, Oxford, 1970

J.M. Turner, *Conflict and Reconciliation: Studies in Methodism and Ecumenism in England 1740–1982*, London, 1985

K.M. Wolfe, *The Churches and the British Broadcasting Corporation*, London, 1984

Index of People and Places